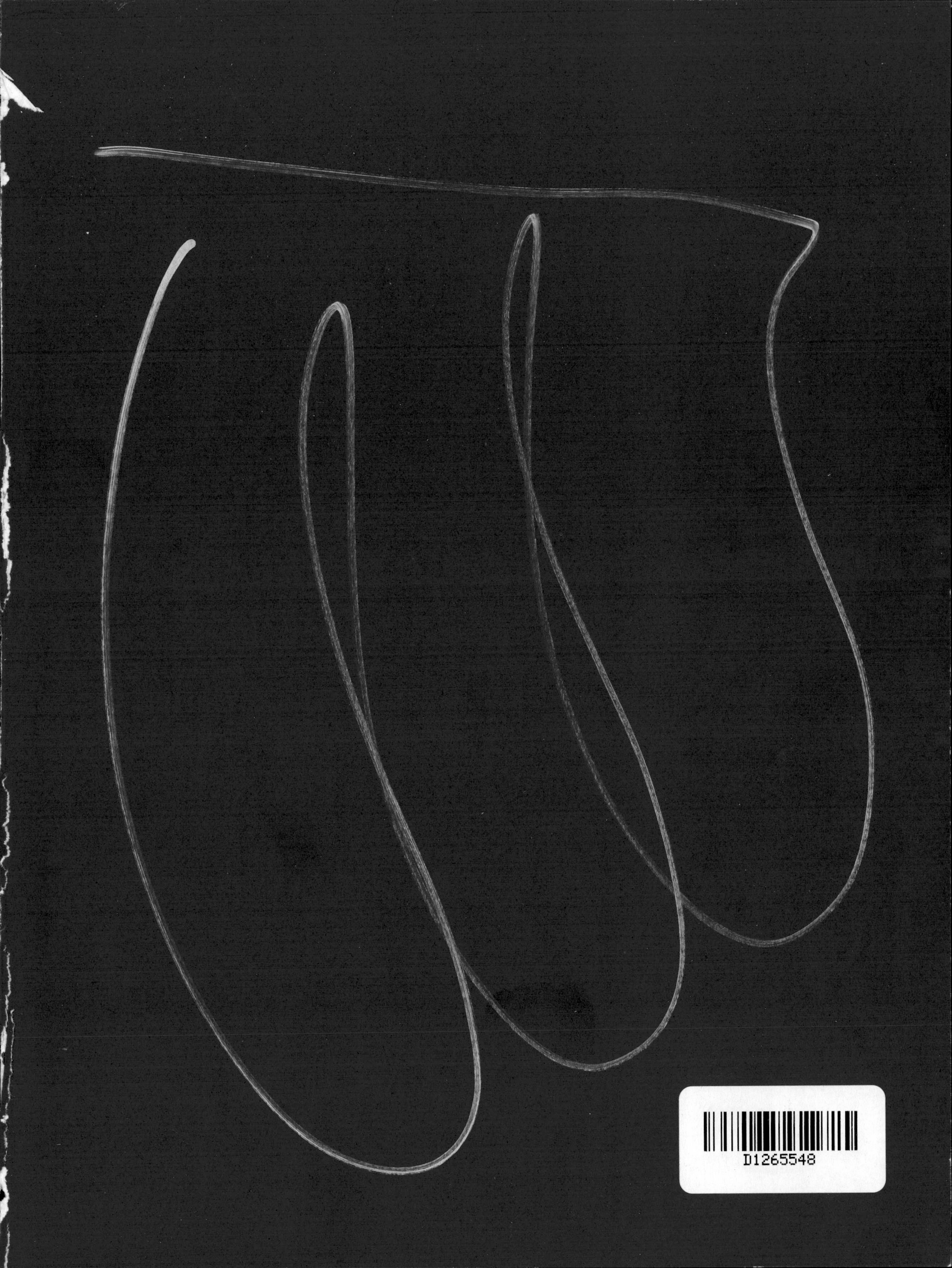

GRAPHIS DESIGN 96

Graphis Design 96

The International Annual of Design and Illustration

Das internationale Jahrbuch über Design und Illustration

Le Répertoire international du Design et de l'Illustration

Edited by • Herausgegeben von • Edité par:

B. Martin Pedersen

Publisher and Creative Director: B. Martin Pedersen

Editors: Heinke Jenssen, Annette Crandall

Associate Editor: Jörg Reimann

Art Directors: B. Martin Pedersen, Randell Pearson

Photographers: Alfredo Parraga, Walter Zuber

Graphis Press Corp. Zürich (Switzerland)

CONTENTS

INHALT

SOMMAIRE

REMARKS

WE EXTEND OUR HEARTFELT THANKS TO CONTRIBUTORS THROUGHOUT THE WORLD WHO HAVE MADE IT POSSIBLE TO PUBLISH A WIDE AND INTERNATIONAL SPECTRUM OF THE BEST WORK IN THIS FIELD.

ENTRY INSTRUCTIONS FOR ALL GRAPHIS BOOKS MAY BE REQUESTED AT:
GRAPHIS PRESS
141 LEXINGTON AVENUE
NEW YORK, NY 10016-8193

ANMERKUNGEN

UNSER DANK GILT DEN EINSENDERN AUS ALLER WELT, DIE ES UNS DURCH IHRE BEITRÄGE ERMÖGLICHT HABEN, EIN BREITES, INTERNATIONALES SPEKTRUM DER BESTEN ARBEITEN ZU VERÖFFENTLICHEN.

TEILNAHMEBEDINGUNGEN FÜR DIE GRAPHIS-BÜCHER SIND ERHÄLTLICH BEIM:
GRAPHIS VERLAG AG
DUFOURSTRASSE 107
8008 ZÜRICH, SCHWEIZ

ANNOTATIONS

TOUTE NOTRE RECONNAISSANCE VA AUX DESIGNERS DU MONDE ENTIER DONT LES ENVOIS NOUS ONT PERMIS DE CONSTITUER UN VASTE PANORAMA INTERNATIONAL DES MEILLEURES CRÉATIONS.

LES MODALITÉS D'INSCRIPTION PEUVENT ÊTRE OBTENUES AUPRÈS DE:
EDITIONS GRAPHIS
DUFOURSTRASSE 107
8008 ZÜRICH, SUISSE

(PRECEDING SPREAD) ILLUSTRATOR: CATHLEEN TOELKE COUNTRY: USA
■ (OPPOSITE) PHOTOGRAPHER: UWE ZISS CONCEPT: WERNER WÜRDINGER COUNTRY: GERMANY
ERRATUM: THE OPPOSITE IMAGE WAS ON THE COVER OF *GRAPHIS BROCHURES 1* AND WAS MISCREDITED THERE. GRAPHIS REGRETS THIS ERROR.

GRAPHIS PUBLICATIONS

GRAPHIS, THE INTERNATIONAL BI-MONTHLY JOURNAL OF VISUAL COMMUNICATION
GRAPHIS SHOPPING BAG, AN INTERNATIONAL COLLECTION OF SHOPPING BAG DESIGN
GRAPHIS MUSIC CD, AN INTERNATIONAL COLLECTION OF CD DESIGN
GRAPHIS BOOKS, AN INTERNATIONAL COLLECTION OF BOOK DESIGN
GRAPHIS DESIGN, THE INTERNATIONAL ANNUAL OF DESIGN AND ILLUSTRATION
GRAPHIS ADVERTISING, THE INTERNATIONAL ANNUAL OF ADVERTISING
GRAPHIS BROCHURES, A COMPILATION OF BROCHURE DESIGN
GRAPHIS PHOTO, THE INTERNATIONAL ANNUAL OF PHOTOGRAPHY
GRAPHIS ALTERNATIVE PHOTOGRAPHY, THE INTERNATIONAL ANNUAL OF ALTERNATIVE PHOTOGRAPHY
GRAPHIS NUDES, A COLLECTION OF CAREFULLY SELECTED SOPHISTICATED IMAGES
GRAPHIS POSTER, THE INTERNATIONAL ANNUAL OF POSTER ART
GRAPHIS PACKAGING, AN INTERNATIONAL COMPILATION OF PACKAGING DESIGN
GRAPHIS LETTERHEAD, AN INTERNATIONAL COMPILATION OF LETTERHEAD DESIGN
GRAPHIS DIAGRAM, THE GRAPHIC VISUALIZATION OF ABSTRACT, TECHNICAL AND STATISTICAL FACTS AND FUNCTIONS
GRAPHIS LOGO, AN INTERNATIONAL COMPILATION OF LOGOS
GRAPHIS EPHEMERA, AN INTERNATIONAL COLLECTION OF PROMOTIONAL ART
GRAPHIS PUBLICATION, AN INTERNATIONAL SURVEY OF THE BEST IN MAGAZINE DESIGN
GRAPHIS ANNUAL REPORTS, AN INTERNATIONAL COMPILATION OF THE BEST DESIGNED ANNUAL REPORTS
GRAPHIS CORPORATE IDENTITY, AN INTERNATIONAL COMPILATION OF THE BEST IN CORPORATE IDENTITY DESIGN
GRAPHIS TYPOGRAPHY, AN INTERNATIONAL COMPILATION OF THE BEST IN TYPOGRAPHIC DESIGN

GRAPHIS PUBLIKATIONEN

GRAPHIS, DIE INTERNATIONALE ZWEIMONATSZEITSCHRIFT DER VISUELLEN KOMMUNIKATION
GRAPHIS SHOPPING BAG, TRAGTASCHEN-DESIGN IM INTERNATIONALEN ÜBERBLICK
GRAPHIS MUSIC CD, CD-DESIGN IM INTERNATIONALEN ÜBERBLICK
GRAPHIS BOOKS, BUCHGESTALTUNG IM INTERNATIONALEN ÜBERBLICK
GRAPHIS DESIGN, DAS INTERNATIONALE JAHRBUCH ÜBER DESIGN UND ILLUSTRATION
GRAPHIS ADVERTISING, DAS INTERNATIONALE JAHRBUCH DER WERBUNG
GRAPHIS BROCHURES, BROSCHÜRENDESIGN IM INTERNATIONAL ÜBERBLICK
GRAPHIS PHOTO, DAS INTERNATIONALE JAHRBUCH DER PHOTOGRAPHIE
GRAPHIS ALTERNATIVE PHOTOGRAPHY, DAS INTERNATIONALE JAHRBUCH ÜBER ALTERNATIVE PHOTOGRAPHIE
GRAPHIS NUDES, EINE SAMMLUNG SORGFÄLTIG AUSGEWÄHLTER AKTPHOTOGRAPHIE
GRAPHIS POSTER, DAS INTERNATIONALE JAHRBUCH DER PLAKATKUNST
GRAPHIS PACKAGING, EIN INTERNATIONALER ÜBERBLICK ÜBER DIE PACKUNGSGESTALTUNG
GRAPHIS LETTERHEAD, EIN INTERNATIONALER ÜBERBLICK ÜBER BRIEFPAPIERGESTALTUNG
GRAPHIS DIAGRAM, DIE GRAPHISCHE DARSTELLUNG ABSTRAKTER TECHNISCHER UND STATISTISCHER DATEN UND FAKTEN
GRAPHIS LOGO, EINE INTERNATIONALE AUSWAHL VON FIRMEN-LOGOS
GRAPHIS EPHEMERA, EINE INTERNATIONALE SAMMLUNG GRAPHISCHER DOKUMENTE DES TÄGLICHEN LEBENS
GRAPHIS MAGAZINDESIGN, EINE INTERNATIONALE ZUSAMMENSTELLUNG DES BESTEN ZEITSCHRIFTEN-DESIGNS
GRAPHIS ANNUAL REPORTS, EIN INTERNATIONALER ÜBERBLICK ÜBER DIE GESTALTUNG VON JAHRESBERICHTEN
GRAPHIS CORPORATE IDENTITY, EINE INTERNATIONALE AUSWAHL DES BESTEN CORPORATE IDENTITY DESIGNS
GRAPHIS TYPOGRAPHY, EINE INTERNATIONALE ZUSAMMENSTELLUNG DES BESTEN TYPOGRAPHIE DESIGN

PUBLICATIONS GRAPHIS

GRAPHIS, LA REVUE BIMESTRIELLE INTERNATIONALE DE LA COMMUNICATION VISUELLE
GRAPHIS SHOPPING BAG, UNE COMPILATION INTERNATIONALE SUR LE DESIGN DES SACS À COMMISSIONS
GRAPHIS MUSIC CD, UNE COMPILATION INTERNATIONALE SUR LE DESIGN DES CD
GRAPHIS BOOKS, UNE COMPILATION INTERNATIONALE SUR LE DESIGN DES LIVRES
GRAPHIS DESIGN, LE RÉPERTOIRE INTERNATIONAL DE LA COMMUNICATION VISUELLE
GRAPHIS ADVERTISING, LE RÉPERTOIRE INTERNATIONAL DE LA PUBLICITÉ
GRAPHIS BROCHURES, UNE COMPILATION INTERNATIONALE SUR LE DESIGN DES BROCHURES
GRAPHIS PHOTO, LE RÉPERTOIRE INTERNATIONAL DE LA PHOTOGRAPHIE
GRAPHIS ALTERNATIVE PHOTOGRAPHY, LE RÉPERTOIRE INTERNATIONAL DE LA PHOTOGRAPHIE ALTERNATIVE
GRAPHIS NUDES, UN FLORILÈGE DE LA PHOTOGRAPHIE DE NUS
GRAPHIS POSTER, LE RÉPERTOIRE INTERNATIONAL DE L'AFFICHE
GRAPHIS PACKAGING, LE RÉPERTOIRE INTERNATIONAL DE LA CRÉATION D'EMBALLAGES
GRAPHIS LETTERHEAD, LE RÉPERTOIRE INTERNATIONAL DU DESIGN DE PAPIER À LETTRES
GRAPHIS DIAGRAM, LE RÉPERTOIRE GRAPHIQUE DE FAITS ET DONNÉES ABSTRAITS, TECHNIQUES ET STATISTIQUES
GRAPHIS LOGO, LE RÉPERTOIRE INTERNATIONAL DU LOGO
GRAPHIS EPHEMERA, LE GRAPHISME – UN ÉTAT D'ESPRIT AU QUOTIDIEN
GRAPHIS PUBLICATION, LE RÉPERTOIRE INTERNATIONAL DU DESIGN DE PÉRIODIQUES
GRAPHIS ANNUAL REPORTS, PANORAMA INTERNATIONAL DU MEILLEUR DESIGN DE RAPPORTS ANNUELS D'ENTREPRISES
GRAPHIS CORPORATE IDENTITY, PANORAMA INTERNATIONAL DU MEILLEUR DESIGN D'IDENTITÉ CORPORATE
GRAPHIS TYPOGRAPHY, LE RÉPERTOIRE INTERNATIONAL DU MEILLEUR DESIGN DE TYPOGRAPHIE

PUBLICATION NO. 247 (ISBN 3-85709-196-7)

PRINTED IN JAPAN BY TOPPAN PRINTING CO., LTD.

COMMENTARIES

KOMMENTARE

COMMENTAIRES

Commentary by David Hillman

Portrait by Fi McGhee

We Are All Artists Now

Graphic design was invented as an industry and as a business in order to establish, consolidate and promote the value of art to the world of commerce and communications. Until then the precursors of graphic designers—the commercial artists—had been lowly folk.

They knew their value was underrated. They knew how influential the power of their imagery could be in the wider world. Calling their art graphic design was the first step in realising their worth.

The people who invented thus distinguished graphic design did not come from business, engineering or humanities backgrounds. They came from art schools and print schools. As their business evolved and grew, it was in the interests of graphic designers to continue distancing themselves from art—the kind of art that hung in galleries—in order to make themselves more accessible to sceptical clients. Clients knew they needed the skills of artists to promote and communicate their own notions and interests, but they did not want the temperamental difficulties or the highbrow associations that had become part of the artist stereotype. And the people who called themselves artists acquiesced, not wanting to be associated with the 'impure' world of commerce.

In Britain at least, where modern fine art has been practically starved out of existence, contemporary art has now come off (some would say fallen off) the walls of galleries. Consequently there is a growing unease that the distinction between graphic design and contemporary art is a false one—just a matter of declaring one's colours and hawking one's work either to advertising agencies, magazines and design groups or to galleries, depending which way you want to jump.

A glance through *Who's Who in Graphic Design* makes the point. It is full of people we call illustrators who, rather than designing modernist logotypes, have made their names as artists with acute imagination, style, historical sense, technique, and craft. So who is to say that the posters of Mucha, Toulouse-Lautrec or Hockney are not graphic design? Could not David Carson ride his reputation and be hung in a gallery if he wanted? Could not Mark Wallinger design posters for Shell if he wanted? Of course many have been making a nonsense of the distinction for years. Is not Milton Glaser an artist? And surely much of Andy Warhol's output was graphic design. Where do you draw the line; why do you draw the line at all? If the graphic designer heroes such as Kandinsky and Magritte had arrived on the scene today, could they not just as easily 'classified' as graphic designers as contemporary artists?

Of course these questions become meaningless if we all become simply artists again. Not for nothing are the visual wizards on magazines called art directors. Not for nothing is graphic design responsible for producing art work for the printer, and the design department called the art department in American parlance. If there's no difference there's no problem. But then what would become of graphic design? By becoming an industry, graphic design has put a stop to the exploitation of artists by clients who capitalise on their imagery in commerce and industry, and in the process has become more powerful and therefore better off than bands of artists roaming the land looking for commissions could ever have hoped to be.

These problems of spurious definitions extend beyond two dimensional art and design. My partner at Pentagram, Daniel Weil, is a professor of industrial design at the Royal College of Art. Theo Crosby, not only an architect but a sculptor of some merit, was also a professor there. For many, working in a design company disqualifies people such as these from being artists. Yet the cars, furniture, lighting and other products of great designers sit happily alongside the sculpture of artists in the museums of modern art.

The false distinction came home to me personally when I designed a sign system for the Tate Gallery, and it was turned down because it was 'it was too much like art'. In other words they were worried that people might think it was art—heaven forbid.

Graphic designers have demonstrated that they understand what their clients need and why. They know that there is something beguiling about their world and work, producing for clients imagery and function that bind together aspiration and style. So their value has continued to grow. The truth is, graphic design is art. But maybe we have to look at ourselves and the implications for our businesses before we tell the world that graphic designers have been artists all along. ■

David Hillman joined Pentagram London in 1978 after working for *Nova* magazine as art director and deputy editor and as a freelance designer. At Pentagram, he continued his editorial design work with numerous publications and carried out C.I. design programs, sign programs and retail designs for various important clients. He has won numerous design awards, he has served on juries of a number of major international competitions and is work was exhibited at the University of Essen, Germany, as well as at the V&A Museum and the Whitechapel Art Gallery, London.

Wir sind jetzt alle Künstler
von David Hillman

Graphik-Design ist zu einer Branche geworden, mit dem Ziel, den Wert der Kunst in der Wirtschaft und Kommunikationsbranche zu etablieren, zu konsolidieren und zu fördern. Die Vorläufer der Graphik-Designer – die kommerziellen Künstler – waren wenig geachtet. Sie wussten, dass ihre Arbeit unterschätzt wurde. Sie wussten, wie einflussreich ihre Bilder auf breiter Ebene sein könnten. Die Bezeichnung ihrer Kunst als Graphik-Design war der erste Schritt zur richtigen Einschätzung ihres Wertes.

Die Leute, die auf diese Art das Graphik-Design erfunden haben, hatten keinen wirtschaftlichen, technischen oder geisteswissenschaftlichen Hintergrund. Sie kamen von Kunstschulen oder aus der Druckbranche. Ihre eigene Branche entwickelte sich und wuchs, und es war ganz im Interesse der Graphik-Designer, sich weiterhin von der Kunst zu distanzieren – von der Art Kunst, die an den Wänden von Galerien hängt –, um für skeptische Kunden zugänglicher zu sein. Die Auftraggeber wussten, dass sie das Können von Künstlern für die wirkungsvolle Verbreitung ihrer eigenen Vorstellungen und Interessen brauchten, aber sie wollten nichts mit den Launen oder der intellektuellen Arroganz der Künstler zu tun haben, denn so sah ihr Klischee aus. Und jenen, die sich Künstler nannten, war das ganz recht, denn sie wollten nichts mit der «schmutzigen» Welt des Kommerzes zu tun haben.

In Grossbritannien zumindest, wo die moderne Kunst praktisch ausgehungert wurde, ist die zeitgenössische Kunst von den Wänden der Galerien verschwunden («gefallen» würden manche sagen). Dementsprechend gibt es ein wachsendes Unbehagen hinsichtlich der Unterscheidung zwischen Graphik-Design und zeitgenössischer Kunst – es ist einfach eine Frage der Interpretation und des Feilbietens – ob man sich an Werbeagenturen, Zeitschriften und Designateliers wendet oder an Gallerien, je nachdem, auf welches Boot man springen will.

Ein Blick ins *Who's Who in Graphic Design* besagt alles. Es ist voll von Leuten, die wir als Illustratoren bezeichnen, die aber statt moderne Logos zu entwerfen, sich ihren Ruf als Künstler mit Phantasie, Stil, Geschichtsbewusstsein, Technik und handwerklichem Können erworben haben. Wer will behaupten, dass die Plakate von Mucha, Toulouse-Lautrec oder Hockney nicht Graphik-Design sind? Könnte David Carson, wenn er wollte, nicht seinen Ruf nutzen und in einer Galerie ausstellen? Könnte Mark Wallinger, wenn er wollte, nicht Plakate für Shell entwerfen? Natürlich haben viele über Jahre hinweg bewiesen, wie unsinnig die Unterscheidung ist. Ist Milton Glaser kein Künstler? Ganz sicher war ein grosser Teil von Andy Warhols Produktion Graphik-Design. Wo ziehen wir die Grenze – warum überhaupt? Wenn Kandinsky und Magritte heute lebten, könnte man sie nicht ebensogut als Graphik-Designer wie als zeitgenössische Künstler «einordnen»°?

Natürlich werden solche Fragen bedeutungslos, wenn wir alle ganz einfach wieder Künstler werden. Nicht umsonst werden die visuellen Zauberer bei Zeitschriften «Art Directors» genannt. Nicht umsonst spricht man bei Druckvorlagen von «art work», und in den USA wird die Graphik-Abteilung allgemein «art department» genannt. Wenn es keinen Unterschied gibt, gibt es auch kein Problem. Aber was würde dann aus Graphik-Design werden? Indem es zu einem Berufszweig wurde, hat Graphik-Design der Ausbeutung der Künstler durch die Auftraggeber, die mit ihren Bildern Geld machen, ein Ende gesetzt, und dabei wurde die Branche stark und besser gestellt, als die Grüppchen von Künstlern, die Aufträgen nachlaufen mussten, je hoffen konnten.

Diese Probleme falscher Definitionen betreffen nicht nur zweidimensionale Kunst und Graphik. Mein Partner bei Pentagram, Daniel Weil, ist Professor für Industrie-Design am Royal College of Art. Theo Crosby, der nicht nur Architekt, sondern auch ein recht anerkannter Bildhauer ist, war dort auch Professor. In den Augen vieler sind jene, die in Graphikateliers arbeiten, als Künstler disqualifiziert. Und doch stehen in den Museen für moderne Kunst Autos, Möbel, Leuchten und andere Produkte von grossen Designern ganz selbstverständlich neben den Skulpturen von Künstlern.

Auch ich selbst habe erfahren, wie unsinnig die Unterscheidung ist. Ich hatte für die Tate Gallery ein Orientierungssystem entworfen, das mit der Begründung abgelehnt würde, es sähe zu sehr nach «Kunst» aus. In anderen Worten, sie befürchteten, dass die Leute es für Kunst halten würden – um Himmels willen!

Graphik-Designer haben bewiesen, dass sie verstehen, was ihre Kunden brauchen und warum sie es brauchen. Sie wissen, dass ihre Welt und ihre Arbeit etwas Betörendes hat: die Verbindung von Phantasie und Zweckgebundenheit, von Stil und Zielsetzung. Und so wuchs ihr Wert. In Wahrheit ist Graphik-Design Kunst. Aber vielleicht müssen wir uns und die Auswirkungen auf unsere Branche genau betrachten, bevor wir der Welt sagen, dass Graphik-Designer schon immer Künstler waren. ■

DAVID HILLMAN KAM 1978 ALS PARTNER ZU PENTAGRAM, LONDON, NACHDEM ER ALS ART DIRECTOR UND STELLVERTRETENDER CHEFREDAKTEUR FÜR DIE ZEITSCHRIFT NOVA UND SPÄTER SELBSTÄNDIG TÄTIG GEWESEN WAR. BEI PENTAGRAM ARBEITETE ER WEITERHIN IN DER ZEITSCHRIFTENGESTALTUNG, ENTWICKELTE C.I.-DESIGN-PROGRAMME, BESCHILDERUNGEN UND LADENGESTALTUNGEN FÜR BEDEUTENDE KUNDEN. ER ERHIELT ZAHLREICHE AUSZEICHNUNGEN; ER WAR JURYMITGLIED BEI WICHTIGEN INTERNATIONALEN DESIGN-WETTBEWERBEN UND SEINE ARBEITEN WURDEN IN VERSCHIEDENEN MUSEEN UND GALERIEN AUSGESTELLT.

Maintenant, nous sommes tous desartistes
par David Hillman

Le design graphique a été créé comme activité industrielle et commerciale dans l'optique d'établir, de consolider, de promouvoir la valeur de l'art aussi bien dans le secteur de l'économie que dans celui de la communication. Les précurseurs des designers graphiques – les artistes commerciaux – ne récoltaient que peu d'éloges. Ils savaient leur travail sous-estimé. Mais ils savaient aussi à quel point leurs images pouvaient influencer le vaste monde. En intitulant leur art «design graphique», ils posèrent le premier jalon vers la reconnaissance de leur valeur.

Les inventeurs du design graphique sortaient soit des écoles d'arts appliqués, soit du monde de l'imprimerie. Alors que leur propre branche se développait, grandissait, il était dans leur intérêt de se distancer de l'art – ce genre d'art que l'on voyait dans les galeries – pour vaincre le scepticisme des clients. Ces derniers n'ignoraient pas qu'ils devaient recourir au savoir-faire des artistes pour promouvoir et communiquer leurs propres idées, sauvegarder leurs intérêts, mais ils refusaient de supporter les sautes d'humeur et l'arrogance intellectuelle des artistes, car c'est ainsi que le stéréotype les décrivait. Pourtant, ceux qui se disaient artistes ne s'en formalisaient pas le moins du monde, ne voulant en aucun cas avoir affaire au monde «pourri» du commerce.

En Grande-Bretagne au moins, où les bastions de l'art moderne ont pratiquement cédé, l'art contemporain a disparu aujourd'hui («est tombé» diraient certains) des murs des galeries. Aussi, le fait de vouloir distinguer le design graphique de l'art contemporain suscite un malaise de plus en plus profond, la démarche étant fausse par nature. Car il s'agit en fait d'une question d'interprétation, de relations de travail selon que l'on s'adresse à des agences de publicité, à des magazines, à des ateliers de design ou à des galeries. Suivant le bord que l'on a décidé de rejoindre, on coule ou on émerge.

Il suffit de feuilleter le *Who's Who in Graphic Design* pour en avoir le cœur net. Il fourmille de personnes que nous désignons sous le terme d'illustrateurs et qui, au lieu de créer des logos modernistes, se sont fait un nom dans le monde de la création grâce à leur imagination débordante, à leur style, à leur sens de l'histoire, à leur technique et à leur savoir-faire. Qui oserait prétendre que les affiches de Mucha, de Toulouse-Lautrec ou de Hockney ne sont pas du design graphique? David Carson, s'il s'en donnait la peine, ne pourrait-il pas user de sa réputation et faire exposer ses œuvres dans une galerie? Mark Allinger ne pourrait-il pas réaliser des affiches pour Shell? Certes, nombreux sont ceux qui ont montré à quel point cette distinction tient du ridicule. Milton Glaser n'est-il pas un artiste? Et, bien sûr, une grande partie de la production d'Andy Warhol était bien du design graphique. Où fixer les limites? Et faut-il le faire? Si les maîtres du design graphique, tels que Kandinsky et Magritte, vivaient à notre époque, ne pourrait-on pas les faire entrer aussi bien dans la «catégorie» des designers graphiques que dans celle des artistes contemporains?

Bien sûr, ces questions perdent tout leur sens si nous redevenons tout simplement des artistes. Ce n'est pas pour rien si dans les magazines, ces magiciens de l'image apparaissent sous le nom de directeurs artistiques. Et ce n'est pas pour rien non plus si le travail livré par un designer graphique pour l'impression est qualifié d'art work? Au même titre, on peut se demander pourquoi, aux Etats-Unis, le département graphisme s'appelle 'art department'. S'il n'y a pas de différence, il n'y a pas de problème. Mais qu'adviendra-t-il alors du design graphique? Parce que le design graphique est devenu une branche à part entière, il a pu mettre un terme à l'exploitation des artistes par leurs clients qui se sont faits fort d'amasser des capitaux sur leur dos, que ce soit dans le commerce ou l'industrie. Leur branche en est sortie plus forte, grandie; un résultat inespéré que les petits groupes d'artistes, toujours à l'affût de contrats, n'auraient jamais osé imaginer.

Ces problèmes de définition ne touchent pas uniquement l'art en deux dimensions ou le graphisme. Mon associé à Pentagram, Daniel Weil, est professeur en design industriel au Royal College of Art. Theo Crosby, architecte mais aussi sculpteur reconnu, y a également enseigné. Pour beaucoup, ceux qui travaillent dans des ateliers de graphisme sont disqualifiés d'office lorsqu'il en va de la définition «d'artiste», même si les voitures, les meubles, les lampes et autres produits de grands designers ont trouvé leur place dans les musées d'art moderne, à côté des sculptures d'artistes.

Les designers graphiques ont démontré qu'ils comprennent ce que veulent leurs clients et pourquoi. Ils savent que leur monde et leur travail ont quelque chose d'envoûtant: la synergie entre imagination et fonction, aspiration et style. Et c'est ainsi que leur valeur a continué d'augmenter. En vérité, le design graphique, c'est de l'art. Mais peut-être devrions-nous nous tendre un miroir, nous sonder, et examiner les conséquences que cela implique pour notre branche avant de dire au monde entier que de tout temps, les designers graphiques ont été des artistes. ■

DAVID HILLMAN A REJOINT LES EFFECTIFS DE PENTAGRAM LONDRES EN 1978 APRÈS AVOIR TRAVAILLÉ EN TANT QUE DIRECTEUR ARTISTIQUE ET RÉDACTEUR ADJOINT POUR LE MAGAZINE NOVA ET GRAPHISTE INDÉPENDANT. A PENTAGRAM, IL A CONTINUÉ DANS LA MÊME VOIE, SOIT LA CONCEPTION GRAPHIQUE DE NOMBREUSES PUBLICATIONS, ET A EFFECTUÉ DE NOMBREUX PROGRAMMES D'IDENTITÉ VISUELLE ET DE SYSTÈMES D'ORIENTATION POUR D'IMPORTANTS CLIENTS. IL S'EST VU DÉCERNER DE NOMBREUSES DISTINCTIONS POUR SES RÉALISATIONS ET A PARTICIPÉ EN TANT QUE JURÉ À DE NOMBREUSES COMPÉTITIONS INTERNATIONALES.

Commentary by Robin Rickabaugh in collaboration with everyone at Principia Graphica: Brian Kerr, Kimberly Lew, Jon Olsen, Heidi Rickabaugh, Qiana Rickabaugh and Jerry Soga

The Tickling of the Clock in the All

An effort to recover the montage lost which unites all things to all things

Symbols themselves are experiences of the absolute in the
Relative. Are there any experiences which are basic forms
Left behind seen as beauty — even the mistakes? It
Would be wrong to stars as they rise back
Seeming to float above the angle agreeable for sitting.
It's also a rewarding point of view to look
In the dot. The emanating point of the unknown,
Discarded, leaves no traces for inspiration. Our mothers nurture
Examples which strictly belong no longer. Spinach should be

Served toward fried apples. You can't be found the
Most brilliant. The process is the wings of our
Airplane. Even the sea and the streams we bathed
And washed. The necessary world where old guides erased
A neutralized bloom is very miserable. There's fire in
His examples when he spits. Tablecloths written in change —
Eat from them. Our inward wind and rain affect
Levels of meaning embodied in examining the artistic deconstructing
And decoding of leaves' experience in the world. Designers
Realize the artifact culture. Posters that break every good
Taste. Sometimes he thinks he's been a pencil — but
He's not. Seeking to identify the variegated picture into
Simple form equations, perfection seems imperfectly itself. The rivers
Are then the seas. Fullness seems emptiness fully present.
There is a new before ever considering a new.
Principles lie at the apparently immobile points which
Receive permission on a blank page. All truth calls to
Quality in shaping the visible wit. Reading did as

Much for design as old cooking oil. Computers should
Celebrate designers' options to choose paths that defy. It
Seems we are living decisions to demonstrate from flint
To light, until we're able to unfold through the
Dim. Then a great wind will seem like a
Whisper encountering elements of values that lead to new
Forms of expression. Even the rocks sweat ceremony. Invisible
Designer, the unseen hand, manifests proportions of unerring perfection
Shaking difficulty. The invisible recalls the sacred of mundane

Existence without doing. From the soffits of windows, selling
The seven continents, reality will always free distractions. Even
The finest craftspeople yield few clues to the simple
Praise. The harp on which you don't tune, you
Get some interesting strange basic truth, a vocabulary, inclusive,
Open to influences from an embroidered shawl. Move to
The knowledge of the question. She's donned it like
An idea expressed by conception, but on her way
A stem looked at them, pulling yellow on the

Others, taking crimson red. Seeing will be just being;
It will be a vision of it. Space and
Silence, condensed to reality, foster independence from objects. Move
To the knowledge of the form where no blame
Rests upon the danger. Where is real for a
Single moment? The culture and our view of ourselves
Dematerialized technology. Creating is never without becoming the timeless
Moment that has susceptible variety. When one understands the
Dry leaf, vitality and aesthetic happens. The ordinary perceives

As being beautiful. In judgement is always the narrow
Critics who complain illegibility and sit on it. We
Are the guardians of reach out. His challenge will
Start where there are none. In order to find
A way, work and worship flicker as much in
Measuring onions. The concept of fusion from every corner
Attempts to indicate where order can find a way
Into the aware. The thin line, a suitable vehicle
For the infinitely prolonged sacred, invoked, from all the

Spaces of reality stretching, the idea of a spiral
Intertwining, trying to reconcile the realm of the conclusion.
In a certain sense, there is another sense. The
Flower, attempting treatment of floral style, faced with the
Task of the present, related all things. The past
Starts projecting itself yesterday. Your future has been your
Entanglement from the outset. The path can be taken
As itself. We fail to read our stomachs. Beside
Us stands the Western mind, yet we are not

Defeated. If the bottom line is profitability, the issue
Becomes a well-made absence of taking risks. If
You don't tune it, the world is so familiar:
Roast turkey — with tomatoes and cauliflower, in which movements
And groupings bring harmony to disparate systems of artistic
Perception. The guarded secret learned from an externalization of
A quite abstract inner sonority — confronting the difficult while
It is still easy. The blanket for the future
Is born woven. Here, too, are the most radical —

With gold and blood. Yet for all this emptiness —
Refuge. In effect, defects can be optimal. Scholar over
The symbols that matter. Its ways are not a
Promise made easily. If "good enough" is good enough,
You lack the time and willingness. Art of art,
And the science between them, exceeds the capabilities
Of both ancient and modern. More, even, than engaging
The visual, beyond the intellectual. Effort to recover the
Montage lost which unites all things to all things.

S.T.TAYLOR 930 B'WAY NEW
NORTON COMPANY
FOLLOW ARROW
INSIDE MEASURE

GRAPHIS

DESIGN

NINETY-SIX

PHOTOGRAPHER: JOYCE OUDKERK POOL

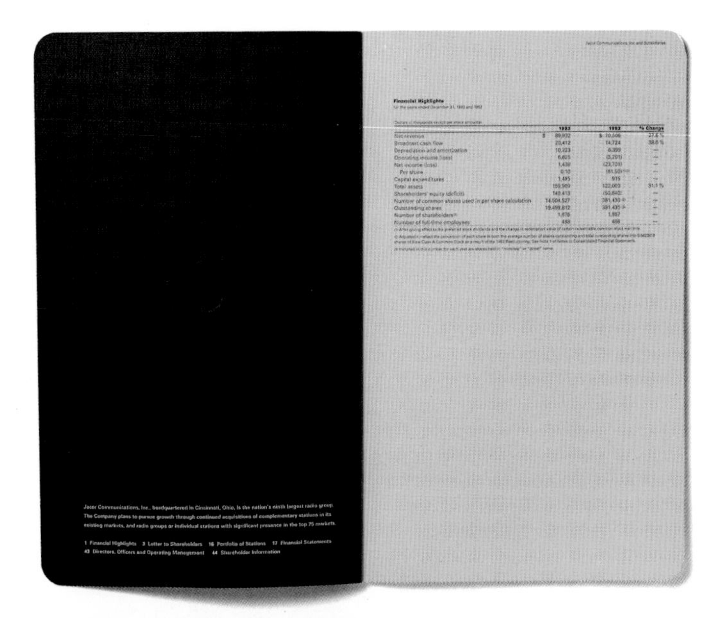

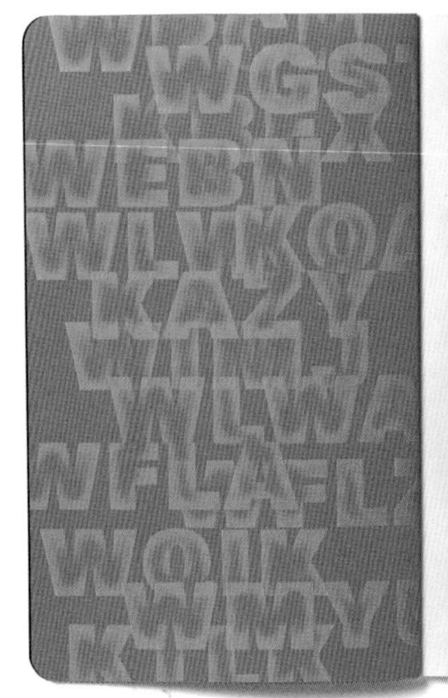

Listen,

1993 was a great, active year for Jacor. We made a few smart decisions, hired some great people, reduced our debt to zero, increased our access to capital, and built share in all of our major markets. Some companies might see those steps as final objectives. But we see them as a new beginning.

Jacor is a "new" company, with new leadership, a new ownership structure, and a highly focused resolve to take full advantage of a

for Jacor to be active in continuing to merge, consolidate and concentrate strength within markets.

The financial strength and flexibility we now have as a result of our public offering last fall gives us the chance to go after acquisitions of individual stations or smaller groups—or even to go for a larger portfolio of stations when it makes sense.

The opportunity to own, operate and represent multiple stations in a given market gives us a chance to pull together

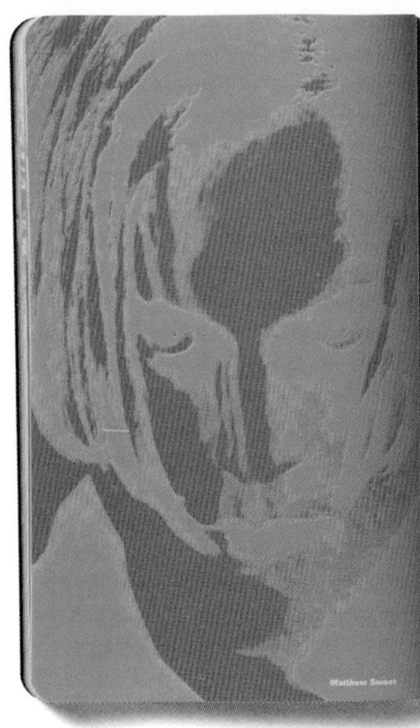

for the listener and the advertiser. Our financial objectives are about increasing our broadcast cash flow—which, as the accompanying financial information shows, we accomplished quite well in 1993.

Our corporate objectives are about building a company that performs for shareholders—in the short and long term. Thanks for joining this program in progress during 1993. We hope you stick around for 1994 and beyond. It'll be radio active.

– Randy Michaels, President

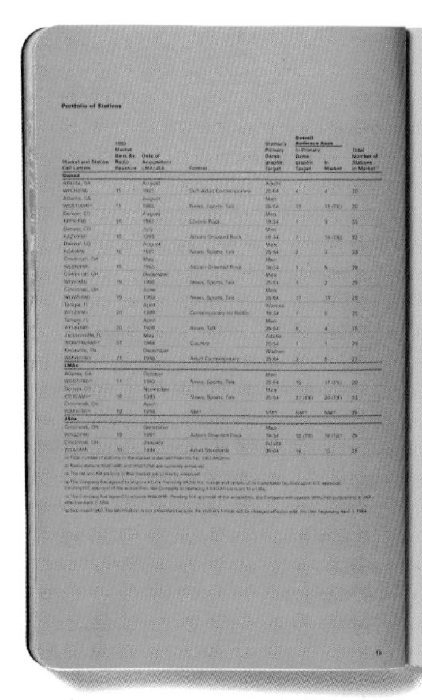

Financial Statements

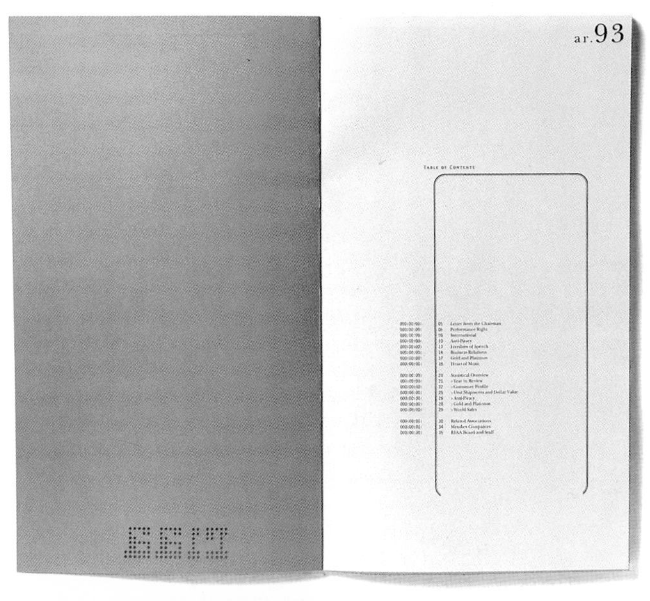

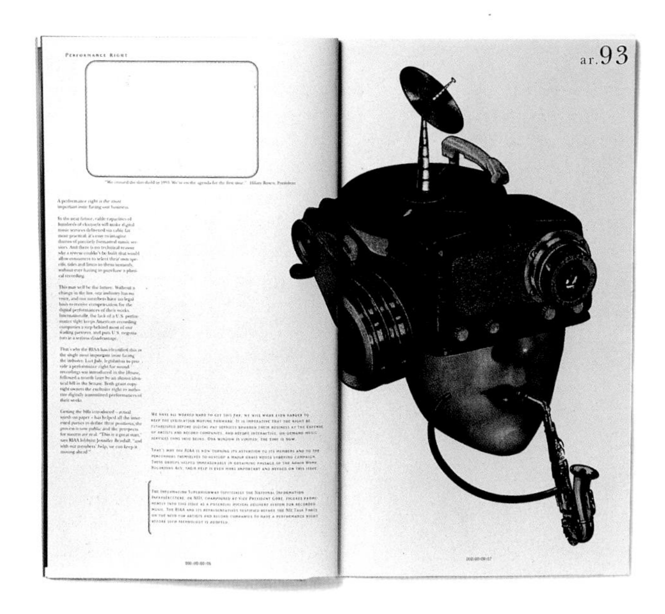

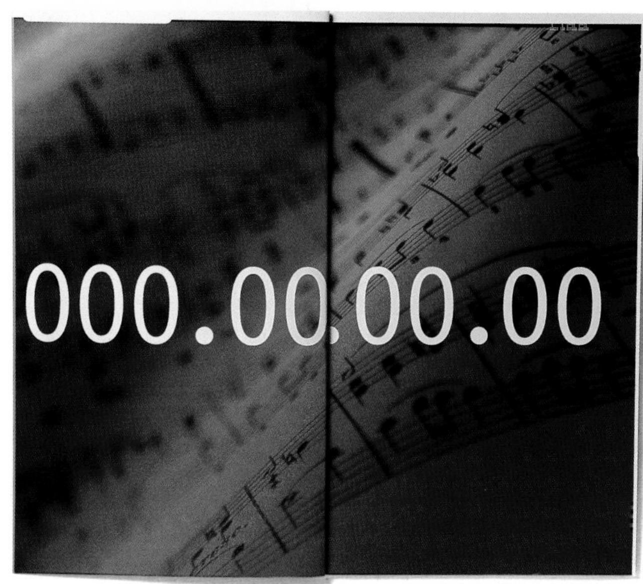

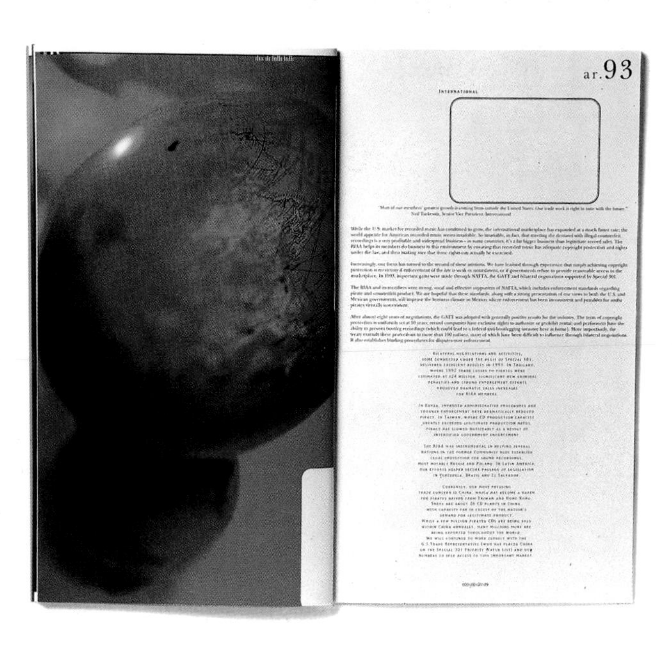

■ 1–6 ART DIRECTOR: ROBERT PETRICK DESIGNER: LAURA RESS PHOTOGRAPHER: VARIOUS DESIGN FIRM: PETRICK DESIGN CLIENT: JACOR COMMUNICATIONS, INC. COUNTRY: USA ■ 7–12 ART DIRECTOR: NEAL ASHBY DESIGNER: NEAL ASHBY ILLUSTRATOR: STEVE BIVER DESIGN FIRM: RECORDING INDUSTRY ASSOCIATION OF AMERICA CLIENT: RECORDING INDUSTRY ASSOCIATION OF AMERICA COUNTRY: USA

■ 1 ART DIRECTORS: LOW POH LI, LIM ENG SEONG DESIGNER: LOW POH LI PHOTOGRAPHER: STUDIO PASHE COPYWRITER: QUEENIE KHOO DESIGN FIRM: BATEY ADS MALAYSIA CLIENT: SIME DARBY BERHAD COUNTRY: MALAYSIA ■ 2–7 ART DIRECTOR: KIT HINRICHS DESIGNER: JACKIE FOSHAUG PHOTOGRAPHERS: TOM GRAVES DESIGN FIRM: PENTAGRAM DESIGN CLIENT: BURLINGTON NORTHERN COUNTRY: USA

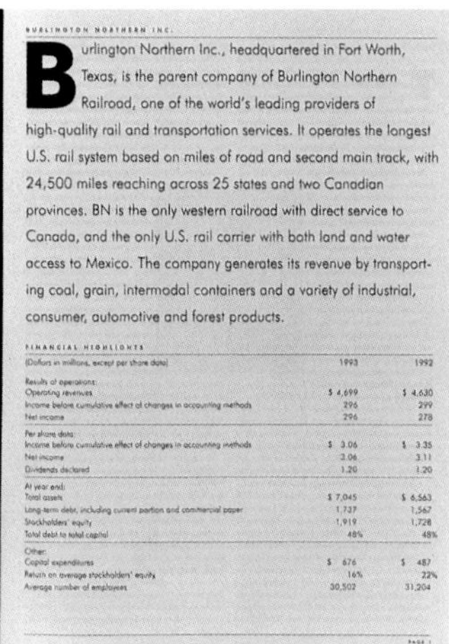

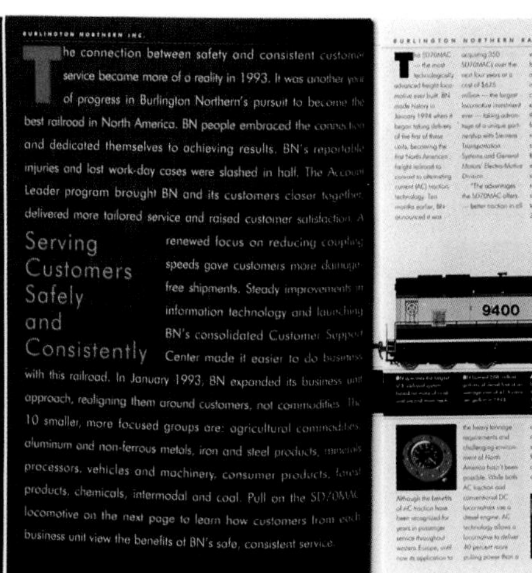

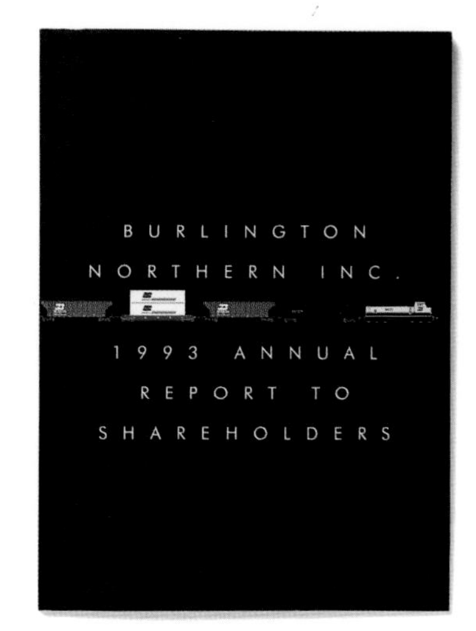

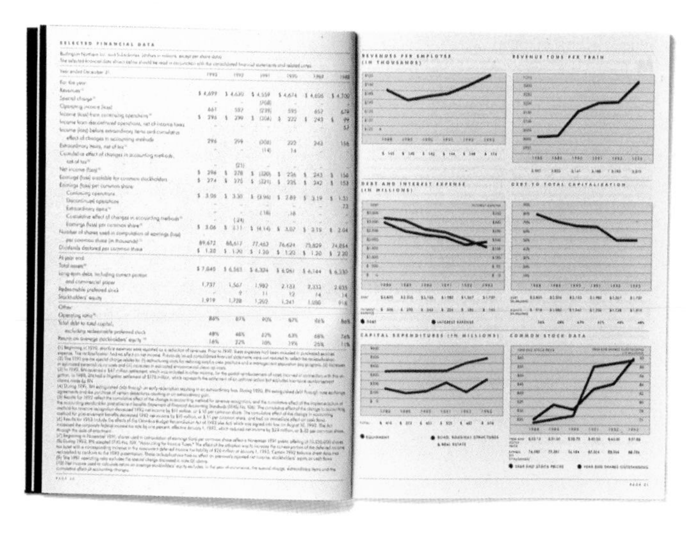

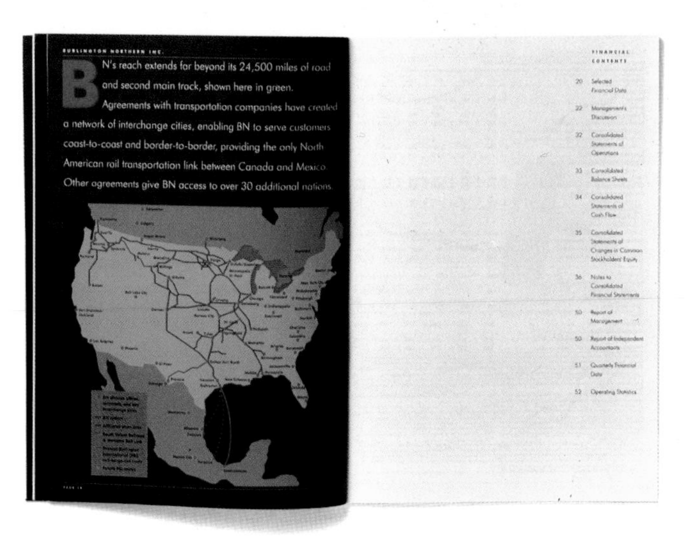

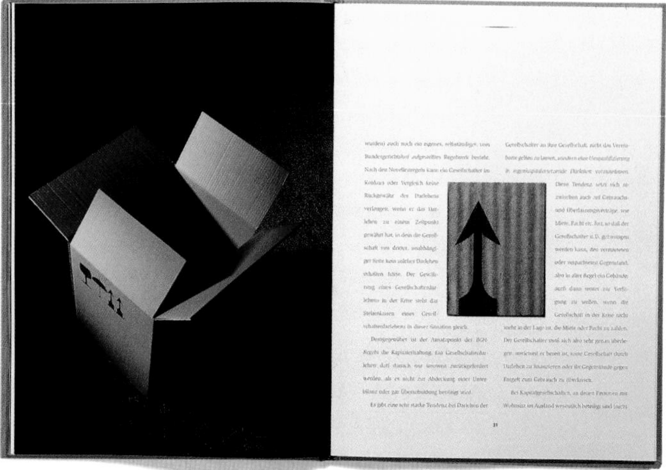

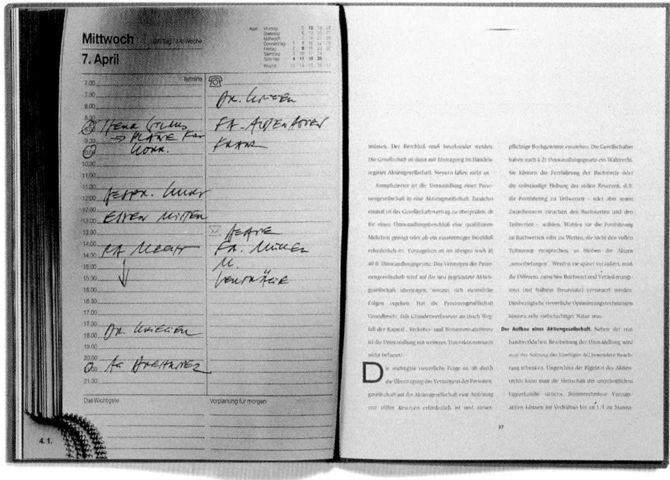

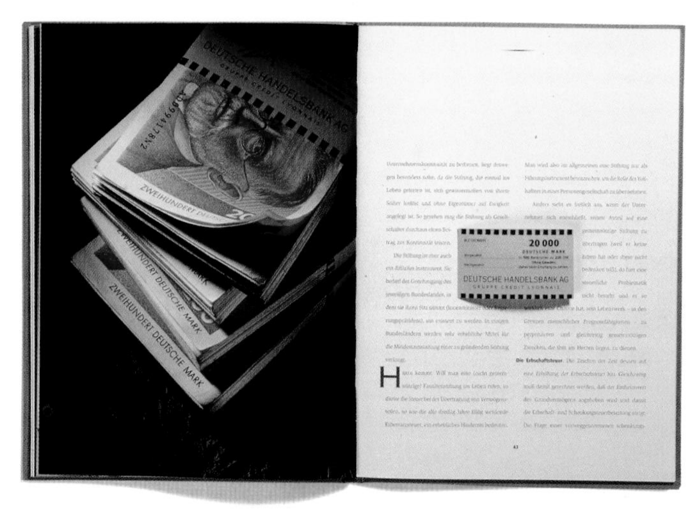

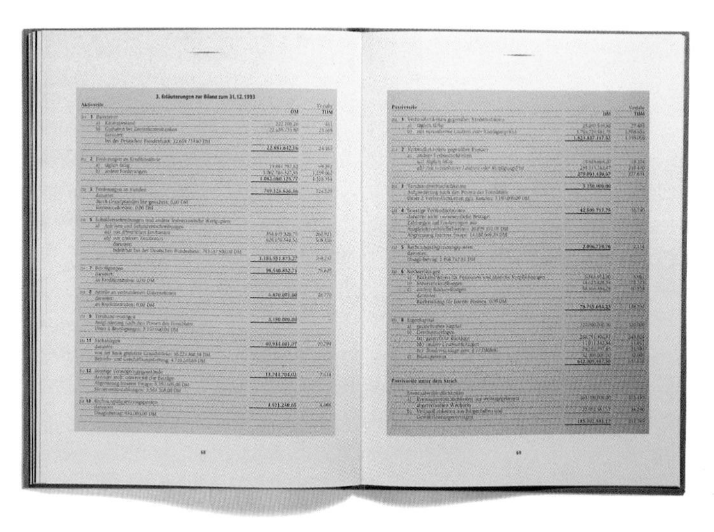

■ 1–6 ART DIRECTOR: KLAUS FEHSENFELD DESIGNER: LIBBY CARTON PHOTOGRAPHER: HUGH JOHNSON COPYWRITER/CLIENT: DEUTSCHE HANDELSBANK AG DESIGN FIRM: W.A.F. WERBEGESELLSCHAFT MBH COUNTRY: GERMANY ■ 7–9 ART DIRECTOR: HOWARD BROWN DESIGNERS: HOWARD BROWN, MIKE CALKINS PHOTOGRAPHER: LANGLEY-PENOYAR CLIENT: URBAN OUTFITTERS COUNTRY: USA

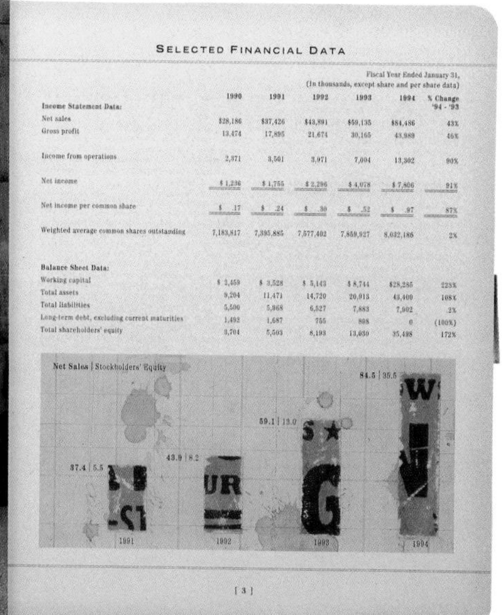

SELECTED FINANCIAL DATA

Fiscal Year Ended January 31,
(In thousands, except share and per share data)

	1990	1991	1992	1993	1994	% Change '94 - '93
Income Statement Data:						
Net sales	$28,186	$37,426	$43,891	$59,135	$84,486	43%
Gross profit	13,474	17,895	21,674	30,165	43,989	46%
Income from operations	2,371	3,501	3,971	7,004	13,302	90%
Net income	$ 1,236	$ 1,755	$ 2,296	$ 4,078	$ 7,806	91%
Net income per common share	$ .17	$ .24	$ .30	$ .52	$ .97	87%
Weighted average common shares outstanding	7,183,817	7,395,885	7,577,402	7,859,927	8,032,186	2%
Balance Sheet Data:						
Working capital	$ 2,459	$ 3,528	$ 5,143	$ 8,744	$28,285	223%
Total assets	9,204	11,471	14,720	20,913	43,400	108%
Total liabilities	5,500	5,968	6,527	7,883	7,902	2%
Long-term debt, excluding current maturities	1,492	1,687	755	898	0	(100%)
Total shareholders' equity	3,704	5,503	8,193	13,030	35,498	172%

[3]

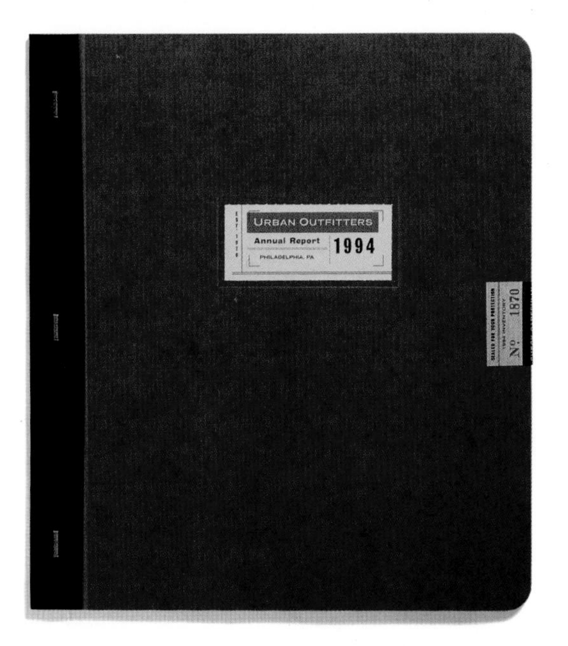

prior fiscal year, a 30.8% increase. As a percentage of net sales, such expenses decreased to 39.2% in fiscal 1993 from 40.3% in the prior fiscal year. The percentage reduction is attributable to the operating leverage resulting from a 34.7% increase in net sales compared to an increase in selling, general and administrative expenses of only 30.8%. The year to year aggregate increase in selling, general and administrative expenses was primarily attributable to the additional infrastructure required to support the increases in comparable store net sales, new stores and Wholesale's increase in net sales.

Net income increased to $4.1 million in fiscal 1993 from $2.3 million in the prior fiscal year, a 77.6% increase. This increase was principally achieved through the increases in net sales and gross profit margins and was partially offset by an increase in the Company's effective income tax rate from 38.1% to 40.5% which was due primarily to higher state income taxes.

LIQUIDITY AND CAPITAL RESOURCES

During the last three years the Company has satisfied its cash requirements through cash flow from operations. The Company's primary uses of cash have been to open new stores, purchase inventories, retire debt and repurchase shares. In addition to cash generated from operations, sources of cash have also included $500,000 of senior long-term borrowing in fiscal 1992 and 1993 and net proceeds from the exercise of certain warrants and employee stock options in each of fiscal 1992, 1993 and 1994. Over the next few years, the Company expects to incur capital expenditures in support of its expansion program. The proceeds from the November 1993 public offering and cash from operations are expected to fund such expansion-related uses of cash.

Although the Company has not borrowed short-term funds during the last three fiscal years, it maintains a line of credit of $6.0 million, of which $1.5 million is available for cash borrowings and $4.5 million is available for issuance of letters of credit. The line is unsecured and any cash borrowings under the line would accrue interest at the prime rate. The Company uses letters of credit primarily to purchase private label and Wholesale's merchandise from offshore suppliers. Outstanding balances of letters of credit at January 31, 1993 and 1994 were $1.7 million and $3.2 million, respectively. As noted above, long-term borrowings were made in fiscal 1992 and fiscal 1993 in the amount of $500,000 each, with an aggregate principal balance outstanding of $1.3 million at January 31, 1993. This debt was repaid in the second quarter of fiscal 1994. Accordingly, there is no principal balance outstanding at January 31, 1994.

The Company expects that the combination of cash from operations and the proceeds from the November 1993 public offering will be sufficient to meet the Company's cash needs for at least the next three years.

SEASONALITY AND QUARTERLY RESULTS

While Urban Outfitters has been profitable in each of its last 16 operating quarters, its operating results are subject to seasonal fluctuations. The Company's highest sales levels have historically occurred during the five month period from August 1 to December 31 of each year. Sales generated during these periods have traditionally had a significant impact on the Company's results of operations for such periods which fall in the "back to school" and holiday seasons, and any decreases in sales for these periods or in the availability of working capital needed in the months preceding these periods could have a material adverse effect on the Company's results of operations. The Company's results of operations in any one fiscal quarter are not necessarily indicative of the results of operations that can be expected for any other fiscal quarter or for the full fiscal year.

The Company's results of operations may also fluctuate from quarter to quarter as a result of the amount and timing of expenses incurred in connection with, and sales contributed by, new stores, store expansions and the integration of new stores into the operations of the Company, as well as other factors. The addition of a large number of new stores can therefore significantly affect results of operations on a quarter to quarter basis.

[10]

QUARTERLY TABLES

The following tables, which are unaudited, set forth the Company's net sales and net income for each quarter during the last three fiscal years and the amount of such net sales and net income, respectively, as a percentage of annual net sales and annual net income.

Fiscal 1992 Quarter Ended (Dollars in thousands)

	April 30, 1991	July 31, 1991	Oct. 31, 1991	Jan. 31, 1992
Net sales	$ 9,002	$10,363	$12,508	$12,018
Net income	455	448	928	465
As a Percentage of Fiscal:				
Net sales	21%	24%	28%	27%
Net income	20	20	40	20

Fiscal 1993 Quarter Ended (Dollars in thousands)

	April 30, 1992	July 31, 1992	Oct. 31, 1992	Jan. 31, 1993
Net sales	$11,033	$12,820	$17,186	$18,096
Net income	495	727	1,840	1,016
As a Percentage of Fiscal:				
Net sales	19%	22%	29%	30%
Net income	12	18	45	25

Fiscal 1994 Quarter Ended (Dollars in thousands)

	April 30, 1993	July 31, 1993	Oct. 31, 1993	Jan. 31, 1994
Net sales	$17,309	$19,431	$24,289	$23,457
Net income	1,346	1,366	3,150	1,944
As a Percentage of Fiscal:				
Net sales	20%	23%	29%	28%
Net income	17	18	40	25

[11]

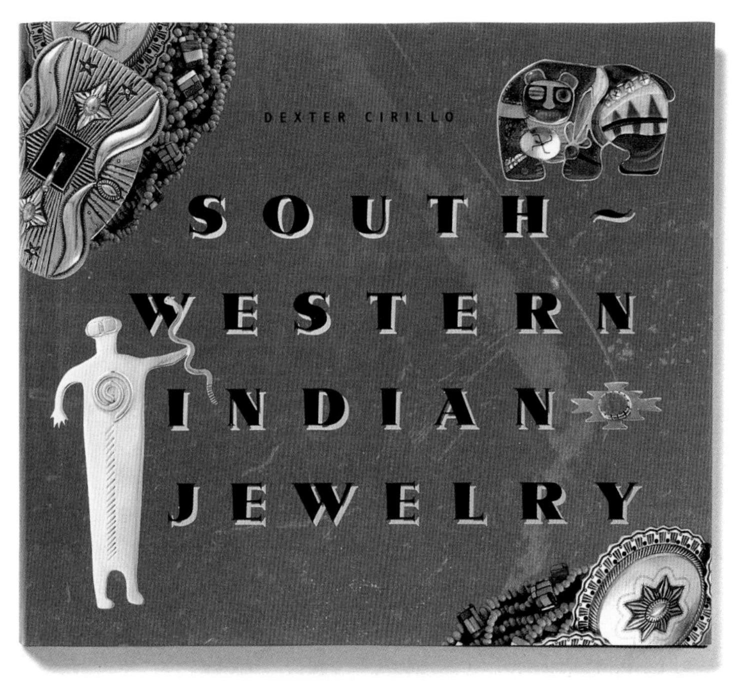

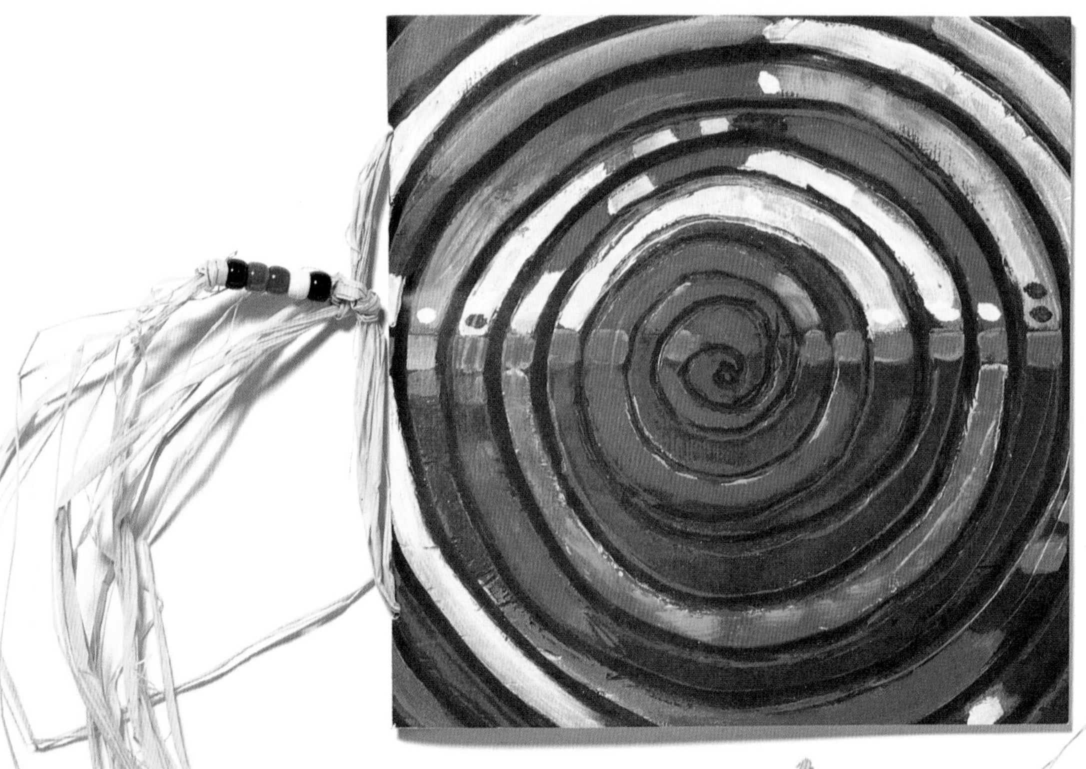

■ 1 Art Director: RENÉE KHATAMI Designer: CELIA FULLER Photographer: MICHEL MONTEAUX Publisher: ABBEVILLE PRESS Country: USA ■ 2 Art Director: MEGAN BARRA Designer: MEGAN BARRA Photographer: ROBLEY DUPLEIX Design Firm: TRINITY DESIGN Publisher: UNIVERSITY ART MUSEUM Country: USA ■ 3–5 Art Direction: CONSTANCE KAINE, WILLIAM A. EWING Editor Original Edition: CATHERINE LAMB Editor U.S. Edition: CAROLINE HERTER Photographers: TONO STANO (3, 5), LUCAS SAMARAS, COURTESY PACE/MACGILL GALLERY, NEW YORK (4) Cover shown: U.S. EDITION Cover Design U.S. Edition: TENAZAS DESIGN Author: WILLIAM A. EWING Orignal Publisher: THAMES AND HUDSON U.S. Publisher: CHRONICLE BOOKS Country: USA

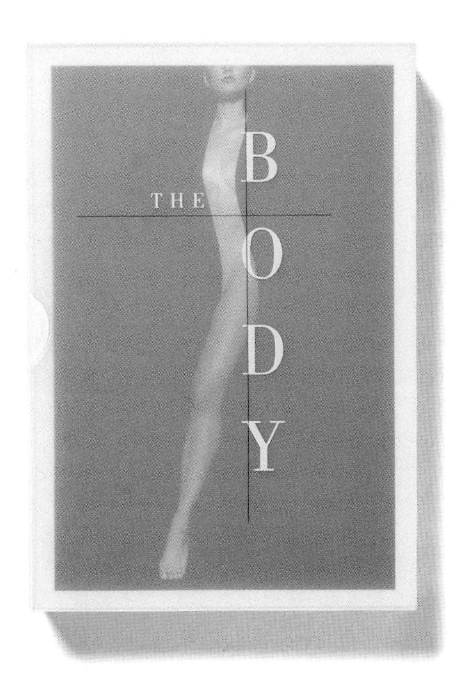
THE
BODY

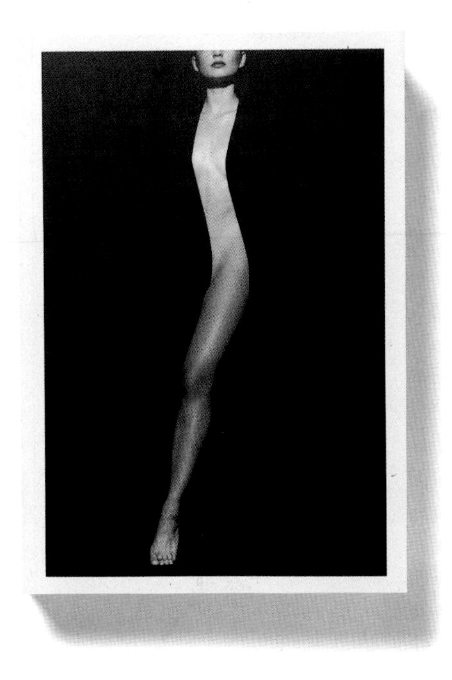

LIGHT LAND

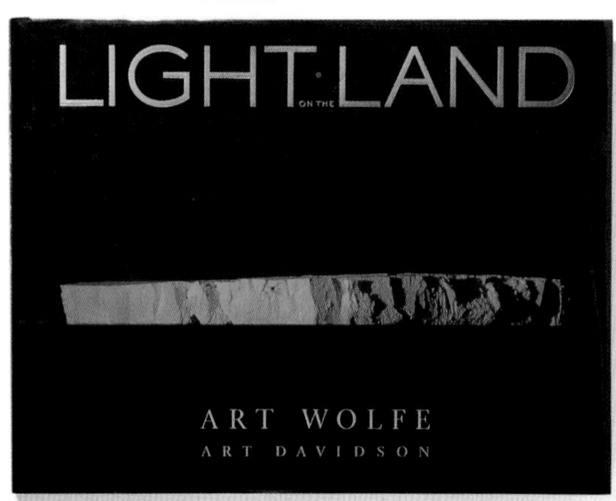
LIGHT ON THE LAND
ART WOLFE
ART DAVIDSON

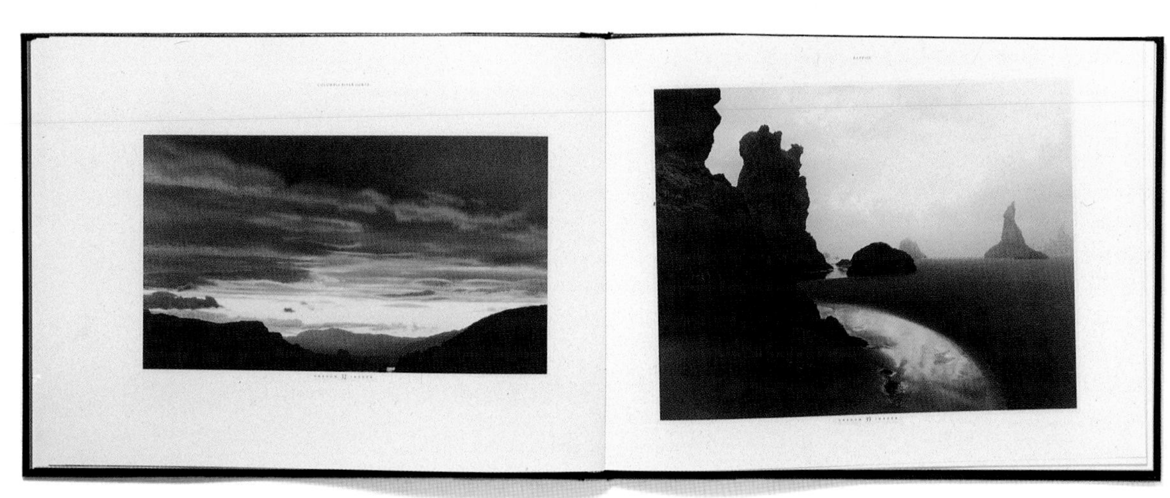

■ (PRECEDING SPREAD) 1–4 ART DIRECTORS: ROBIN RICKABAUGH, HEIDI RICKABAUGH DESIGNERS: PAUL MORT, ROBIN RICKABAUGH PHOTOGRAPHER: ART WOLFE DESIGN FIRM: PRINCIPIA GRAPHICA PUBLISHER: BEYOND WORDS PUBLISHING, INC. COUNTRY: USA ■ 5–8 ART DIRECTORS: ROBIN RICKABAUGH, HEIDI RICKABAUGH DESIGNERS: JON OLSEN, ROBIN RICKABAUGH PHOTOGRAPHER: JERRY V. HUNT

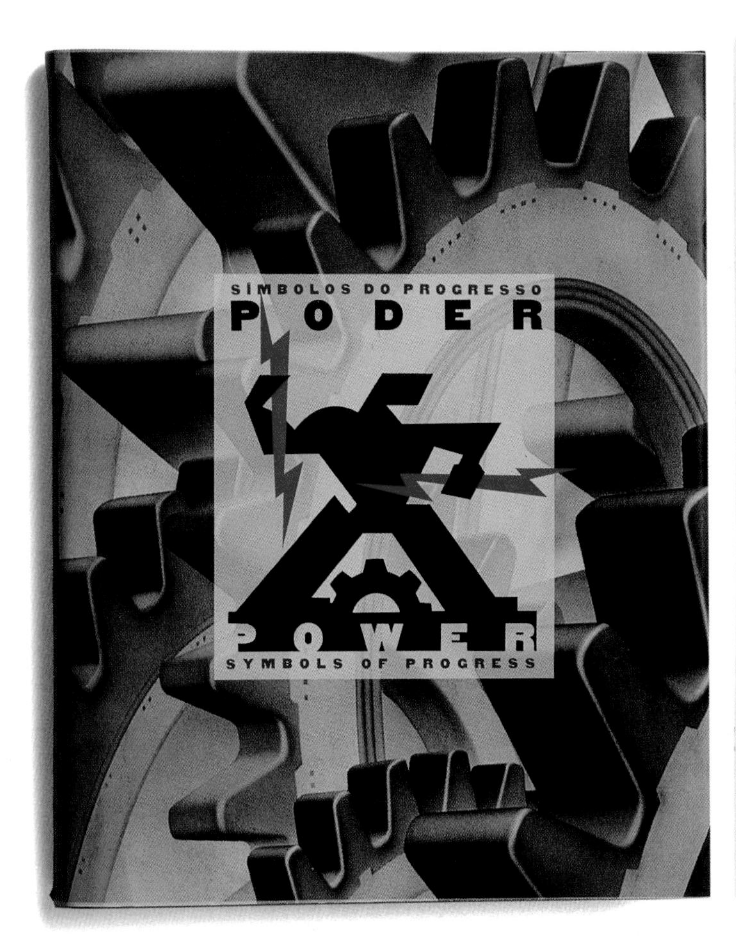

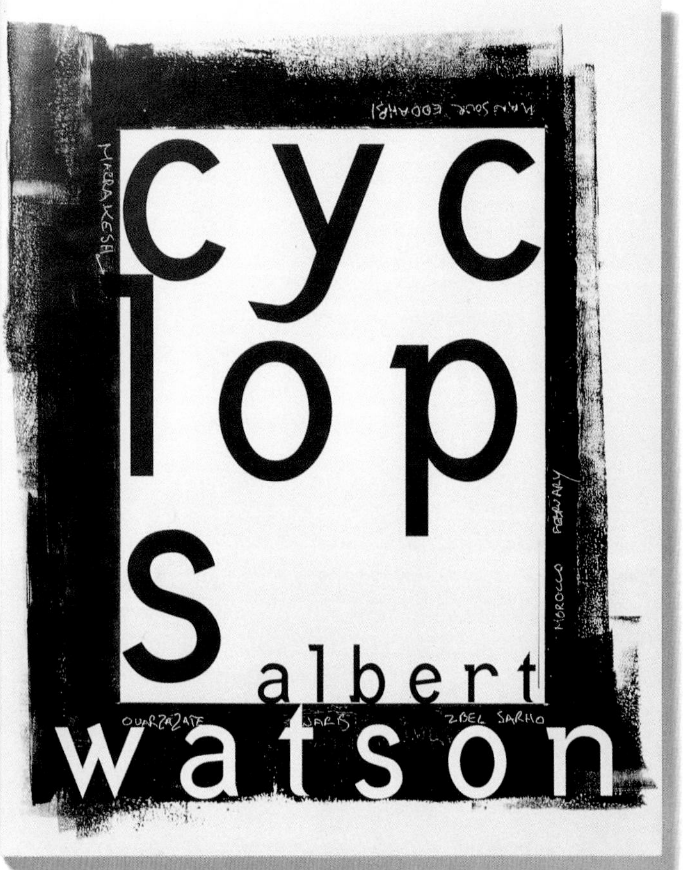

PUBLISHER: JERRY V. HUNT DESIGN FIRM: PRINCIPIA GRAPHICA COUNTRY: USA ■ (THIS SPREAD) 1 ART DIRECTOR/DESIGNER: OSWALDO MIRANDA STUDIO: CASA DE IDE'IAS PUBLISHER: CASA DE IDE'IAS EDITORA COUNTRY: BRASIL ■ 2–8 ART DIRECTOR/DESIGNER: DAVID CARSON PHOTOGRAPHER: ALBERT WATSON PHOTO EDITOR: LAURIE KRATOCHVIL PUBLISHER: CALLAWAY EDITIONS COUNTRY: USA

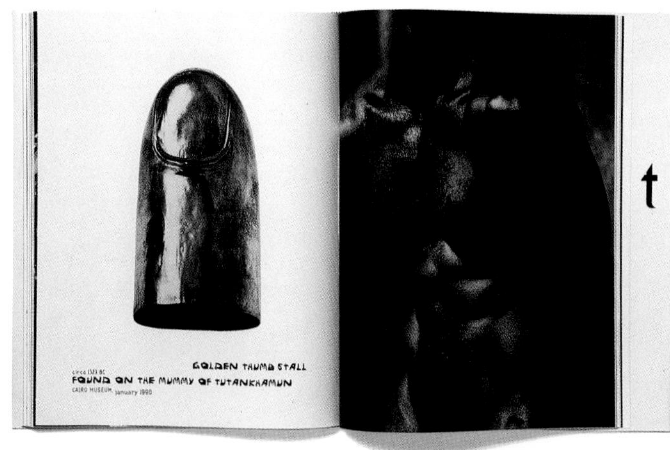
GOLDEN THUMB STALL
FOUND ON THE MUMMY OF TUTANKHAMUN
t

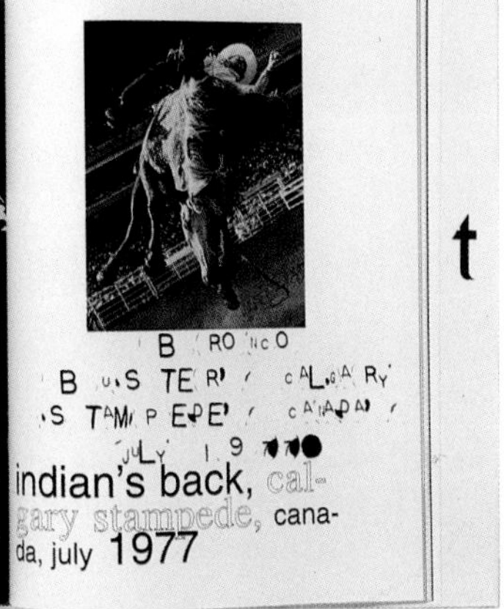
t
indian's back, calgary stampede, canada, july 1977

< bobby brown,

■ 1, 2 DESIGNER: MICHELLE MARTINO PHOTOGRAPHERS: DAVID HEALD, LEE EWING DESIGN FIRM: GUGGENHEIM MUSEUM DESIGN DEPT. PUBLISHER: GUGGENHEIM MUSEUM/SOLOMON R. COUNTRY: USA ■ 3, 4 ART DIRECTOR: LINDA COLE ART EDITOR/DESIGNER: TINA NEVILLE MANAGING ART

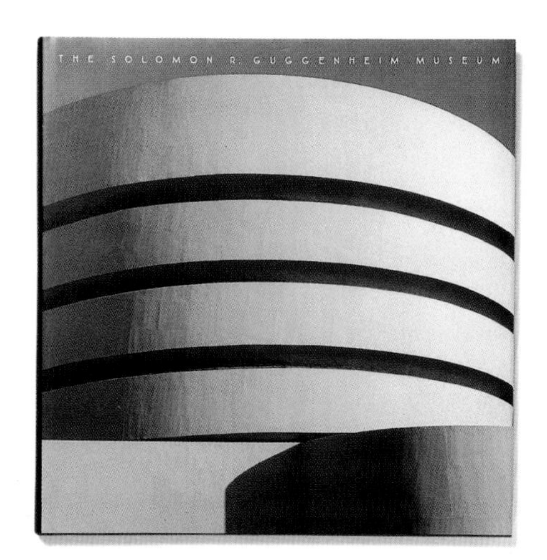

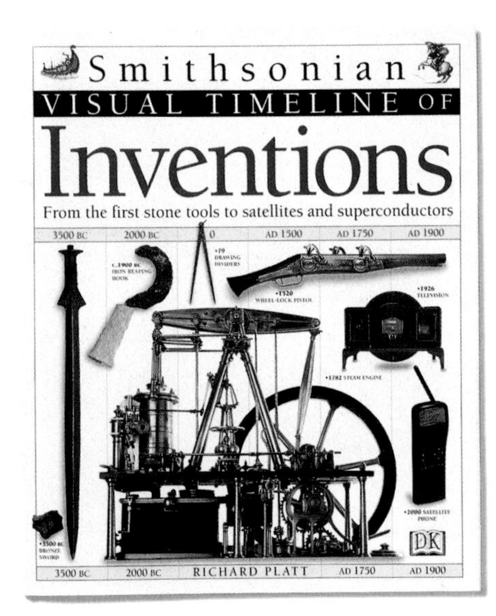

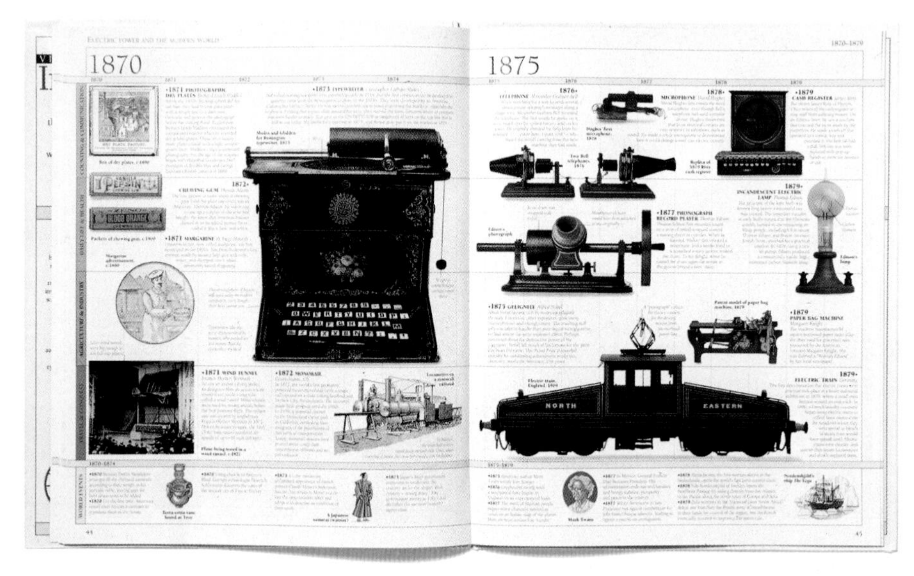

EDITOR: PETER BAILEY PHOTOGRAPHER: MARK GULEZIAN/QUICKSILVER PHOTOGRAPHERS ILLUSTRATORS: RUSSELL BARNETT, NICK SHEWRING DESIGN FIRM/PUBLISHER: DORLING KINDERSLEY PUBLISHING INC. COUNTRIES: GREAT BRITAIN, USA ■ 5–11 ART DIRECTOR: SAM SHAHID PHOTOGRAPHER: HERB RITTS PHOTO EDITOR: LAURIE KRATOCHVIL PUBLISHER: LITTLE, BROWN & COMPANY/BULFINCH PRESS COUNTRY: USA

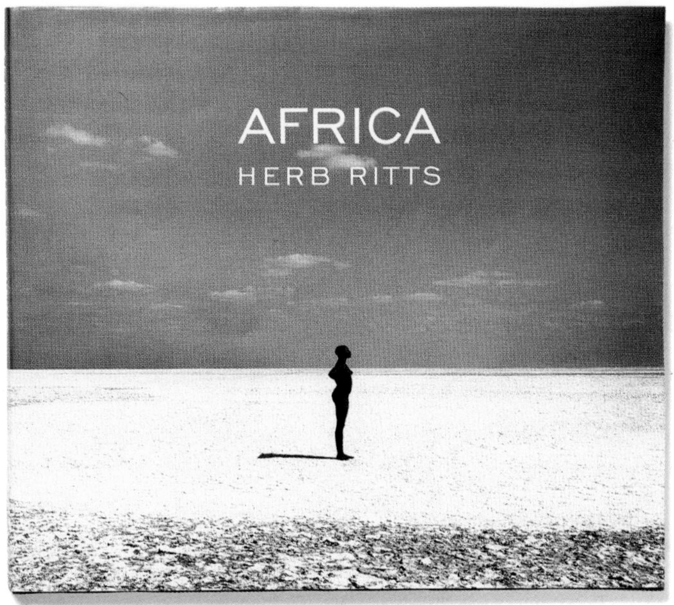
AFRICA
HERB RITTS

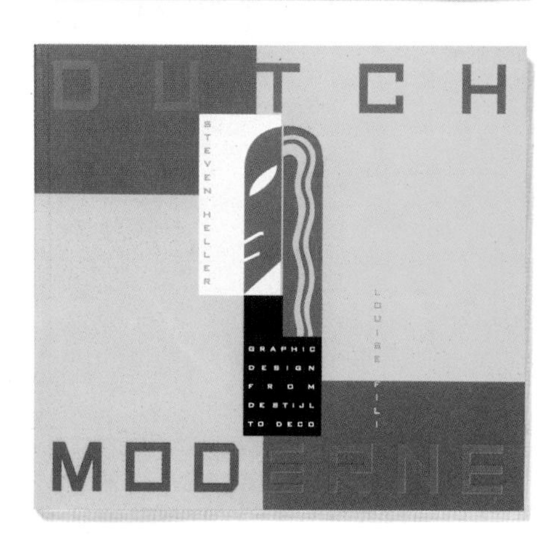

THE RENAISSANCE OF DUTCH TYPOGRAPHY IN THE EARLY TWENTIETH CENTURY SPRANG FROM BOTH THE RESURGENCE OF TRADITIONAL FORMS AND THE DEVELOPMENT OF AVANT-GARDE APPROACHES. THE TRADITIONALISTS BELIEVED THAT THE MOST FUNCTIONAL TYPOGRAPHY WAS ELEGANT **TYPOGRAPHY** AND "INVISIBLE." THEY REEVALUATED TYPOGRAPHIC STANDARDS WITH THE PRIMARY GOAL OF PROVIDING THE WRITER WITH THE TOOLS OF COMMUNICATION. THE AVANT-GARDE BELIEVED THAT TYPE HAD AN AUTONOMOUS FUNCTION, AND THEY USED ALL AVAILABLE MEANS TO EMPHASIZE "EXPRESSIVE, ASSOCIATIVE, AND PLASTIC POSSIBILITIES WITH THE FORMS OF LETTERS THEMSELVES" (KEES BOOS, IN FRIEDMAN, 1982). THE TRADITIONALISTS REESTABLISHED ORDER AND CREATED A NEED FOR SERIOUS TYPOGRAPHERS IN A FIELD DEBASED BY POOR AESTHETICS; THE MODERNISTS TESTED THE LIMITS OF TYPOGRAPHIC EXPRESSION AND PUSHED THE BOUNDARIES OF PLASTIC FORM. TUCKED BETWEEN THE TWO EXTREMES WAS AN ECLECTIC MANNER USED BY THE MAJORITY OF DUTCH BUSINESSES FOR ADVERTISING AND LOGOS. SOME TYPOGRAPHIC INNOVATIONS WERE INFLUENCED BY THE TWO FORMAL SCHOOLS, BUT MOST WERE UNTHEORETICAL SOLUTIONS TO COMMERCIAL PROBLEMS. THE LETTERING RANGED FROM THE UNREPENTANTLY OLD-FASHIONED TO THE PROUDLY EXPRESSIONISTIC. OF THESE, THE ONES THAT WERE DISTINCTLY DUTCH EVOLVED FROM WENDINGEN STYLE DECORATIVISM.

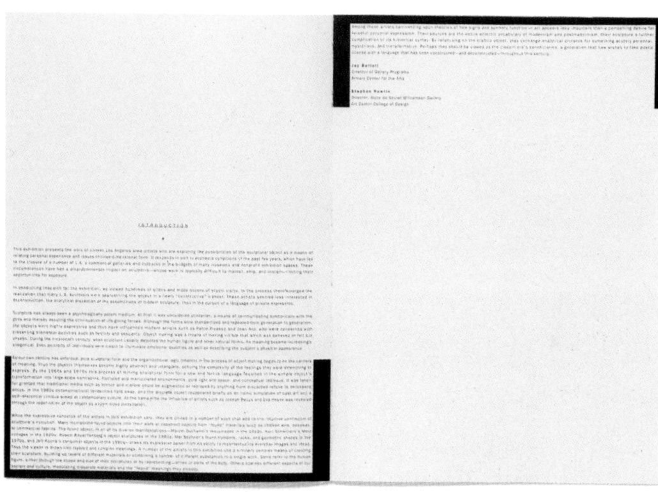

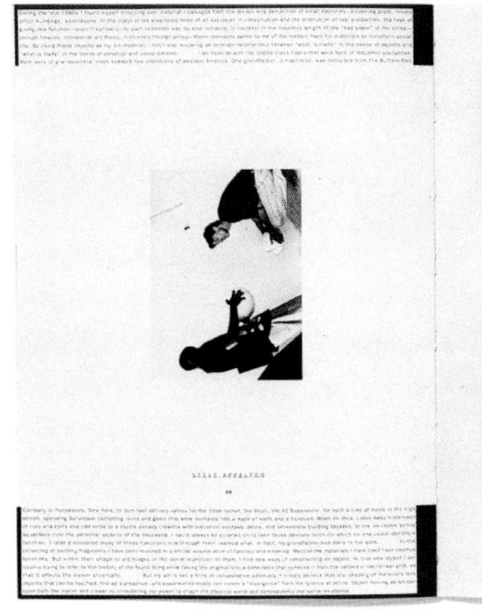

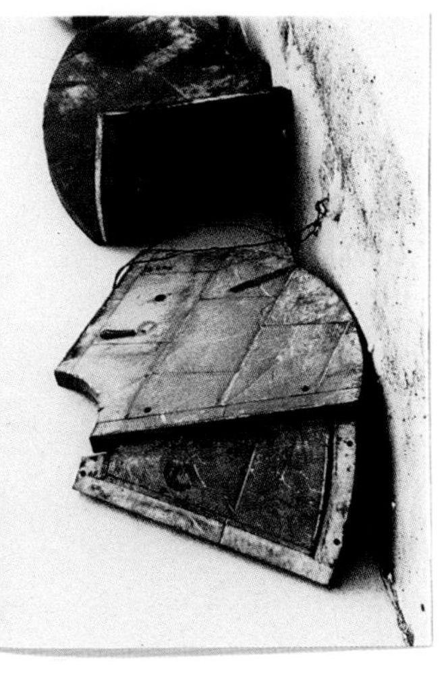

■ 1, 2 DESIGNER: MITSUO KATSUI DESIGN FIRM: KATSUI DESIGN OFFICE INC. CLIENT: PHILADELPHIA MUSEUM OF ART COUNTRY: USA ■ 3, 4 ART DIRECTORS: ROBIN RICKABAUGH, HEIDI RICKABAUGH DESIGNERS: JON OLSEN, ROBIN RICKABAUGH PHOTOGRAPHER: ART WOLFE DESIGN FIRM: PRINCIPIA GRAPHICA PUBLISHER: BEYOND WORDS PUBLISHING, INC. COUNTRY: USA ■ 5, 6 ART DIRECTOR: LOUISE FILI DESIGNERS: LOUISE FILI, LEAH LOCOCO PUBLISHER: CHRONICLE BOOKS COUNTRY: USA ■ 7–10 ART DIRECTOR: REBECA MENDEZ DESIGNER: DARIN BEAMAN DESIGN FIRM: ART CENTER DESIGN OFFICE COUNTRY: USA

■ 1, 2 ART DIRECTOR: GARRY EMERY DESIGNER: EMERY VINCENT ASSOCIATES CLIENT: ASIALINK COUNTRY: AUSTRALIA ■ 3 ART DIRECTOR/DESIGNER: MICHAEL JOHNSON DESIGN FIRM: JOHNSON DAVIES CLIENT: THE DESIGNERS AND ART DIRECTORS ASSOCIATION OF THE UNITED KINGDOM COUNTRY: GREAT BRITAIN ■ 4 ART DIRECTOR/DESIGNER: KLAUS BIETZ DESIGN FIRM: HWL + PARTNER DESIGN CLIENT: MANNHEIMER VERSICHERUNG COUNTRY: GERMANY ■ 5-12 AUSTRIA ART DIRECTORS ANNUAL ART DIRECTORS: PETER SCHMID, MIKE HIRSCHL PHOTOGRAPHERS: ROBERT STRIEGL, GERHARD MERZEDER PUBLISHER/CLIENT: CREATIV CLUB AUSTRIA COUNTRY: AUSTRIA

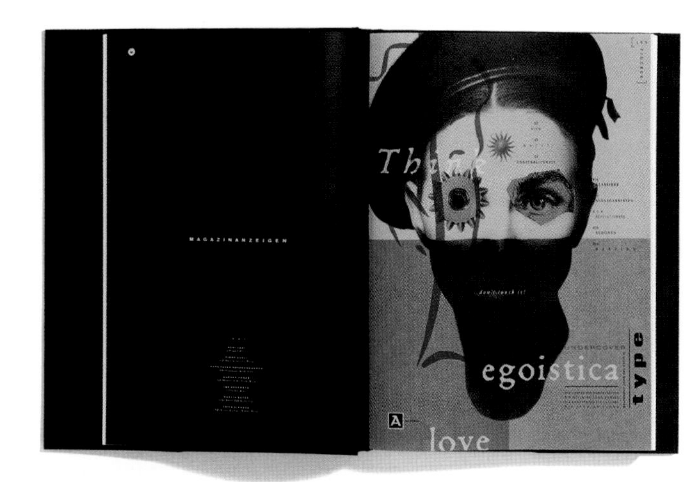
MAGAZINANZEIGEN
egoistica
type
love

FOTO · ILLUSTRATION
spielen
Mit Licht

PLAKATE
新三共胃腸薬（顆粒）
£4.44
POP CORN

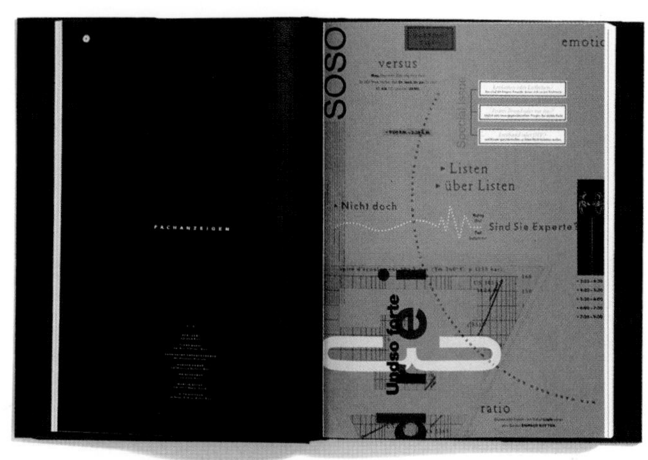
FACHANZEIGEN
soso
versus
Listen
über Listen
Nicht doch
Sind Sie Experte?
ratio

DESIGN

PACKAGING
Barbie
Ken

TV-SPOTS
JETZT: DIE

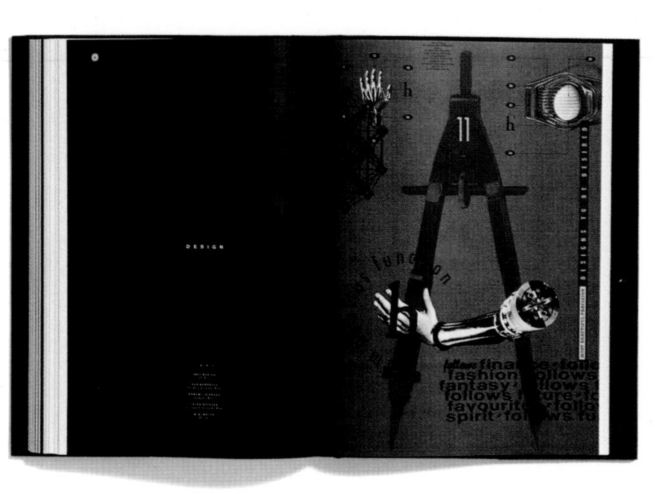
DESIGN

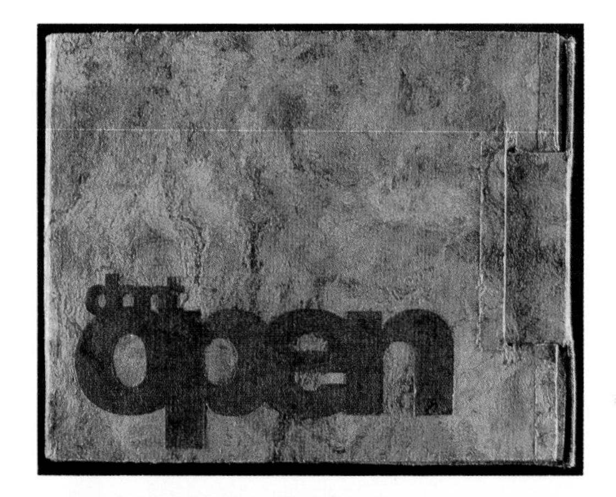

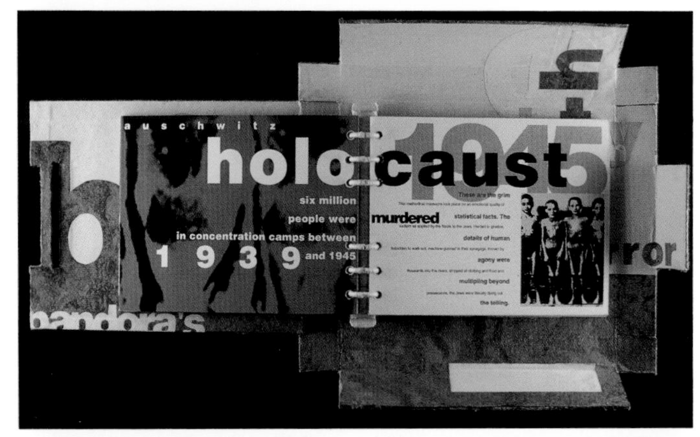

■ 1–8 DESIGNER: SPIROS DRAKATOS COUNTRY: GREAT BRITAIN ■ 9, 10 ART DIRECTOR: DAVID POCKNELL DESIGNERS: DAVID POCKNELL, MANDY NOLAN PHOTOGRAPHER: COLIN TURNER (10) DESIGN FIRM: PENTAGRAM DESIGN PUBLISHER: PHAIDON PRESS COUNTRY: GREAT BRITAIN ■ 11, 12 ART DIRECTOR: SEAN PERKINS DESIGNER: WENDELIN HESS PHOTOGRAPHER: RICHARD J. BURBRIDGE PUBLISHER: BOOTH-CLIBBORN EDITIONS COUNTRY: GREAT BRITAIN

'contemporary'
architecture and interiors of the 1950s
Lesley Jackson
PHAIDON

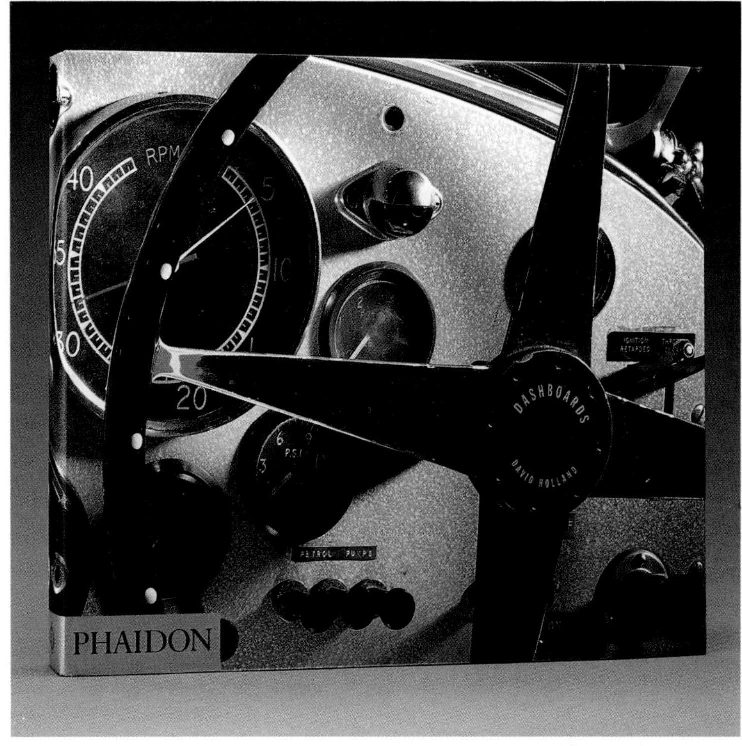
RPM
DASHBOARDS
DAVID HOLLAND
PETROL PUMPS
PHAIDON

rick poynor

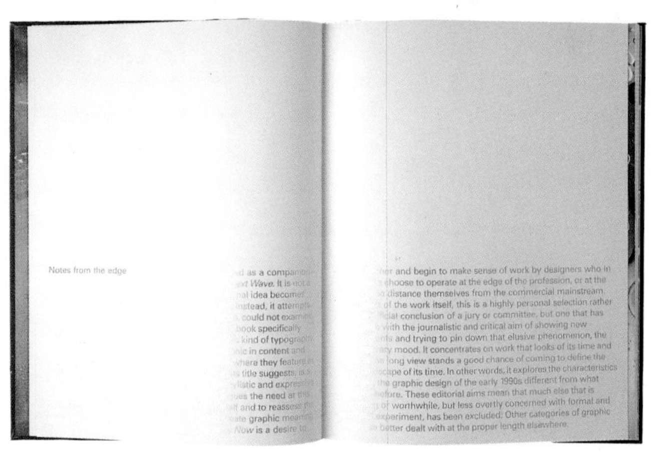
Notes from the edge

■ 1 ART DIRECTOR: VICTOR WEAVER DESIGNER/ILLUSTRATOR: MICHAEL SCHWAB STUDIO: MICHAEL SCHWAB PUBLISHER: HYPERION/DISNEY PUBLISHING COUNTRY: USA ■ 2 ART DIRECTOR/DESIGNER: PAUL BUCKLEY ILLUSTRATOR: COURTESY OF BATTLE CREEK

ADVENTISTS HOSPITAL/GARTH "DUFF" STOLTZ PUBLISHER: PENGUIN USA COUNTRY: USA ■ 3–5 ART DIRECTOR: STÉPHANIE BOLLIGER DESIGNER: STÉPHANIE BOLLIGER CLIENT: STÉPHANIE BOLLIGER DESIGN FIRM: BOLLIGER DESIGN STUDIO COUNTRY: SWITZERLAND

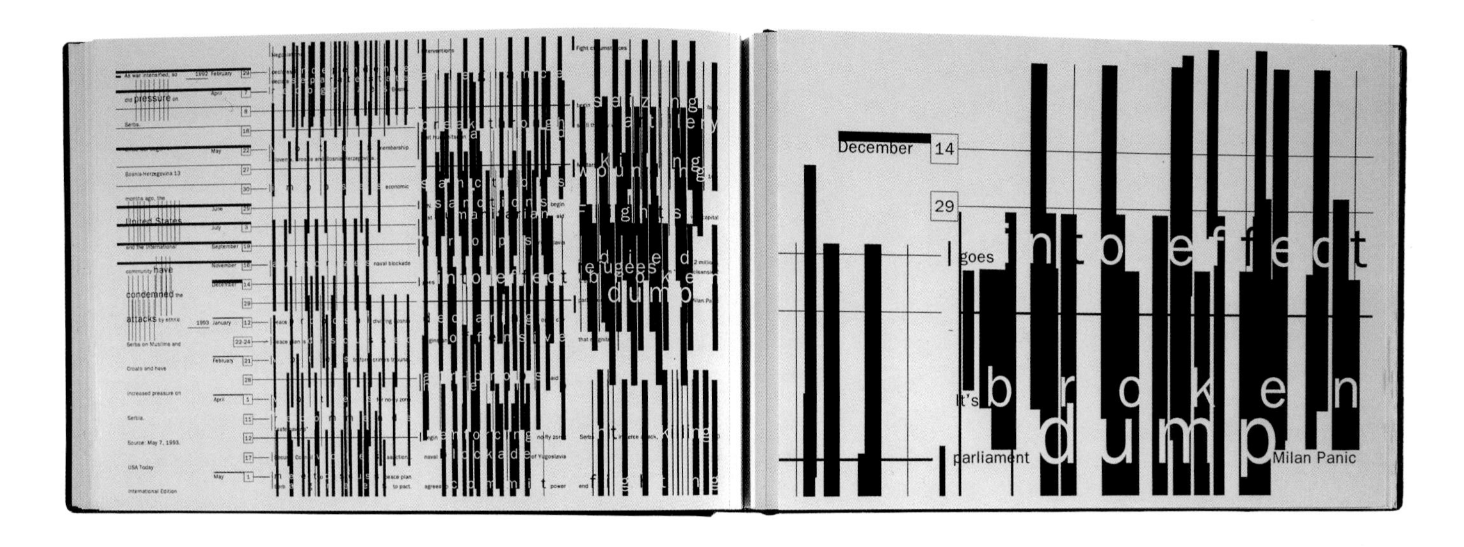
December
14
29
goes
into effect
it's
broken
dump
parliament
Milan Panic

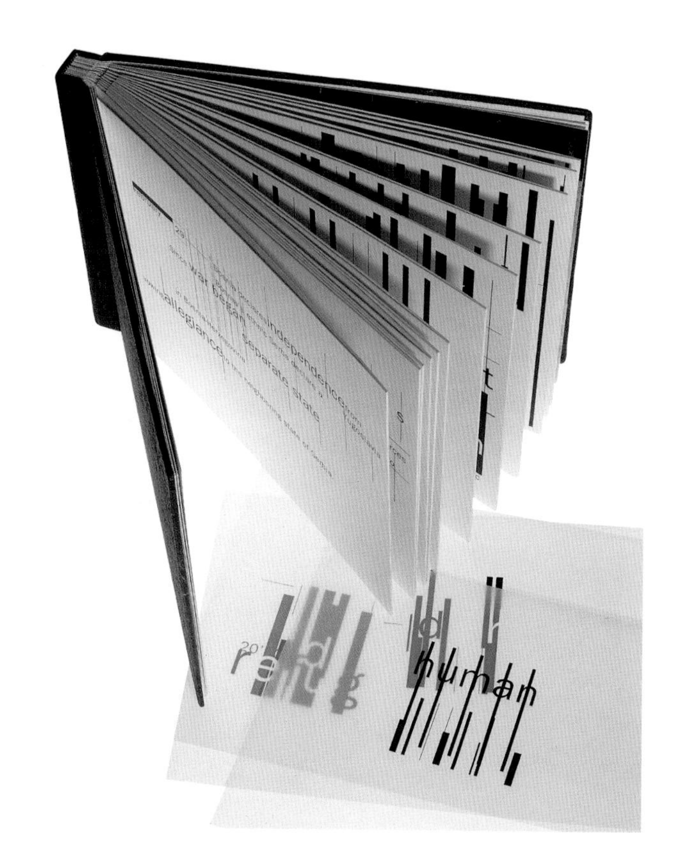
human

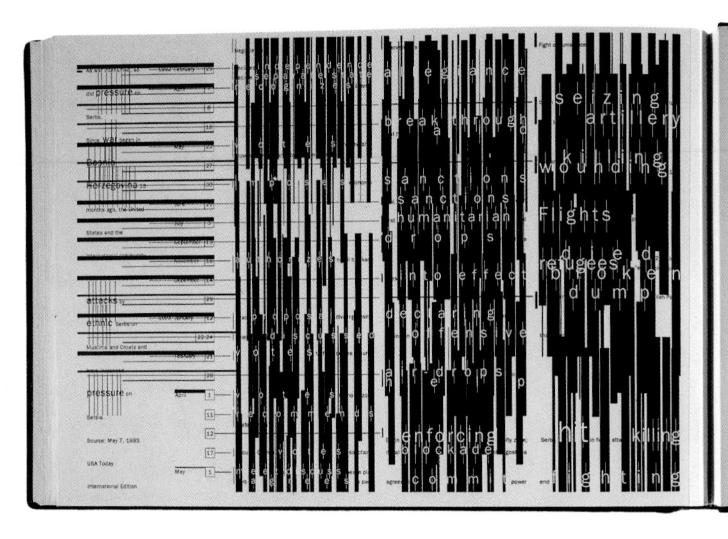
pressure
seizing
artillery
break through
killing
wounding
sanctions
humanitarian
Flights
drops
refugees
into effect
broken
dump
declaring
offensive
air drops
enforcing
blockade
hit
killing

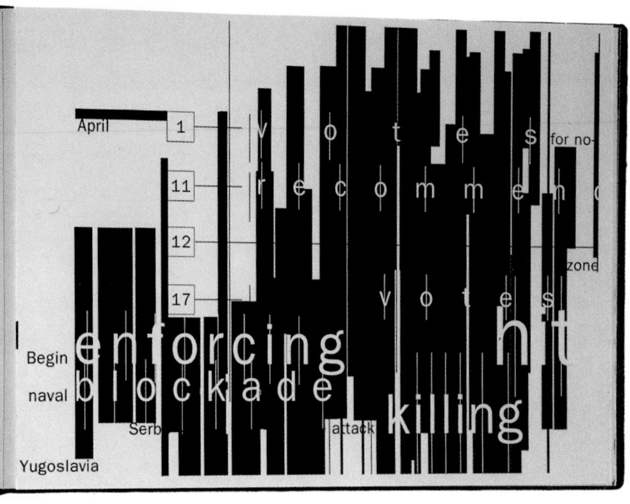
April
1
votes
for no-
11
recommend
12
zone
17
votes
Begin
enforcing
hit
naval
blockade
killing
Serb
attack
Yugoslavia

■ 1 ART DIRECTOR/DESIGNER: MICHAEL TOBIN PHOTOGRAPHER: PETER MOREHAND DESIGN FIRM: RITTA & ASSOCIATES CLIENT: BMW OF NORTH AMERICA, INC. COUNTRY: USA ■ 2-9 ART DIRECTOR: ANTHONY RUTKA DESIGNER: PRISCILLA HENDERER PHOTOGRAPHER: DAVID ZICKL ILLUSTRATOR: VARIOUS DESIGN FIRM: RUTKA WEADOCK DESIGN CLIENT: HARTWICK COLLEGE COUNTRY: USA

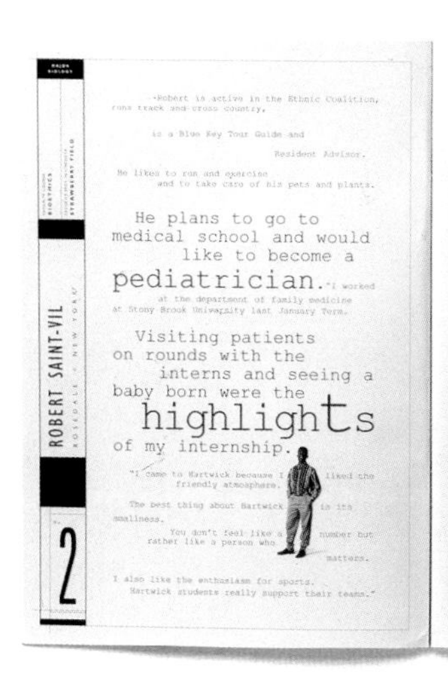
He plans to go to medical school and would like to become a pediatrician.
Visiting patients on rounds with the interns and seeing a baby born were the highlights of my internship.
ROBERT SAINT-VIL
2

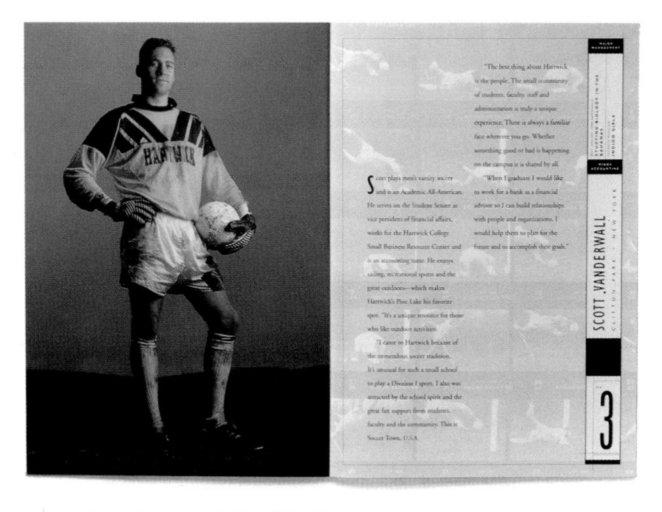
SCOTT VANDERWALL
3

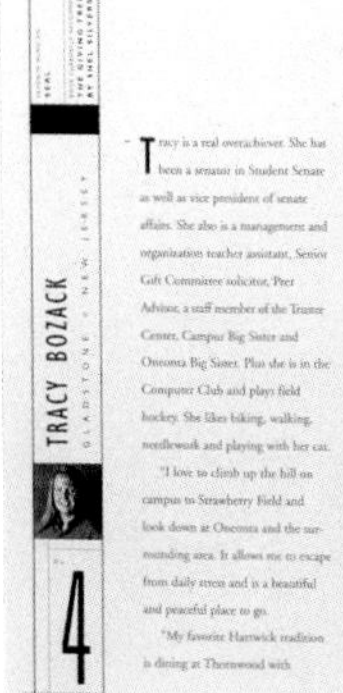
TRACY BOZACK
4

GREGG IS MANAGER OF ARTHAUS; PRESIDENT OF THE MEN'S VOLLEYBALL CLUB; PRESIDENT OF UNTITLED, THE ART CLUB; A PEER COUNSELOR; AND SERVES ON THE SPECIAL HEARING BOARD OF THE COLLEGE JUDICIAL SYSTEM. HE LIKES TO READ, PLAY DRUMS, WRITE SUBVERSIVE CAMPUS NEWSPAPERS, DRAW, TEACH ART AND WORK WITH CHILDREN. IN FACT, HIS BEST JANUARY TERM EXPERIENCE WAS PAINTING AND DRAWING IN THE CARIBBEAN WHICH HE SPENT "DRAWING, PAINTING, TEACHING AND LEARNING FROM A LARGE GROUP OF CHILDREN WHO GATHERED AROUND ME AT GROS-ISLET, ST. LUCIA. WHEN I GRADUATE I WOULD LIKE TO CONTINUE MY ART AND TO TEACH AND SHARE WITH OTHERS. "I CAME TO HARTWICK BECAUSE I FELL IN LOVE WITH THE FACILITIES AND STAFF AT THE SUMMER STUDIO ARTS WORKSHOP I ATTENDED HERE. THE BEST THING ABOUT HARTWICK IS THE CLOSE RELATIONSHIPS WHICH DEVELOP BETWEEN THE PROFESSORS AND STUDENTS."
GREGG VANCE EMERY
5

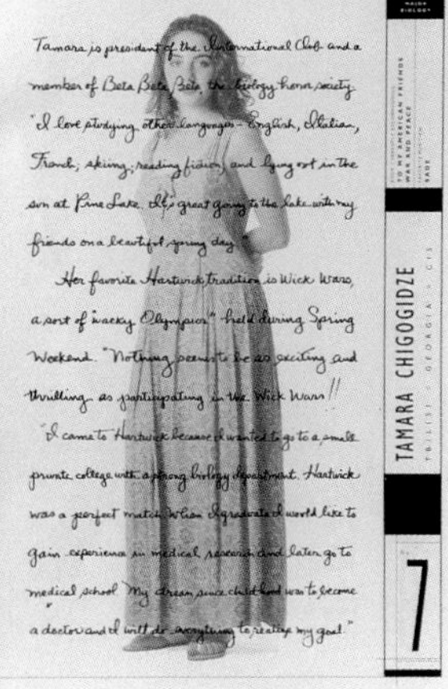
TAMARA CHIGOGIDZE
7

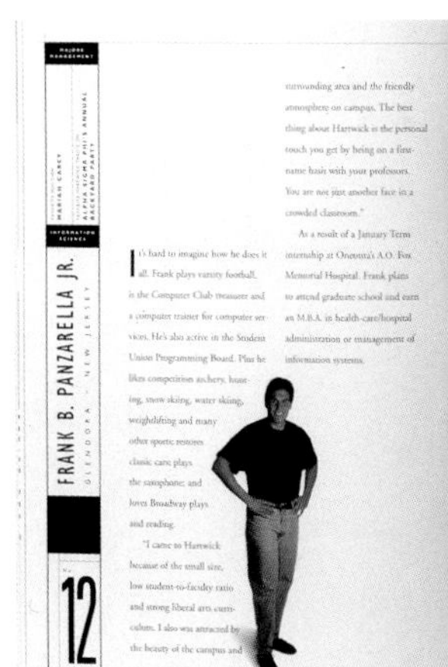
FRANK B. PANZARELLA JR.
12

YAGER HALL
ETHICS & RELIGION
FRIENDSHIP
BLUE KEY
FALL
TRAVELING
STUDENT SENATE
VICE PRESIDENT
LAW
SCHOOL
HOLIDAY DINNERS
WORKING OUT
SPRING
DANCING
YAGER HALL
ETHICS
RELIGION
FRIENDSHIP · BLUE KEY
FALL · TRAVELING
STUDENT SENATE
VICE PRESIDENT
LAW SCHOOL

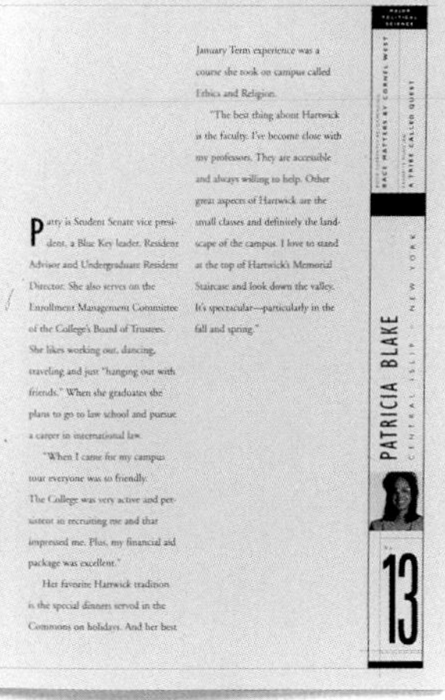
PATRICIA BLAKE
13

AMY ROWE
14

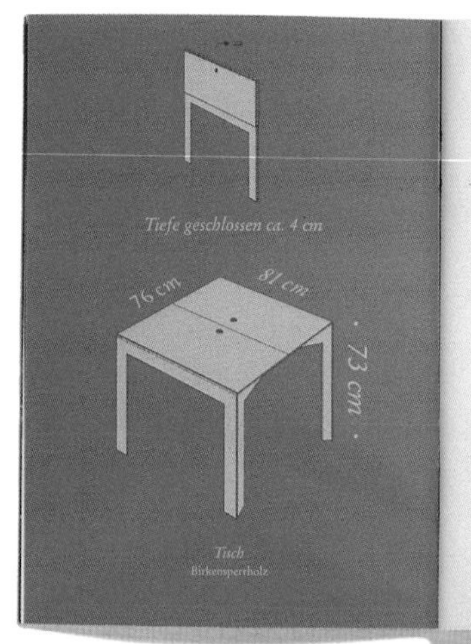

Gut Holz!
Der Klapptisch LAST MINUTE
Für gewöhnlich haftet jeder Art von Klappmöbel etwas wackeliges, und damit immer der Hautgoût des billig, provisorischen an, wobei dieser Negativ-Touch jedoch in den gekonnten Modellen durch praktische Handhabung, geringeres Gewicht und damit verbunden günstigem Preis wettgemacht wird. Bei Hauke Murkens Klapptisch LAST MINUTE hingegen sucht man das markante Gestellimage dieser Möbelspezies vergeblich. Nichts da mit Scharnieren, klapperdürren Tischbeinen oder quietschendem Scherengitter. Und auch die Tischoberfläche gibt keine unmittelbaren Hinweise auf die raumsparende Faltqualität. Stattdessen von oben und von der Seite flächige Ansichten. Die Beine und der an zwei Seiten an die Tischoberfläche bündig anschließende Unterbau messen in der Breite immerhin 8 cm und auch die Tischplatte selbst ist lediglich einmal geteilt. Alles in allem also eine gestandene Erscheinung, die uns der junge Berliner Designer Hauke Murken da hinstellt, bzw. hinhängt. Das raffinierte an der Sache liegt darin, daß die breiten Tischelemente nicht nur dem Tisch das Wackelimage nehmen, sondern daß damit eine für ein Klappmöbel überdurchschnittliche Stabilität erreicht wird und sich so eine Art Gattungsspagat vollzieht. Der Tisch vereint das Bedürfnis nach Standfestigkeit mit den »Platz da!« Wünschen in jeder Art beengter Arbeits- und Wohnumgebung. Zudem ist dieses Teil durch die intelligente Kantenausbildung fugenlos mit seinesgleichen zu kombinieren: große Festtafel, Familienspieltisch, Trinkgelage »Oans, zwoa, gsufa!«, oder Präsentation von meterlangen Planexzessen. Alles machbar! Hier läßt sichs spielen, speisen und zechen!
Also denn: Gut Holz!

Volker Albus

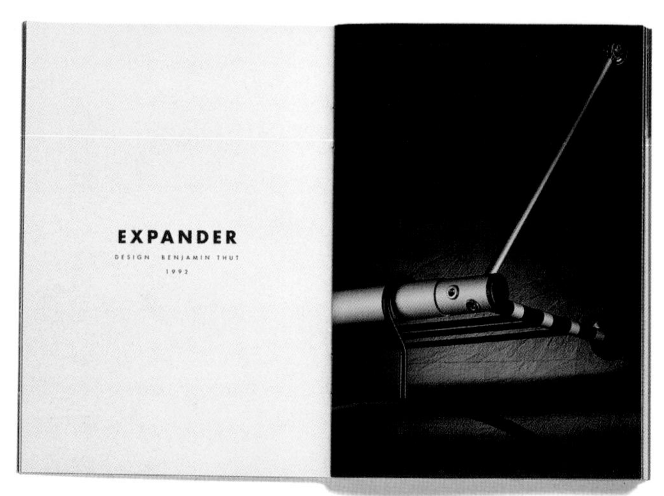

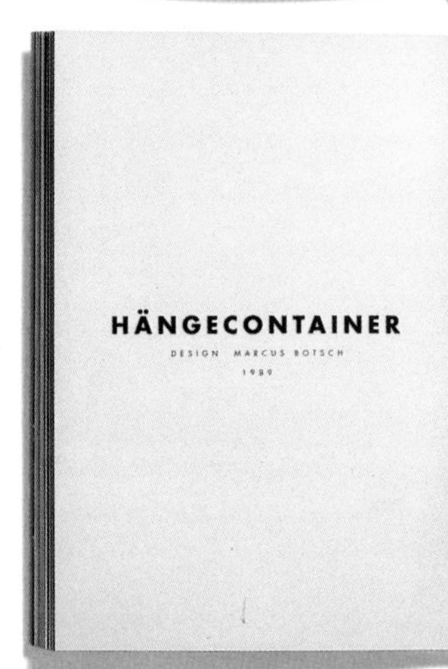

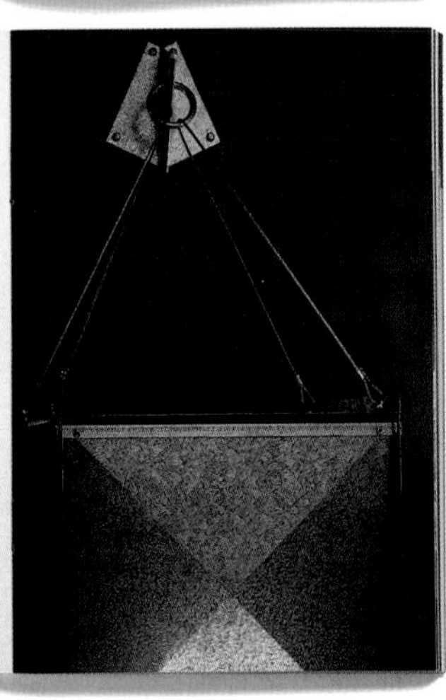

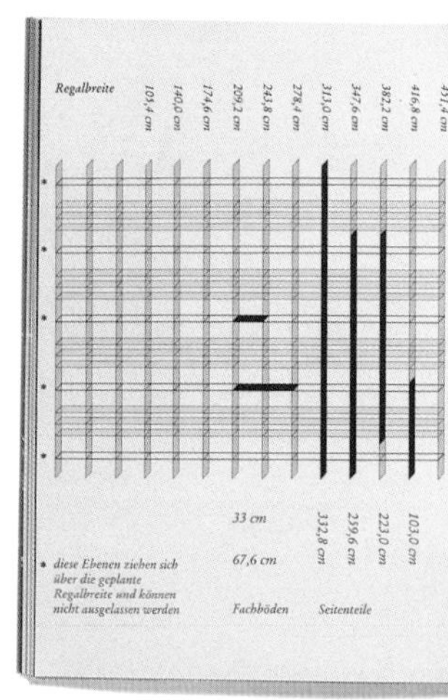

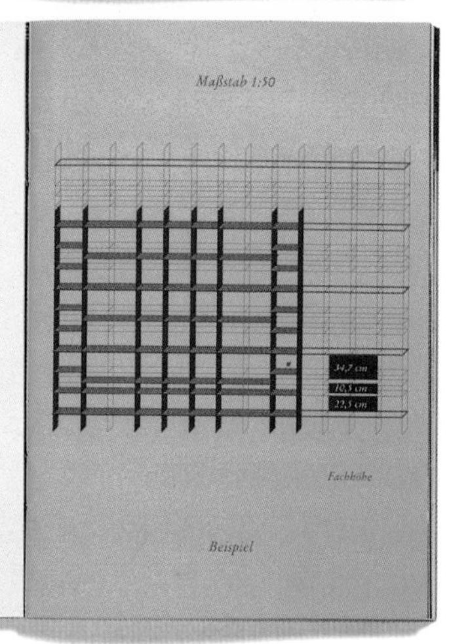

Die Seite hält die Schiene.
Die Schiene hält den Boden.
Der Boden hält die Schiene.
Die Schiene hält die Seite.
29 cm
332,8 cm
259,6 cm
223 cm
103 cm
34 cm
67,6 cm
33 cm

Regalsystem
Das Material ermöglicht die einfache Konstruktion: zu Platten gepreßte Holzfasern, MDF 16 mm, in Steckverbindung mit Aluminium-Schienen

*Das Raster gliedert Höhe und Breite: in der Planungsmappe mit * gekennzeichnete Ebenen ziehen sich über die geplante Regalbreite und können nicht ausgelassen werden. Der Raum zwischen den * Ebenen ist variabel. Halbiert ergeben sich A4-Fächer für Ordner, Bücher, Schallplatten – gedrittelt A5-Fächer für Bücher/Taschenbücher. Die Seitenteile legen die Regalhöhe fest: 103 cm, 223 cm, 259,6 cm oder 332,8 cm. Seitenteil 223 cm basiert auf derselben Rasterteilung wie Seitenteil 259,6 cm, wurde aber für Raumhöhen unter 260 cm unten auf 223 cm gekürzt. Das unterste Fach bei 223 cm hohen Regalen ist dadurch immer ein 34,7 cm hohes Fach (siehe Zeichnung in der Planungsmappe). Die Fachböden bestimmen die Regalbreite: Mindestbreite ist 105,4 cm, Maximalbreite 451,4 cm. Vertikal stehen entweder schmale oder breite Fächer übereinander. Mit Hilfe des FNP - Spannseils kann das Regal auch frei in den Raum gestellt werden.*

Das Regalsystem FNP kann als Quintessenz des bisherigen Schaffens von Axel Kufus gelten – als eine reine Struktur ist es reduziert auf die Funktionen Wangen, Böden und den Verbund mit Alu-Schienen, die ohne Werkzeug eingesteckt werden. Es ist in seinen Proportionen absolut ausgeglichen. Dieser souveräne Entwurf von 1989 wurde von den Juroren des Design Zentrums Nordrhein Westfalen im Wettbewerb »Design-Innovationen '91« für hohe Design Qualität ausgezeichnet. 1992 wurde die Einsatzmöglichkeit durch eine neuartige Verspannvorrichtung erweitert. Eine Umrüstung auch vorhandener Regale ist einfach. Lediglich vier kleine Bohrungen an genau definierten Stellen sind nötig. Die Stahldrähte verspannen jeweils 3x3 FNP-Fächer. Axel Kufus sieht die Form als unmittelbare Konsequenz aus der Funktion. „Die Proportionen ergeben sich aus der Abmessung des Halbzeugs. Es entsteht bei der Herstellung praktisch kein Verschnitt." Die Grundsätze, Transparenz des Entwurfs und Funktionalität, stehen absolut im Vordergrund. Design wird hier auf seine Grundfunktion des optimalen Dienens für einen definierten Zweck zurückgeführt.

Georg C. Bertsch

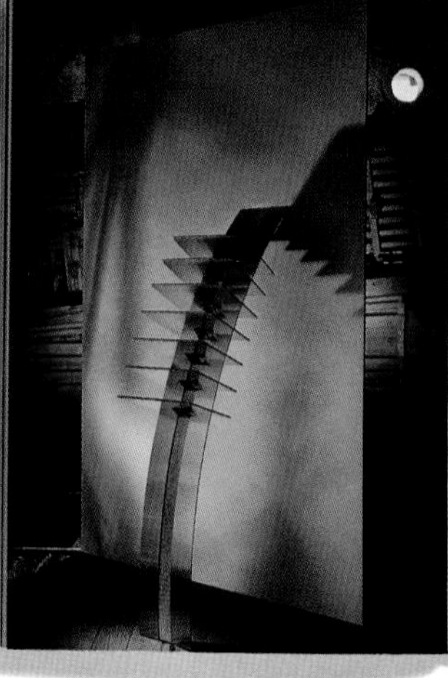

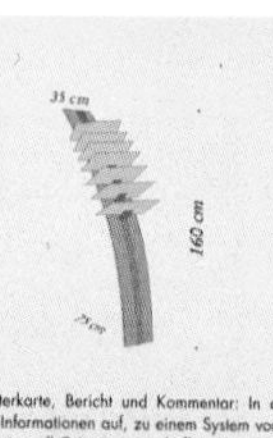

Spielplan und Wetterkarte, Bericht und Kommentar: In der Zeitung fächern sich all die Informationen auf, zu einem System von Kolumnen und Spalten. Das Raster soll Orientierung schaffen. Hier die Reportage, dort die Rezension. Doch die Verwirrung bleibt. Denn Provinz und weite Welt, Lokales und Globales sind kaum noch zu trennen. Börsenbilanz und Stellenangebot, Außen- und Innenpolitik: Die Zusammenhänge liegen auf der Hand. Die Vernetzung schreitet voran. Die Dinge geraten ins Wanken, täglich muß neu geordnet werden. Die Zeitschriftenablage TELL der Gruppe Formfürsorge folgt dem Prinzip Zeitung, schafft Ordnung und Orientierung ohne diese dogmatisch festzuschreiben. Das System ist flexibel, Veränderung problemlos möglich. TELL strukturiert den Raum. Im Großen wie im Kleinen. Das portable Objekt lehnt schlicht an der Wand. Einteilungen lassen sich variieren, die sieben Tablare aus Metawell – einem Aluminium-Halbzeug – sind bequem in der Höhe zu verstellen; sie rasten in der Mitte des Bogens in kleine Rillen ein.

Fabian Wurm

Zeitschriftenablage
Aluminium Metawell

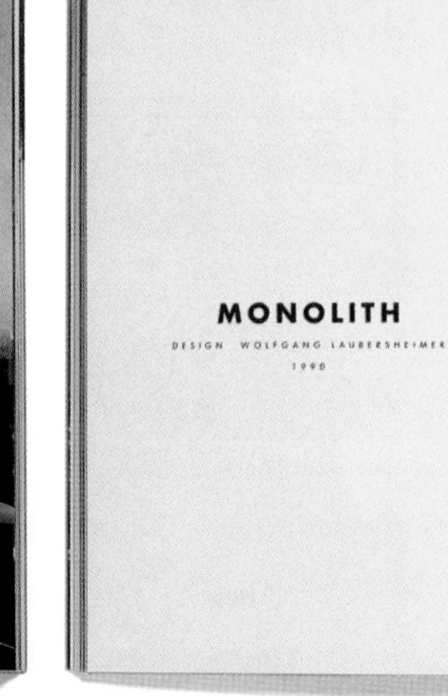

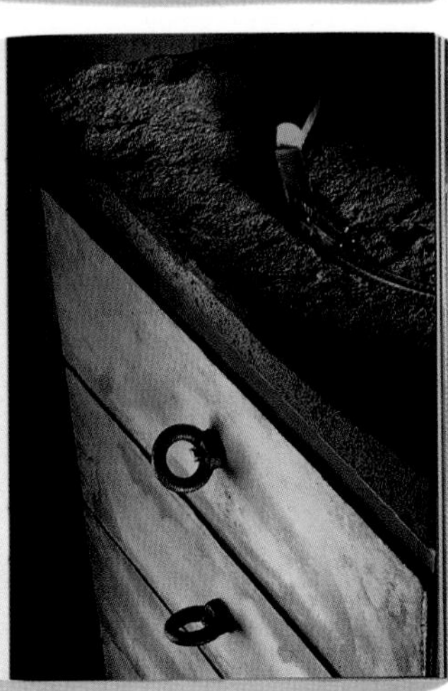

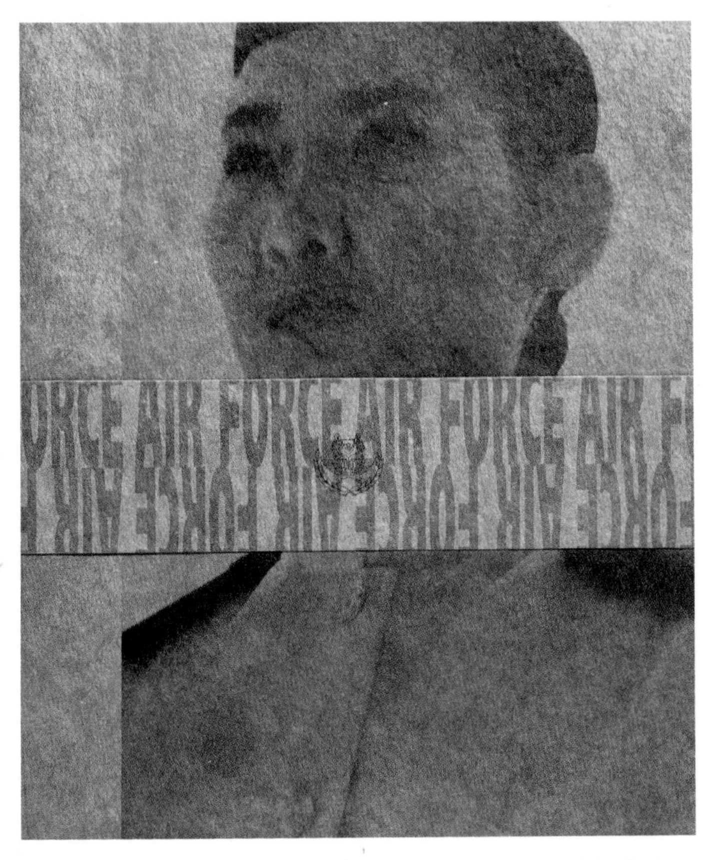

■ 1-8 DESIGNERS: RAFAEL JIMÉNEZ, CLAUDIA CASAGRANDE PHOTOGRAPHERS: TOM VACK, FABIO PADOVESE ILLUSTRATOR: RAFAEL JIMÉNEZ DESIGN FIRM: JIMÉNEZ & CASAGRANDE CLIENT: MOORMANN COUNTRY: GERMANY ■ 9, 10 ART DIRECTOR/DESIGNER/PHOTOGRAPHER: CHUANDA TAM DESIGN FIRM: LEO BURNETT SINGAPORE CLIENT: REPUBLIC OF SINGAPORE AIR FORCE COUNTRY: SINGAPORE

RISTO SUOMI

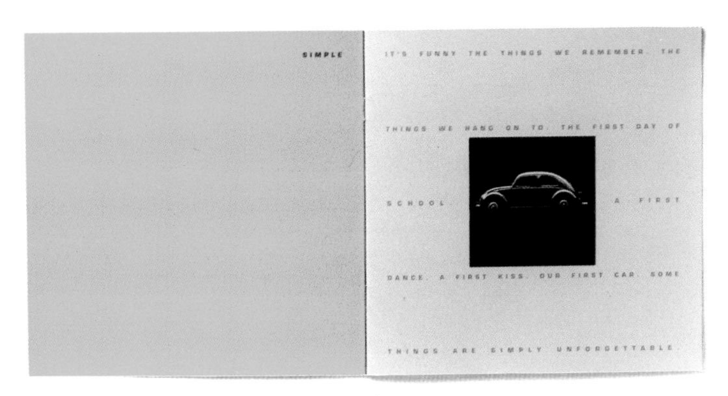

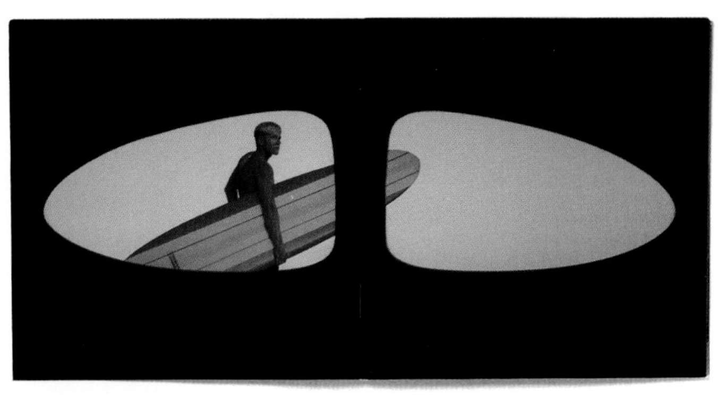

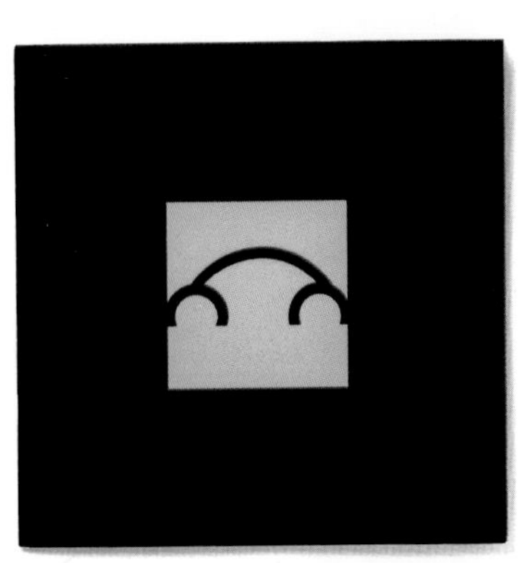

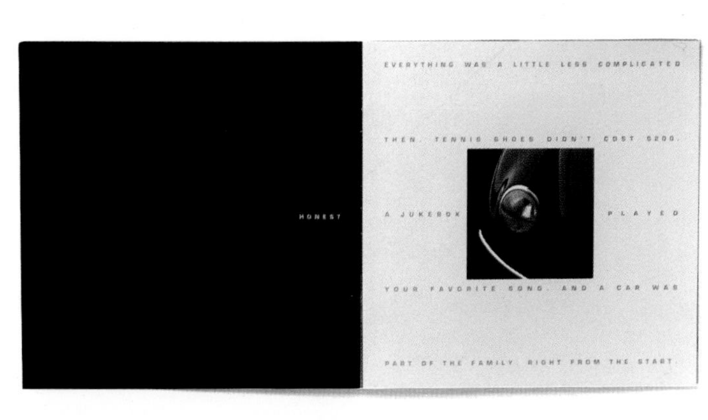

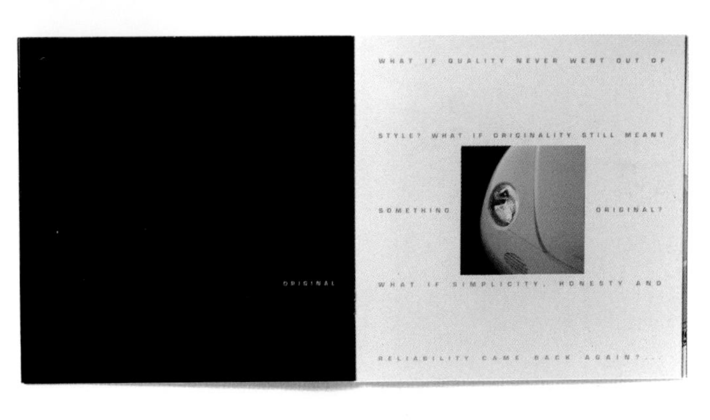

■ 1–7 ART DIRECTOR: EERO AULIO DESIGNER: EERO AULIO PHOTOGRAPHER: VARIOUS EDITOR IN CHIEF: MARJATTA LEVANTO CLIENT: THE NATIONAL GALLERY COUNTRY: FINLAND ■ 8–14 ART DIRECTORS/DESIGNERS: DENNIS MERRITT, KARIN BURKLEIN ARNOLD PHOTOGRAPHER: RODNEY RASCONA DESIGN FIRM: SHR PERCEPTUAL MANAGEMENT CLIENT: VOLKSWAGEN OF AMERICA COUNTRY: USA

■ 1 DESIGNER: BRAD NORR ILLUSTRATOR: BRAD NORR DESIGN FIRM: BRAD NORR DESIGN CLIENT: HSB RELIABILITY TECHNOLOGIES, INC. COUNTRY: USA ■ 2 ART DIRECTORS: NEIL POWELL, KOBE DESIGNERS: NEIL POWELL, KOBE, ALAN LEUSINK, MISSY WILSON DESIGN FIRM:

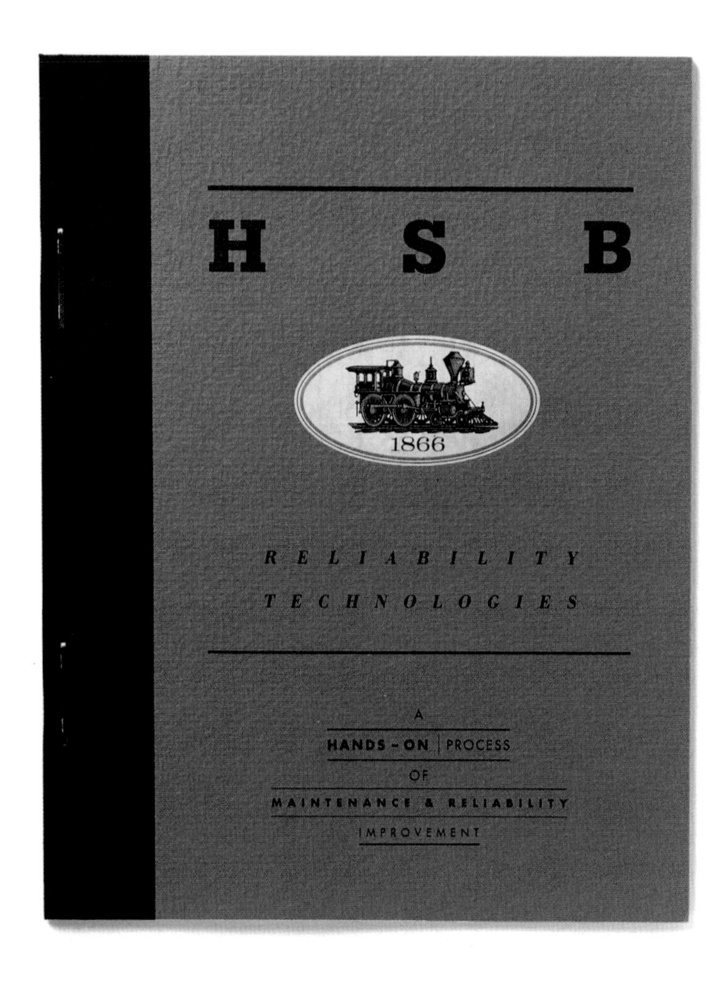

DUFFY DESIGN CLIENT: STRUCTURE COUNTRY: USA ■ 3–6 ART DIRECTOR: REBECA MENDEZ DESIGNER: DARIN BEAMAN PHOTOGRAPHER: STEVEN A. HELLER DESIGN FIRM: ART CENTER DESIGN OFFICE CLIENT: ART CENTER COLLEGE OF DESIGN COUNTRY: USA

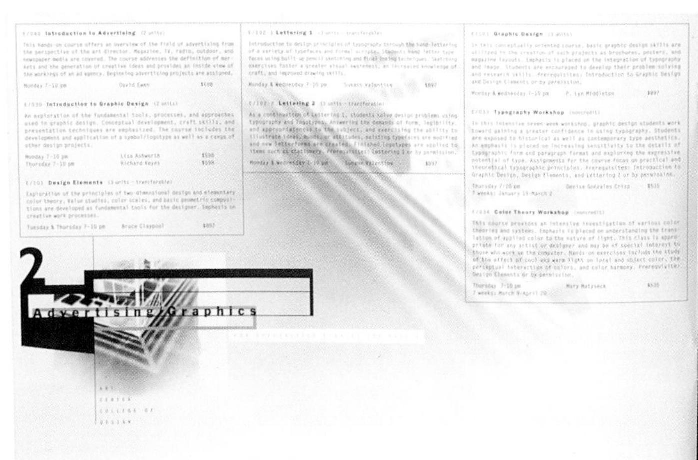

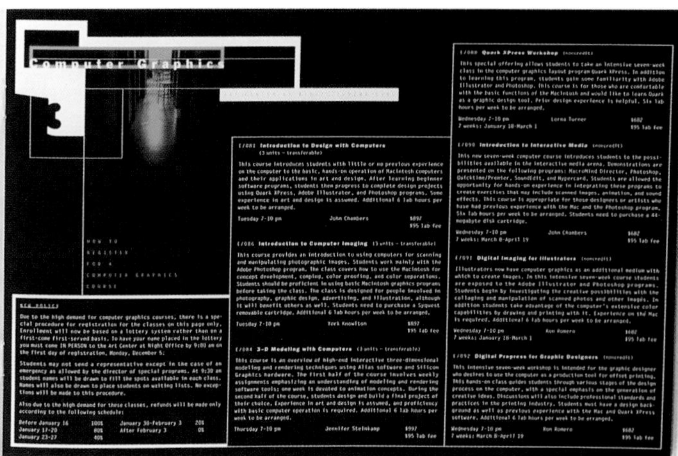

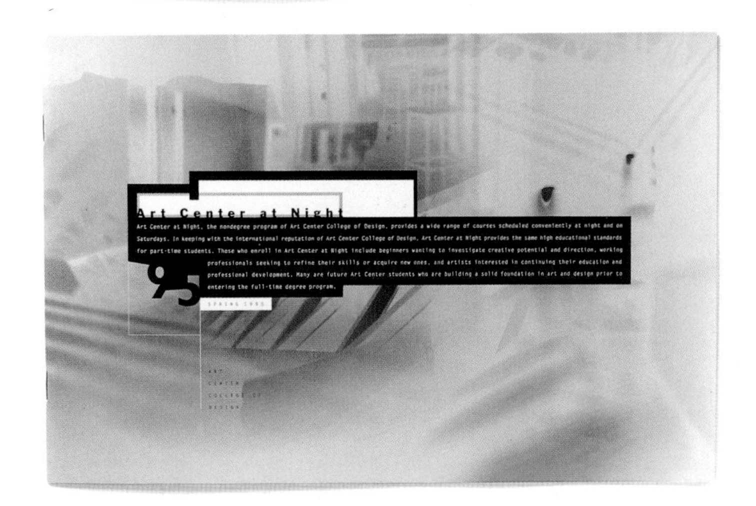

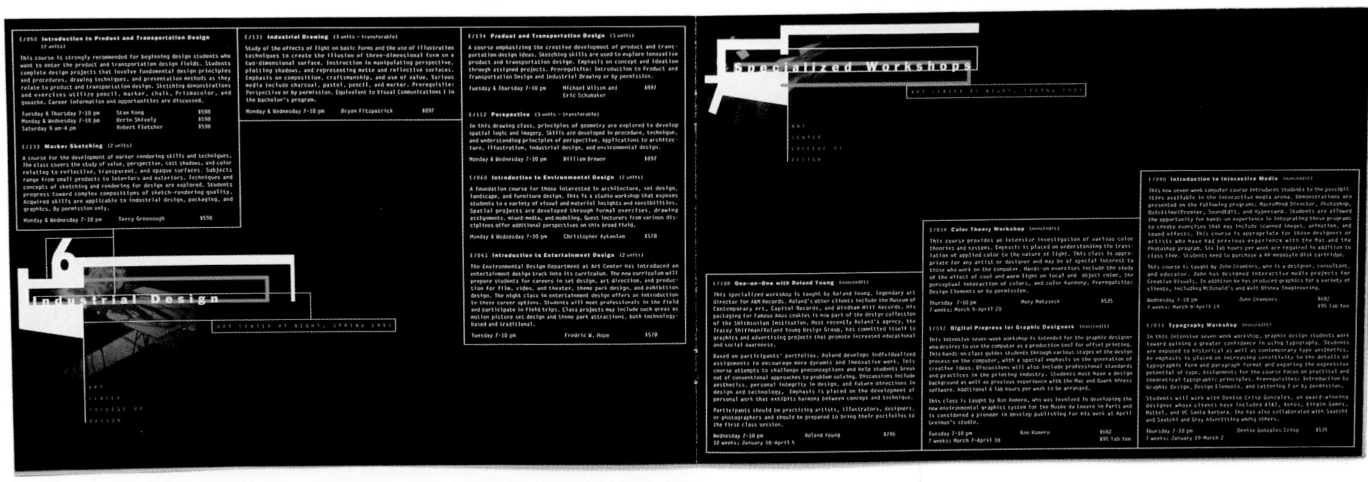

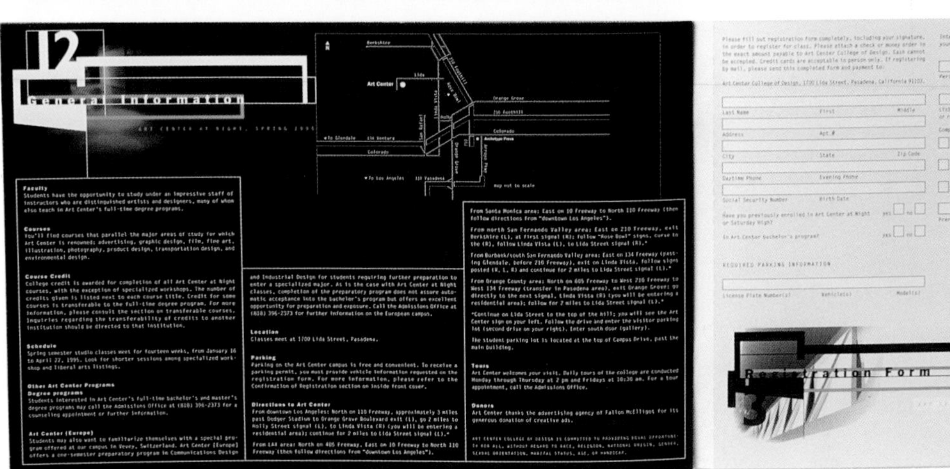

Einige Vorzüge hören Sie besonders gut, andere besonders gerne.

Das Geschäft mit der Nachrüstung von Musiksystemen läuft gut, aber leider oft am Händler vorbei. Die direkte Kooperation von Bose® mit den Automobilherstellern garantiert deshalb, daß sich dieses Musikgeschäft wieder in Ihrem Haus abspielt - ohne zusätzlichen Aufwand. Im Gegenteil, mit ausführlichen Verkäufer-Schulungen und Verkaufsförderungs-Maßnahmen sorgt Bose für das entsprechende Know-how, mit konsequenter Öffentlichkeitsarbeit auch für die Nachfrage.

In der Zusammenarbeit mit den Automobilherstellern setzt Bose dabei ganz auf die Partnerschaft mit Auto-Spezialisten: Reitter & Schefenacker, einer der erfahrendsten Zulieferbetriebe der Automobilindustrie übernimmt, systemverantwortlich Service und Logistik. Dazu kommen die Konstruktion und Fertigung mechanischer Teile, die Montage und die Just-in-Time-Lieferung. Durch diese Verbindung konnte Bose von Anfang an auf 60 Jahre Erfahrung zurückgreifen. Und Sie auf ein Team, das von Autos soviel versteht wie von Musik.

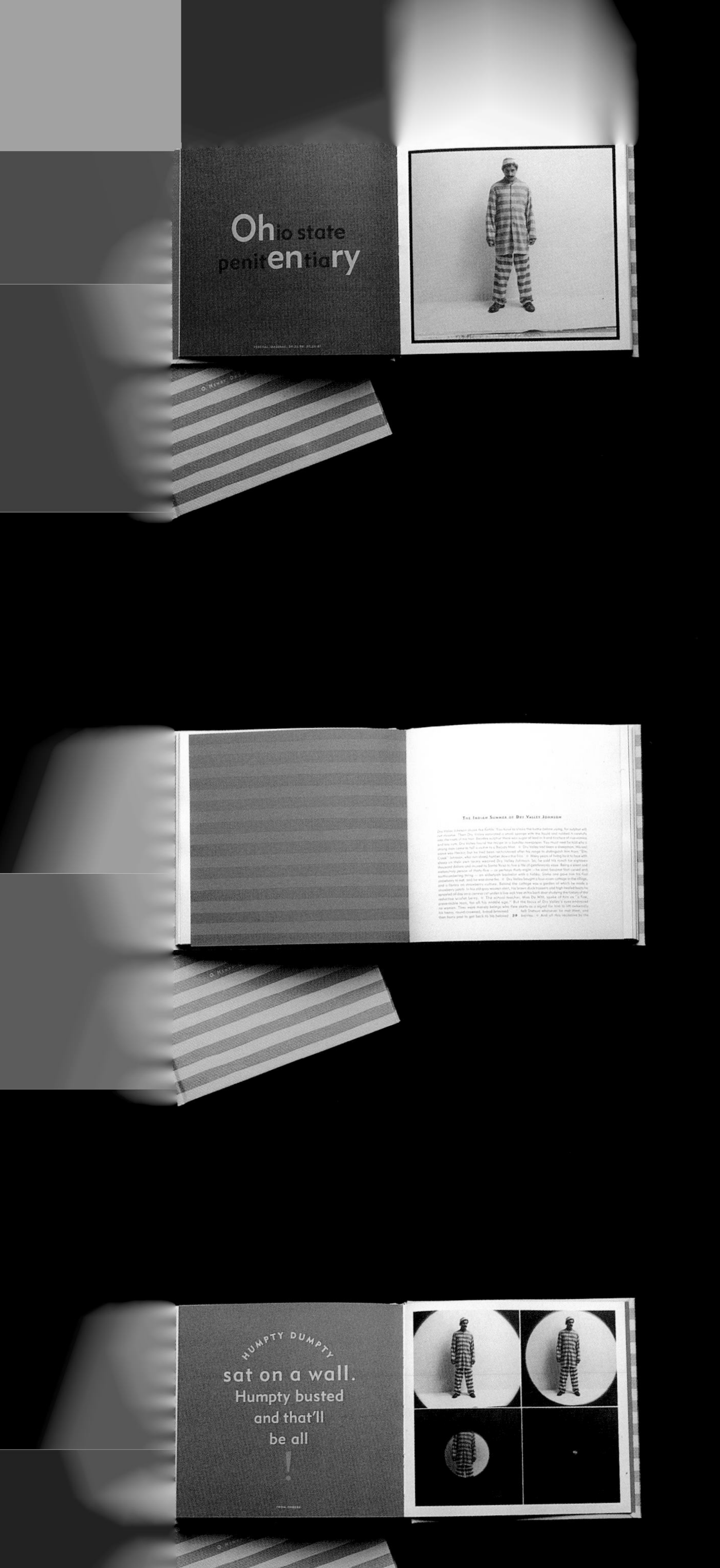

Ohio state penitentiary
The Indian Summer of Dry Valley Johnson
Humpty Dumpty
sat on a wall.
Humpty busted
and that'll
be all
!

SIMPLICITY
LIMITS
STRENGTH
SKILL
flexibility
CREATIVITY
INVENTIVENESS
ELEGANCE
PASSION
COMMUNICATION
CONCRETE

LES FIGURES

■ (PRECEDING SPREAD) **1–3** ART DIRECTORS: RALF SCHMERBERG, JOERG BAUER DESIGNER: JOERG BAUER PHOTOGRAPHER: RALF SCHMERBERG DESIGN FIRM: JUBEL + TRUBEL GESTALTUNGS- UND PROJEKTAGENTUR CLIENT: BOSE GMBH - O.E.M. DIVISION EUROPA COUNTRY: GERMANY ■ **4, 6, 8** ART DIRECTOR: LANA RIGSBY DESIGNERS: LANA RIGSBY, MICHAEL THEDE, TROY S. FORD PHOTOGRAPHER:

GEOF KERN DESIGN FIRM: RIGSBY DESIGN CLIENT: HERITAGE PRESS COUNTRY: USA ■ **5, 7, 9** ART DIRECTOR/DESIGNER: JILLY SIMONS PHOTOGRAPHER: GEOF KERN DESIGN FIRM/CLIENT: CONCRETE COUNTRY: USA ■ (THIS SPREAD) **1** ART DIRECTOR/DESIGNER/DESIGN FIRM: LE PETIT DIDIER PHOTOGRAPHERS: D.H. DANCY, P. BODE CLIENT: APEILOR COUNTRY: FRANCE ■ **2–5** ART DIRECTOR: ALAN CHAN DESIGNERS: ALAN CHAN, PETER LO ILLUSTRATOR: PETER LO DESIGN FIRM: ALAN CHAN DESIGN COMPANY CLIENT: AJIOKA CO. LTD. COUNTRY: JAPAN

CHINESE BUTTON

FOUR HAPPINESS

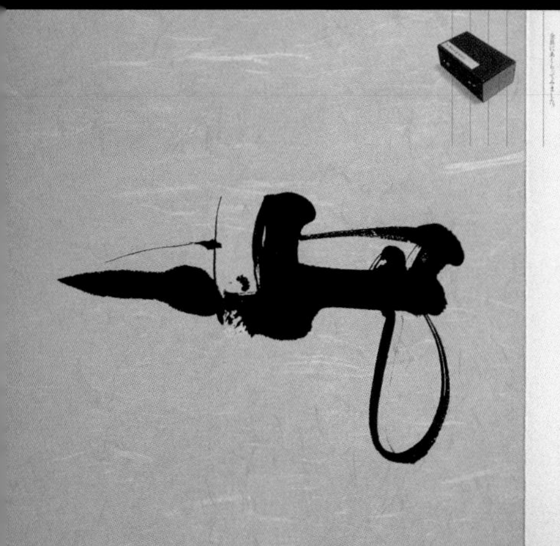

CHINA CONNECTION

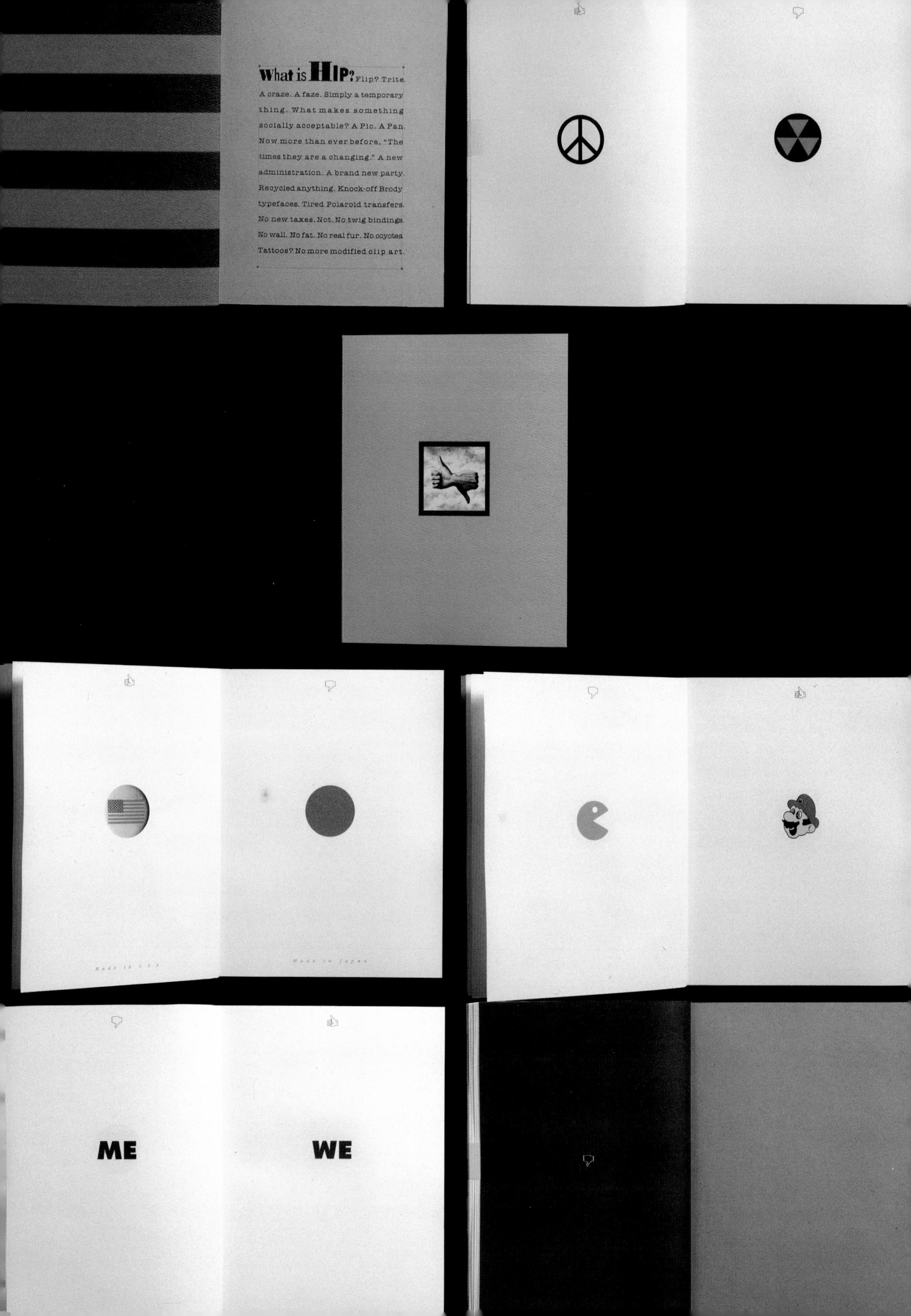
What is HIP? Flip? Trite.
A craze. A faze. Simply a temporary
thing. What makes something
socially acceptable? A Pic. A Pan.
Now more than ever before, "The
times they are a changing." A new
administration. A brand new party.
Recycled anything. Knock-off Brody
typefaces. Tired Polaroid transfers.
No new taxes. Not. No twig bindings.
No wall. No fat. No real fur. No coyotes.
Tattoos? No more modified clip art.
Made in U.S.A
Made in Japan
ME
WE

■ 1–7 Art Director: Rex Peteet Designers: Rex Peteet, Derek Welch Illustrators: Rex Peteet, Derek Welch, Mike Schroeder Design Firm: Sibley/Peteet Design, Inc. Client: Dallas Society of Visual Communications

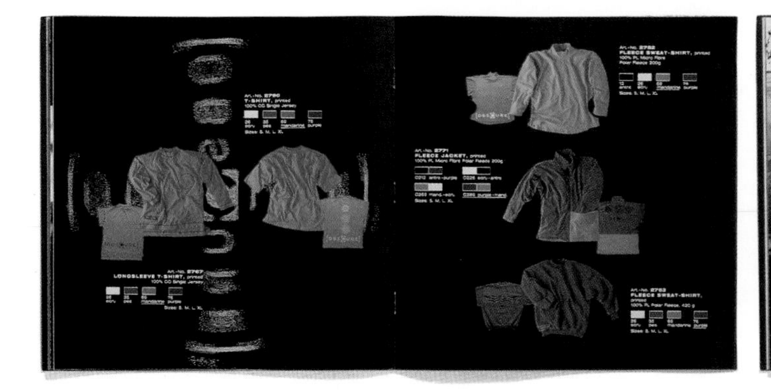

Country: USA ■ 8–12 Art Director: Alexandra Richter Designer: Regina Hocker Photographer: Andreas Loewenhaus Design Firm: Agentur Richter Client: Head Sportwear International GmbH Obscure Country: Germany

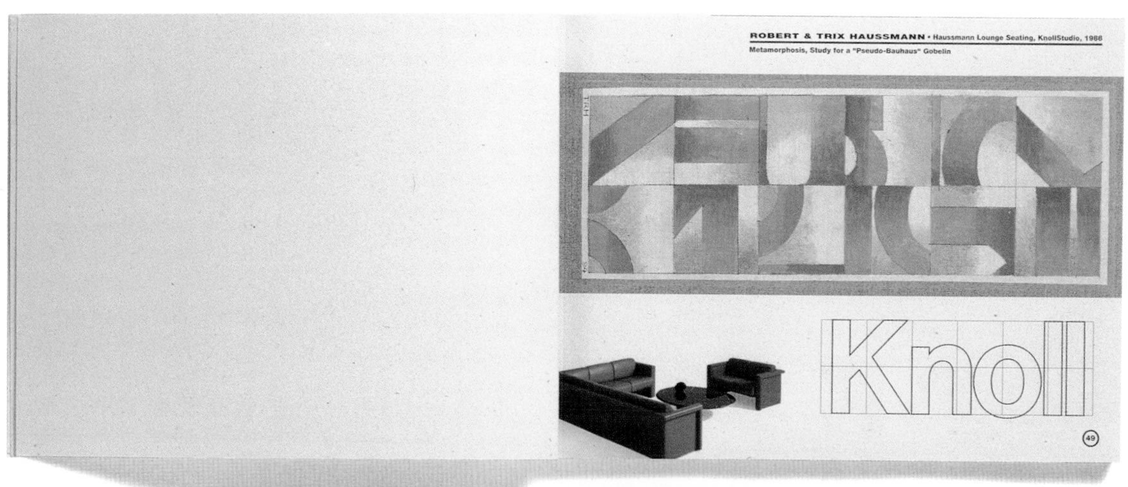

ROBERT & TRIX HAUSSMANN • Haussmann Lounge Seating, KnollStudio, 1988
Metamorphosis, Study for a "Pseudo-Bauhaus" Gobelin
Knoll
49

JOHN RIZZI • Interaction Tables, 1991

t ink

77

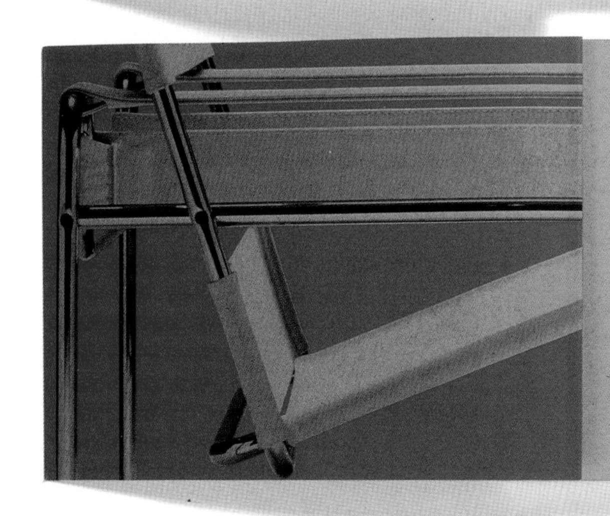

Knoll Celebrates 75 Years Of Bauhaus Design, 1919-1994

spring
1994
Reebok

as the MOST RESPECTED
BRAND
SPORT, IN THE
REEBOK
tennis
is ready for the huge challenge of the major
tennis
NEW
BOOM

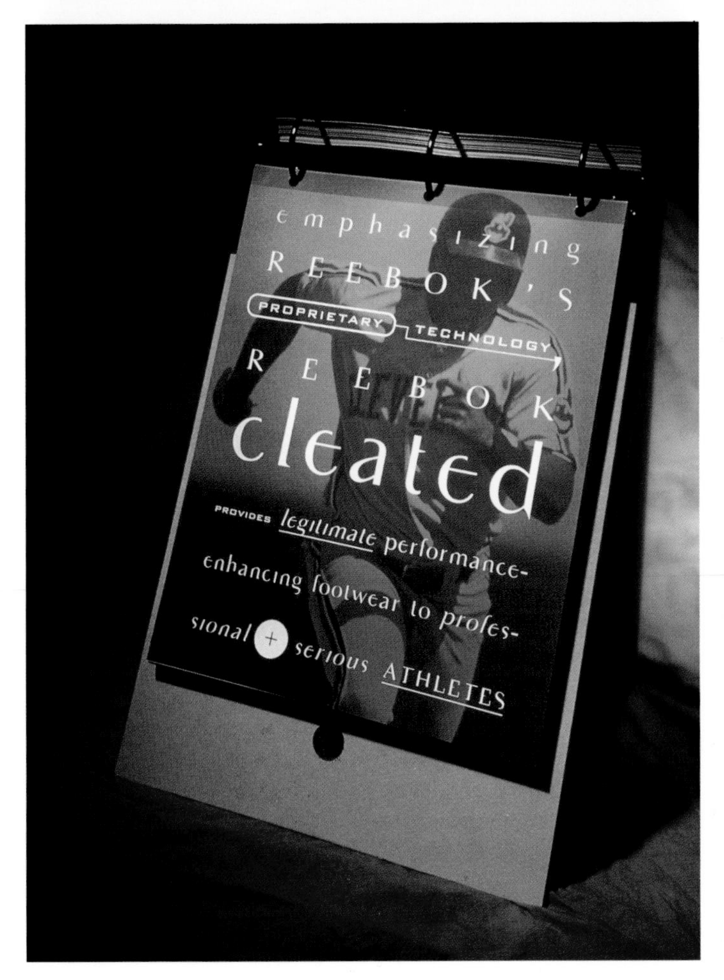
emphasizing
REEBOK'S
PROPRIETARY TECHNOLOGY
REEBOK
cleated
PROVIDES legitimate performance-
enhancing footwear to profes-
sional + serious ATHLETES

marketing spend
TOTAL ADVERTISING, MARKETING
AND PROMOTIONAL SPEND:
US: $150
MILLION
GLOBAL: $250
MILLION
THESE NUMBERS REPRESENT AN
ESTIMATED
30%
OF THE
INDUSTRY SPEND
Reebok

■ (PRECEDING SPREAD) 1–4 ART DIRECTORS/DESIGNERS: CHRIS SOLWAR, LUCY POPE DESIGN FIRM: KNOLL GRAPHICS COUNTRY: USA ■ 5-8 ART DIRECTORS: DANN DE WITT, DAVID CECCHI DESIGNERS: DANN DE WITT, DAVID CECCHI, KEVIN GRADY PHOTOGRAPHER: STOCK DESIGN FIRM: DE WITT ANTHONY CLIENT: REEBOK INTERNATIONAL LTD. COUNTRY: USA ■ (THIS SPREAD) 1 ART DIRECTOR: FRANZ MERLICEK DESIGNER: TINA FEIERTAG COPYWRITER: STEFAN POTT DESIGN FIRM: DEMNER, MERLICEK & BERGMANN WERBEGESELL-

SCHAFT M.B.H. CLIENT: RHENUS AG COUNTRY: GERMANY ■ 2, 5-8 ART DIRECTORS: STEVEN SANDSTROM, CHARLOTTE MOORE DESIGNER: STEVEN SANDSTROM PHOTOGRAPHER: DOUG PETTY ILLUSTRATOR: DANIEL CLOWES DESIGN FIRM: SANDSTROM DESIGN CLIENT: THE COCA COLA COMPANY COUNTRY: USA ■ 3, 4 ART DIRECTORS: BOB HAMBLY, BARB WOOLLEY DESIGNERS: MERCEDES ROTHWELL, GORD WOOLLEY ILLUSTRATORS: BOB HAMBLY, BARRY BLITT DESIGN FIRM: HAMBLY & WOOLLEY CLIENT: THE EDGE SCREEN STUDIO COUNTRY: CANADA

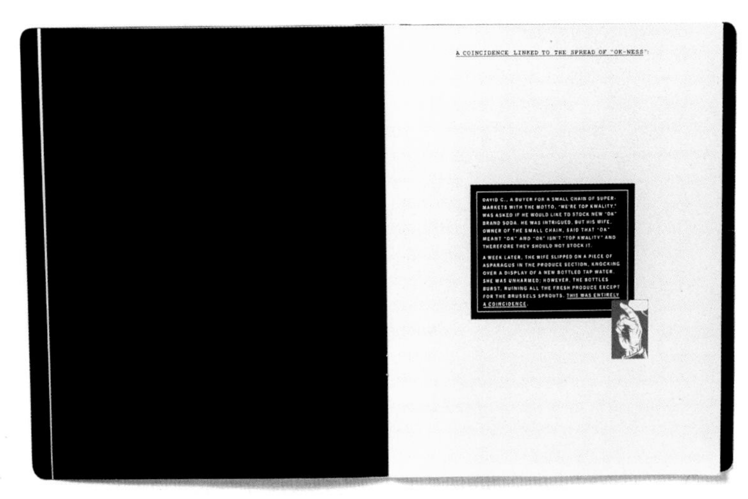
A COINCIDENCE LINKED TO THE SPREAD OF "OK-NESS":
DAVID C., A BUYER FOR A SMALL CHAIN OF SUPERMARKETS WITH THE MOTTO, "WE'RE TOP KWALITY," WAS ASKED IF HE WOULD LIKE TO STOCK NEW "OK" BRAND SODA. HE WAS INTRIGUED, BUT HIS WIFE, OWNER OF THE SMALL CHAIN, SAID THAT "OK" MEANT "OK" AND "OK" ISN'T "TOP KWALITY" AND THEREFORE THEY SHOULD NOT STOCK IT.
A WEEK LATER, THE WIFE SLIPPED ON A PIECE OF ASPARAGUS IN THE PRODUCE SECTION, KNOCKING OVER A DISPLAY OF A NEW BOTTLED TAP WATER. SHE WAS UNHARMED; HOWEVER, THE BOTTLES BURST, RUINING ALL THE FRESH PRODUCE EXCEPT FOR THE BRUSSELS SPROUTS. THIS WAS ENTIRELY A COINCIDENCE.

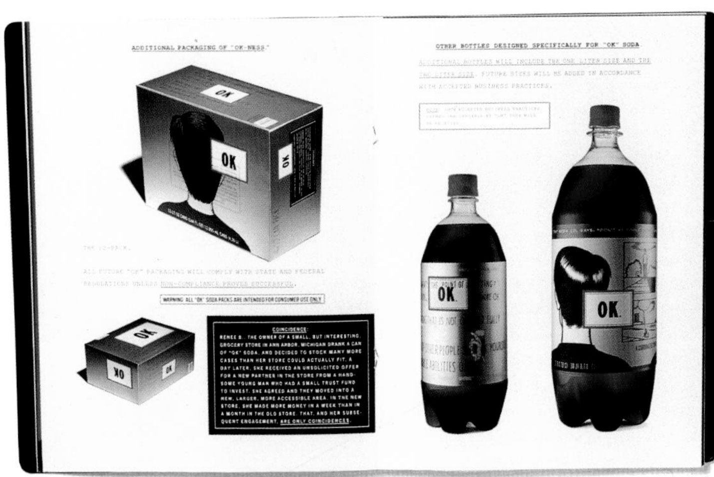
ADDITIONAL PACKAGING OF "OK-NESS."
OK
ALL FUTURE "OK" PACKAGING WILL COMPLY WITH STATE AND FEDERAL REGULATIONS UNLESS NON-COMPLIANCE PROVES SUCCESSFUL.
WARNING: ALL "OK" SODA PACKS ARE INTENDED FOR CONSUMER USE ONLY
COINCIDENCE:
RENEE B., THE OWNER OF A SMALL, BUT INTERESTING, GROCERY STORE IN ANN ARBOR, MICHIGAN DRANK A CAN OF "OK" SODA, AND DECIDED TO STOCK MANY MORE CASES THAN HER STORE COULD ACTUALLY FIT. A DAY LATER, SHE RECEIVED AN UNSOLICITED OFFER FOR A NEW PARTNER IN THE STORE FROM A HANDSOME YOUNG MAN WHO HAD A SMALL TRUST FUND TO INVEST. SHE AGREED AND THEY MOVED INTO A NEW, LARGER, MORE ACCESSIBLE AREA. IN THE NEW STORE, SHE MADE MORE MONEY IN A WEEK THAN IN A MONTH IN THE OLD STORE. THAT, AND HER SUBSEQUENT ENGAGEMENT, ARE ONLY COINCIDENCES.
OTHER BOTTLES DESIGNED SPECIFICALLY FOR "OK" SODA.
WITH ACCEPTED BUSINESS PRACTICES.

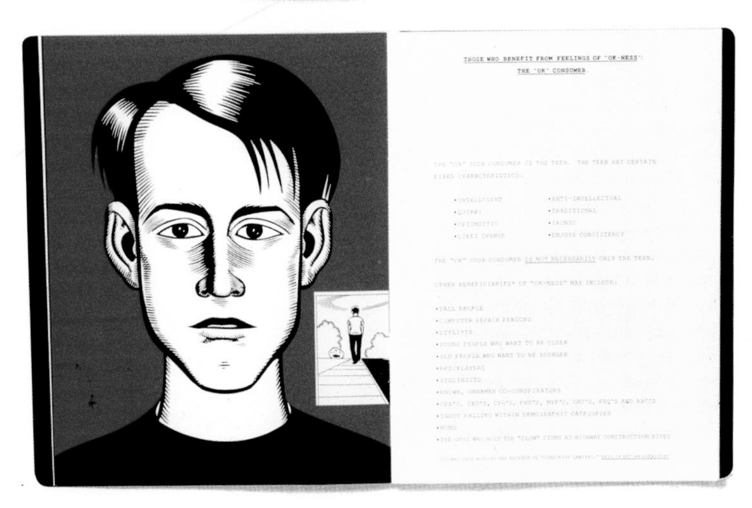
THOSE WHO BENEFIT FROM FEELINGS OF "OK-NESS":
THE "OK" CONSUMER.
•INTELLIGENT
•QUIRKY
•ANTI-INTELLECTUAL
•TRADITIONAL
•IRONIC
•ENJOYS CONSISTENCY

"OK-NESS" AND CAN DESIGNS.
OK
NEW "OK" SODA CAN DESIGNS WILL BE CREATED AT THE SOLE DISCRETION OF "OK" BRAND SODA.
THE REACTION OF THE TEEN CONSUMER MAY BE TAKEN INTO ACCOUNT. THE REACTION OF OTHER "OK" CONSUMERS MAY NOT BE TAKEN INTO ACCOUNT. (SEE PREVIOUS PAGE.)
"OK-NESS" AND BOTTLE DESIGN.
THE 20 OUNCE AND/OR THE SLIGHTLY SMALLER 16 OUNCE BOTTLES.
WHILE BOTTLE AND CAN DESIGNS ARE SUBJECT TO CHANGE WITHOUT PRIOR NOTIFICATION, THE "OK" SODA "CONCOCTION" IS SUBJECT TO NO CHANGE AT ANY TIME.

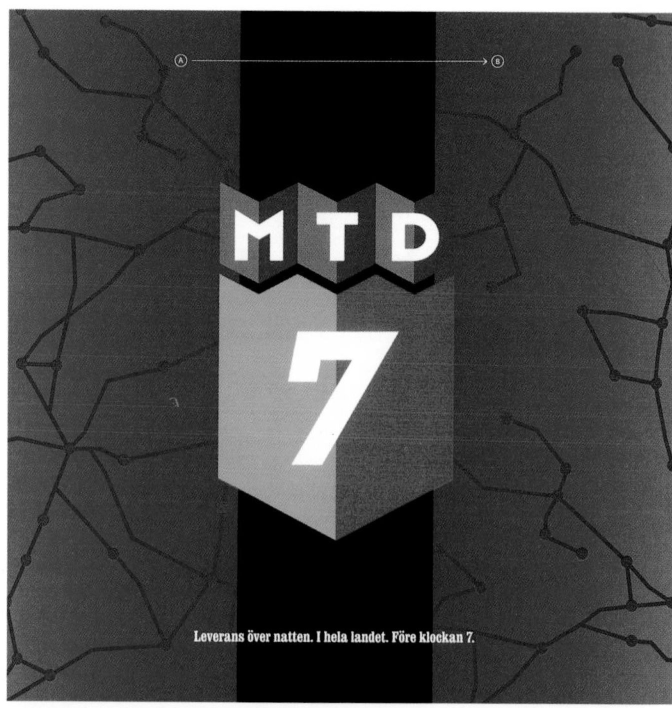
A
B
MTD
7
Leverans över natten. I hela landet. Före klockan 7.

RADFORD UNIVERSITY
SELU

BALLY CLASSICS
BALLY

■ 1 ART DIRECTOR: DAVID FREEMAN DESIGNERS: LEE HODDY, PIP LLEWELLIN PHOTOGRAPHER: MARTIN LANGFIELD DESIGN FIRM: SAMPSON TYRRELL LTD. CLIENT: CASTROL LTD. COUNTRY: GREAT BRITAIN ■ 2 ART DIRECTOR/DESIGNER: KLAS BJÖRKMAN DESIGN FIRM: BJÖRKMAN & MITCHELL CLIENT: MTD COUNTRY: SWEDEN ■ 3 ART DIRECTOR: KITTY IRWIN DESIGNER: SAMANTHA HAND BASS DESIGN FIRM: RADFORD

UNIVERSITY PUBLIC INFORMATION AND RELATIONS CLIENT: UNIVERSITY ADVANCEMENT, RADFORD UNIVERSITY COUNTRY: USA ■ 4 ART DIRECTOR: ANTONIE REINHARD DESIGNERS: MARTIN GABERTHÜEL, ANDREA REINHART PHOTOGRAPHER: JÜRG BERNHARDT DESIGN FIRM: SEILER DDB NEEDHAM BERN CLIENT: BALLY INTERNATIONAL AG COUNTRY: SWITZERLAND ■ 5, 6 ART DIRECTOR: CHRIS HILL DESIGNER: HILL GROUP ILLUSTRATOR: LINDA BLECK DESIGN FIRM: HILL/A MARKETING DESIGN GROUP, INC. CLIENT: MONTERREY TECH COUNTRY: USA

■ 1, 2 CREATIVE DIRECTOR: JAMES A. SEBASTIAN ART DIRECTOR: MICHAEL MCGINN DESIGNERS: JAMES A. SEBASTIAN, FRANK NICHOLS DESIGN FIRM: JAMES LUNG CLIENT: STRATHMORE PAPER COUNTRY: USA ■ 3–9 ART DIRECTORS: STEVEN TOLLESON,

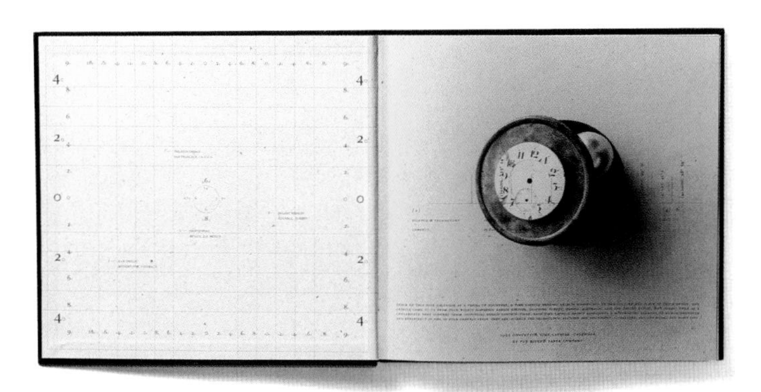

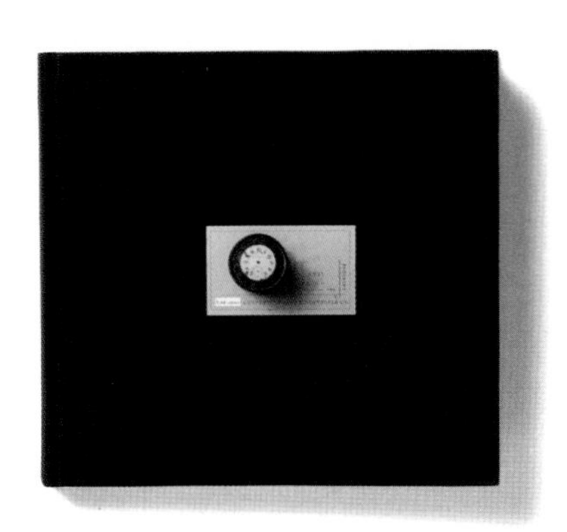

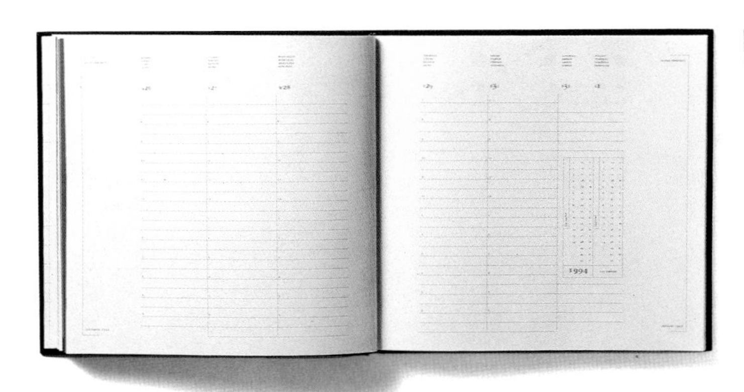

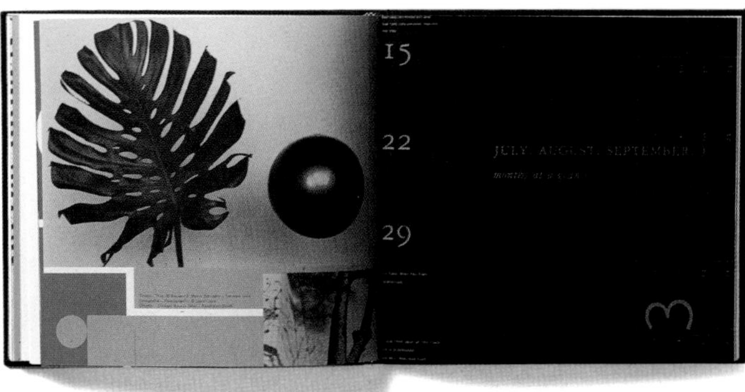

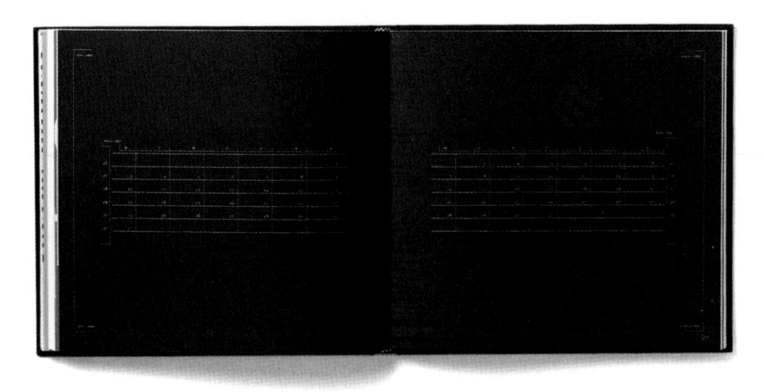

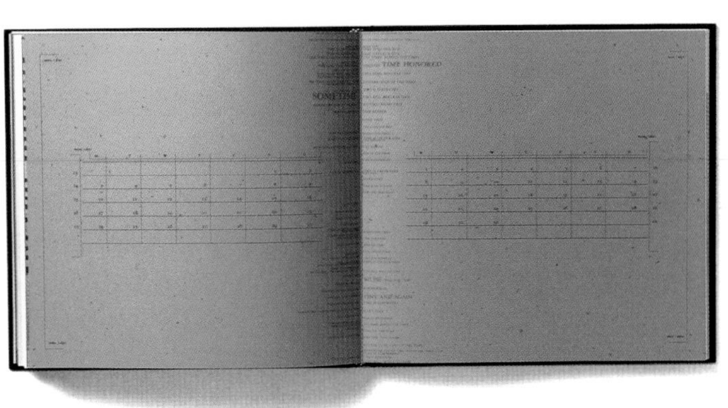

JENNIFER STERLING Designers: STEVEN TOLLESON, JENNIFER STERLING Photographers: JOHN CASADO, DAVID MAGNUSSON Illustrators: JACK MALLOY, JONATHAN ROSEN Design Firm: TOLLESON DESIGN Client: FOX RIVER PAPER COMPANY Country: USA

■ 1–6 ART DIRECTORS: CAROLINE TERRIER, PATRIK BAUME DESIGNER: PATRIK BAUME DESIGN FIRM: KODAK CLIENT: KODAK COUNTRY: FRANCE ■ 7, 8 DESIGNER: IRINA TARKHANOVA ILLUSTRATOR: IRINA TARKHANOVA CLIENT: IMA-PRESS COUNTRY: RUSSIA

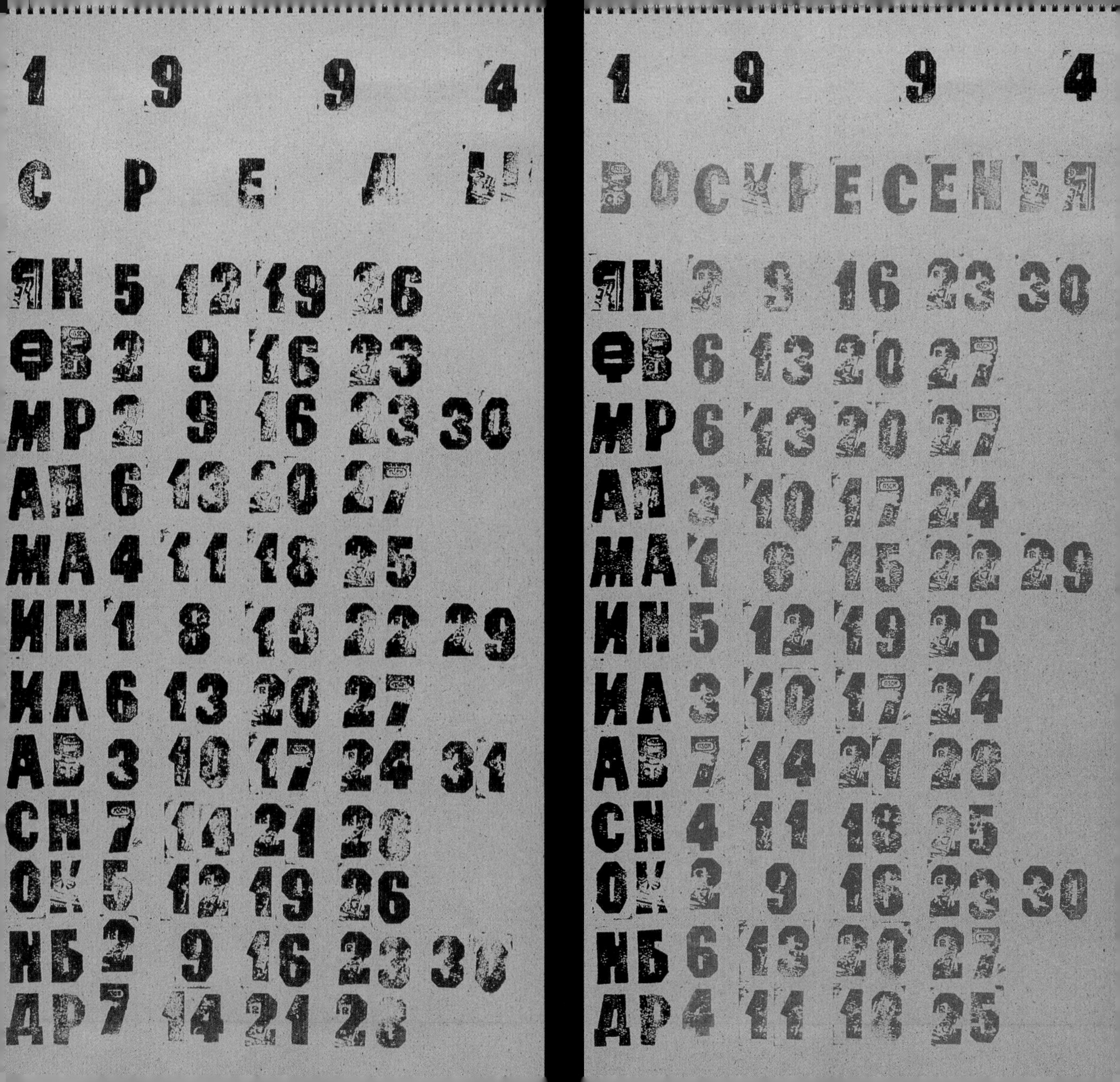
1994
СРЕДЫ
ЯН 5 12 19 26
ФВ 2 9 16 23
МР 2 9 16 23 30
АП 6 13 20 27
МА 4 11 18 25
ИН 1 8 15 22 29
ИА 6 13 20 27
АВ 3 10 17 24 31
СН 7 14 21 28
ОК 5 12 19 26
НБ 2 9 16 23 30
ДР 7 14 21 28
1994
ВОСКРЕСЕНЬЯ
ЯН 2 9 16 23 30
ФВ 6 13 20 27
МР 6 13 20 27
АП 3 10 17 24
МА 1 8 15 22 29
ИН 5 12 19 26
ИА 3 10 17 24
АВ 7 14 21 28
СН 4 11 18 25
ОК 2 9 16 23 30
НБ 6 13 20 27
ДР 4 11 18 25

■ 1–6 ART DIRECTOR: ACHIM GRINTSCH DESIGNER: ACHIM GRINTSCH PHOTOGRAPHERS: PETRA KOMOROWSKI (2), MICHAEL NEUHAUS (3, PORTRAIT), EKKEHARDT REINSCH (3, BACKGROUND), MATHIAS WOLTMANN (4), BERND JONKMANNS (5), MARKUS

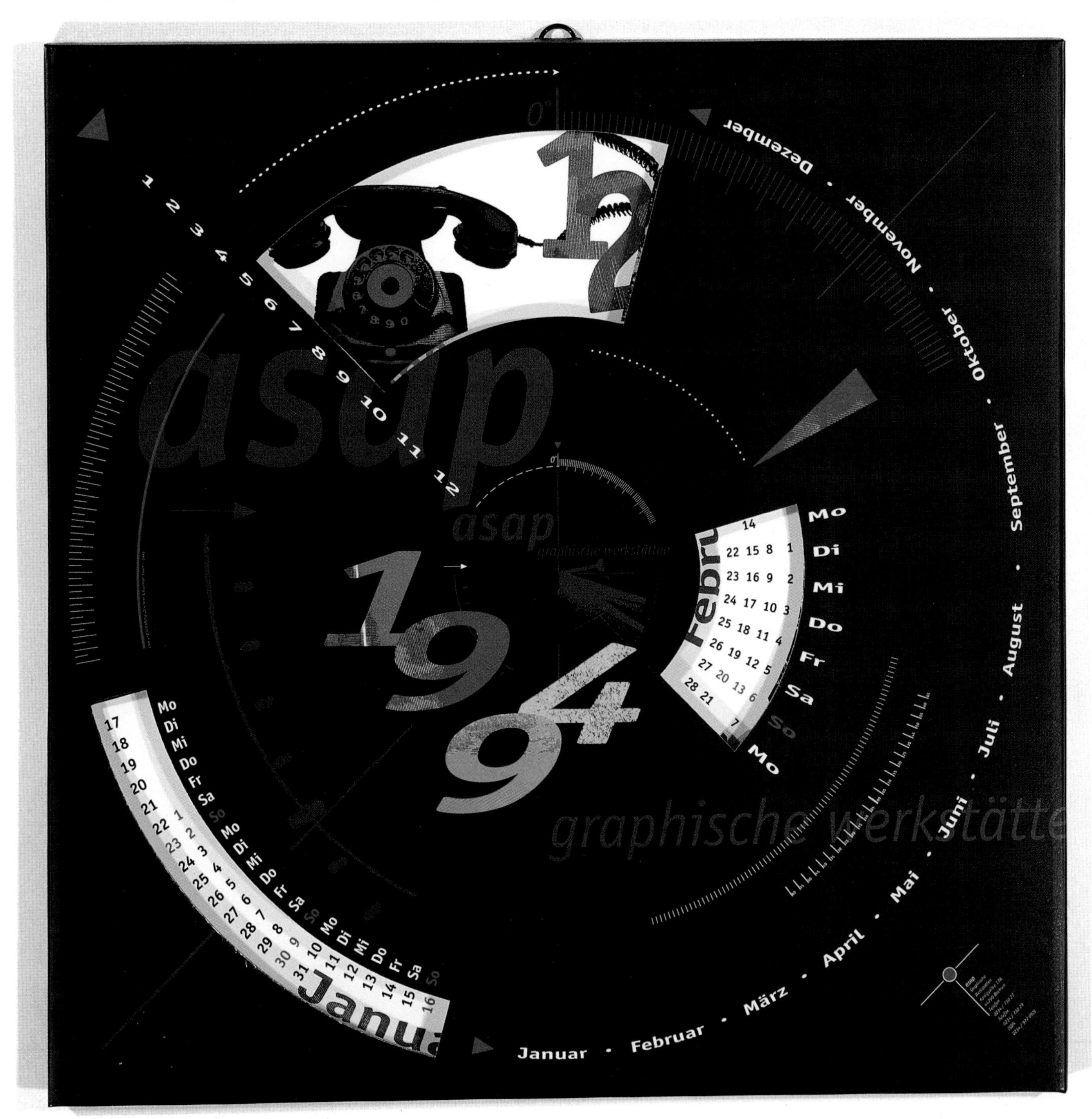

BULLIK (6) CLIENT: STORA BILLERUD AG COUNTRY: GERMANY ■ 7 ART DIRECTOR: ZBIKOWSKI & BUURMAN DESIGN FIRM: ZBIKOWSKI & BUURMAN DESIGNER: CHRISTIANE ZBIKOWSKI CLIENT: ASAP GRAPHISCHE WERKSTÄTTEN COUNTRY: GERMANY

■ 1 ART DIRECTORS: HATSUKO KOBAYASHI, TAKAAKI MATSUMOTO DESIGNER: HATSUKO KOBAYASHI DESIGN FIRM/CLIENT: SAZABY INC. COUNTRY: JAPAN ■ 2 ART DIRECTOR: KEIZO MATSUI DESIGNER: KEIZO MATSUI PHOTOGRAPHER: MASAO CHIBA DESIGN FIRM: KEIZO MATSUI & ASSOCIATES CLIENT: HUNDRED DESIGN INC. COUNTRY: JAPAN ■ 3, 4 ART DIRECTOR/DESIGNER: KAZUMASA NAGAI DESIGN FIRM: NIPPON DESIGN CENTER, INC. CLIENT: MITSUBISHI ELECTRIC CORPORATION COUNTRY: JAPAN ■ 5, 6 ART DIRECTOR/DESIGNER: SHIN MATSUNAGA ARTIST: SHIN MATSUNAGA DESIGN FIRM: SHIN MATSUNAGA DESIGN INC. CLIENT: MONSANTO JAPAN LIMITED COUNTRY: JAPAN

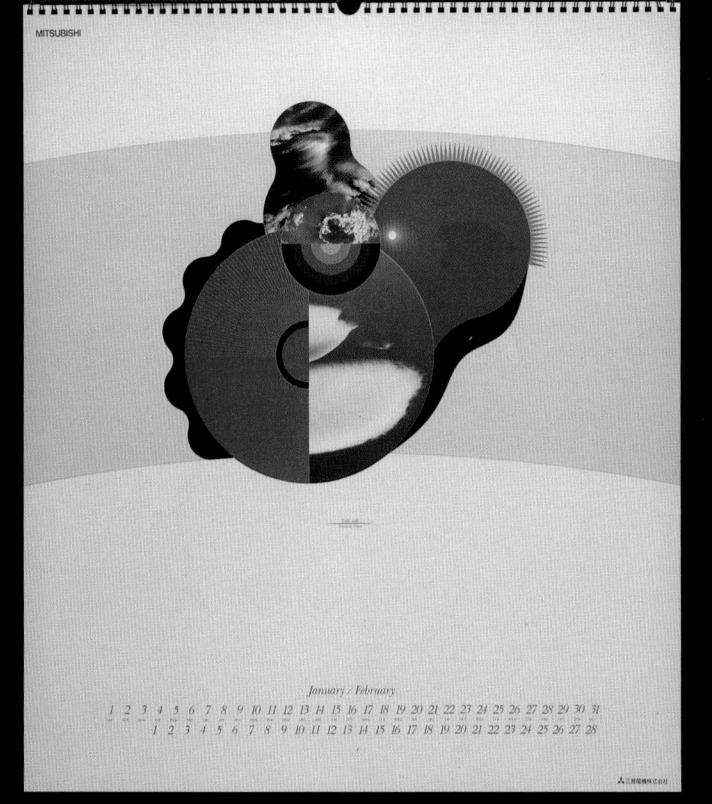
MITSUBISHI
January / February

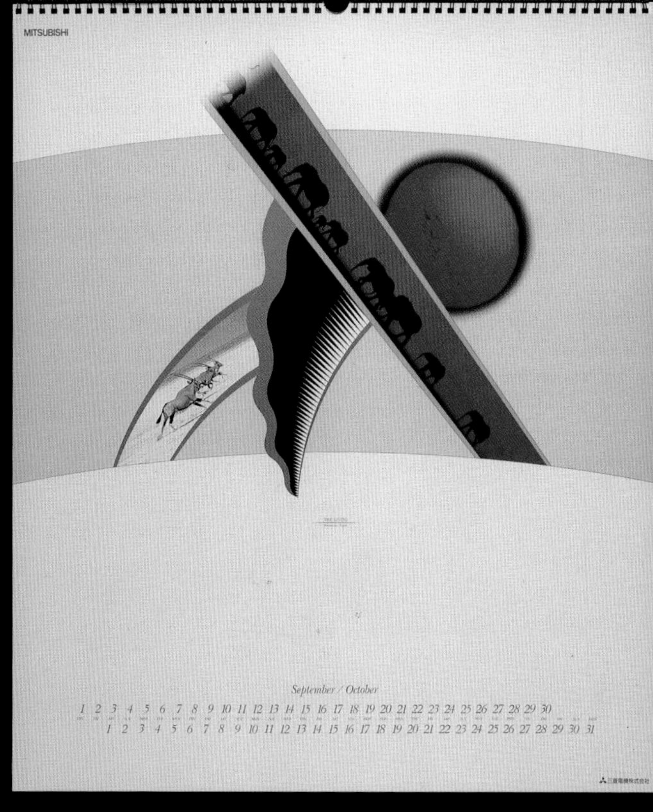
MITSUBISHI
September / October

Art Director: KURT KOEPFLE
Designers: PAULA SCHER, RON LOUIE, LISA MAZUR
Design Firm: PENTAGRAM DESIGN
Client: PUBLIC THEATER
Country: USA

FILM
F
AT THE PUBLIC
THE PUBLIC THEATER
BLADE
TO THE HEAT
SOME PEOPLE
THE DIVA IS DISMISSED
SIMPATICO
THE PETRIFIED PRINCE
HIM
THE MERCHANT
OF VENICE
A LANGUAGE
OF THEIR OWN
SILENCE CUNNING, EXILE
DANCING
ON MOONLIGHT
DOG OPERA
THE PUBLIC THEATER
SHIVA
THEATER
SHIVA
THEATER

PUBLIC
THEATER
THE SEASON BEGINS OCTOBER 12
THE PUBLIC THEATER

■ 1 ART DIRECTOR: MICHAEL DENNY DESIGNERS: HAROLD BATTEN, DEBORAH OSBORNE, JOHN BATESON DESIGN FIRM: ROUNDEL DESIGN GROUP CLIENT: GREAT WESTERN INTERCITY COUNTRY: GREAT BRITAIN ■ 2 ART DIRECTORS/DESIGNERS: TOM ANTISTA,

THOMAS FAIRCLOUGH DESIGN FIRM: ANTISTA FAIRCLOUGH DESIGN CLIENT: CLARK REFINING & MARKETING, INC. COUNTRY: USA ■ 3–6 ART DIRECTOR: NIKKO AMANDONICO DESIGNER: PAUL BARRY DESIGN FIRM: ENERGY PROJECT CLIENT: DOBBER COUNTRY: ITALY

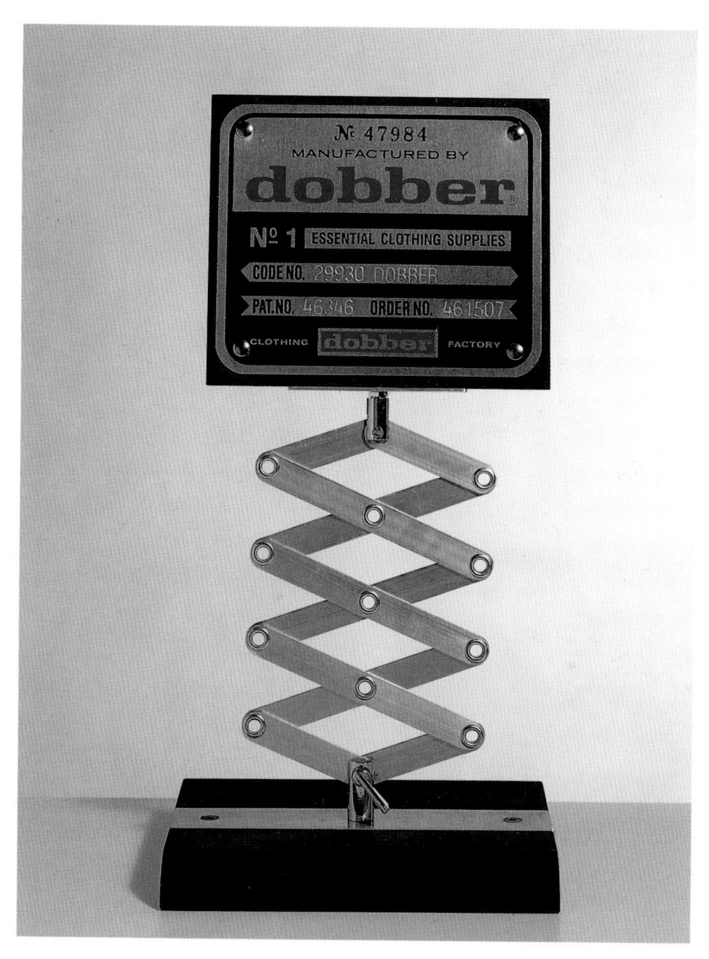
№ 47984
MANUFACTURED BY
dobber
№ 1 ESSENTIAL CLOTHING SUPPLIES
CODE NO. 29930 DOBBER
PAT. NO. 46346 ORDER NO. 461507
CLOTHING dobber FACTORY

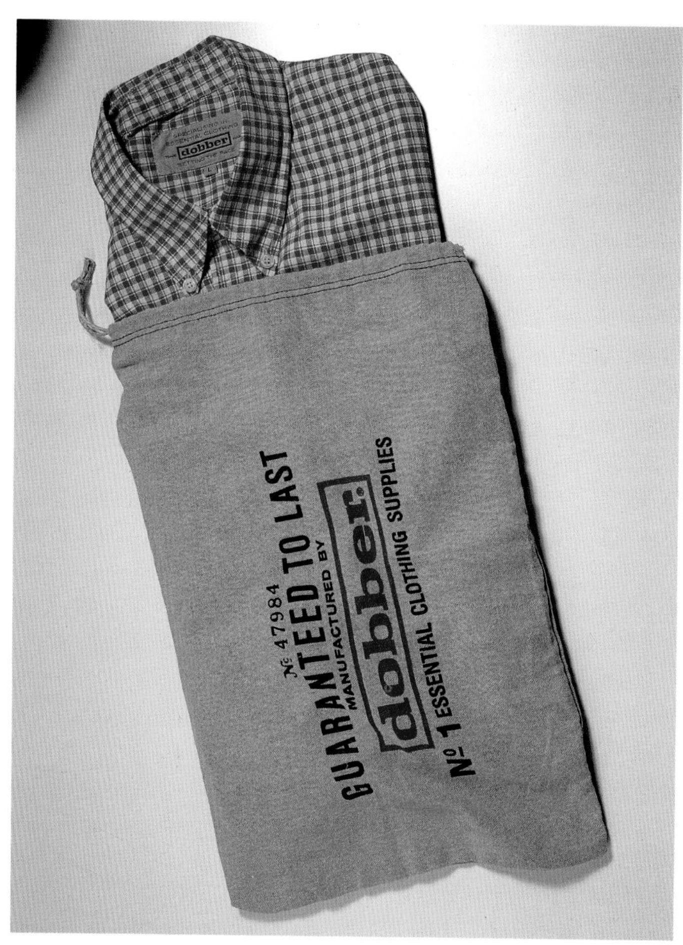
№ 47984
GUARANTEED TO LAST
MANUFACTURED BY
dobber
№ 1 ESSENTIAL CLOTHING SUPPLIES

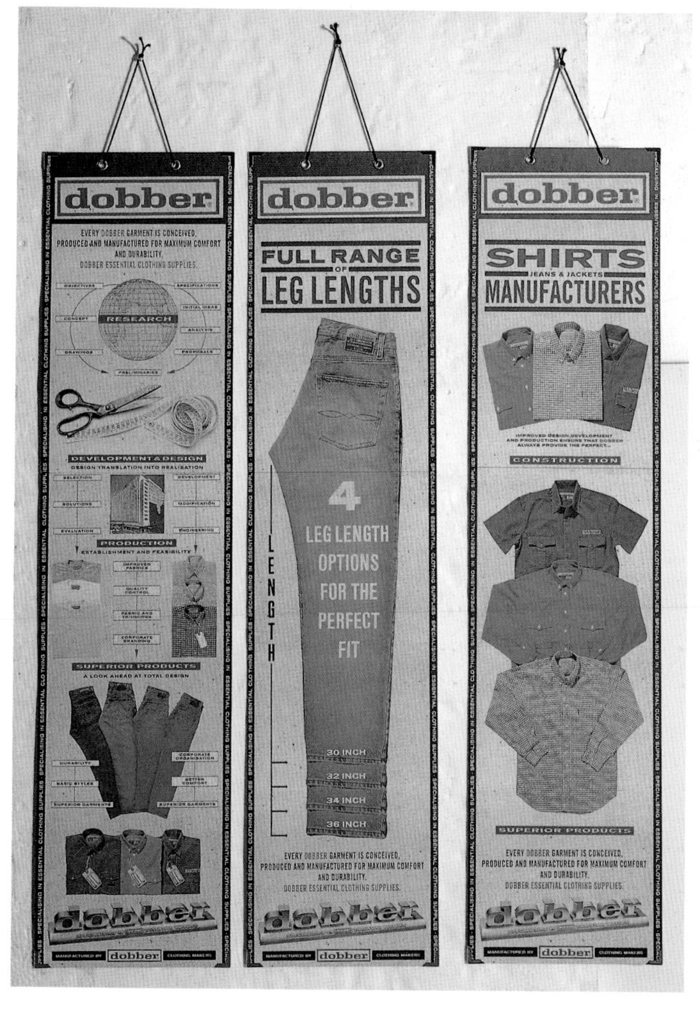
dobber
EVERY DOBBER GARMENT IS CONCEIVED, PRODUCED AND MANUFACTURED FOR MAXIMUM COMFORT AND DURABILITY.
DOBBER ESSENTIAL CLOTHING SUPPLIES.
RESEARCH
DEVELOPMENT & DESIGN
PRODUCTION
SUPERIOR PRODUCTS
dobber
FULL RANGE OF LEG LENGTHS
LENGTH
4 LEG LENGTH OPTIONS FOR THE PERFECT FIT
30 INCH
32 INCH
34 INCH
36 INCH
EVERY DOBBER GARMENT IS CONCEIVED, PRODUCED AND MANUFACTURED FOR MAXIMUM COMFORT AND DURABILITY.
DOBBER ESSENTIAL CLOTHING SUPPLIES.
dobber
SHIRTS
JEANS & JACKETS
MANUFACTURERS
CONSTRUCTION
SUPERIOR PRODUCTS
EVERY DOBBER GARMENT IS CONCEIVED, PRODUCED AND MANUFACTURED FOR MAXIMUM COMFORT AND DURABILITY.
DOBBER ESSENTIAL CLOTHING SUPPLIES.
dobber

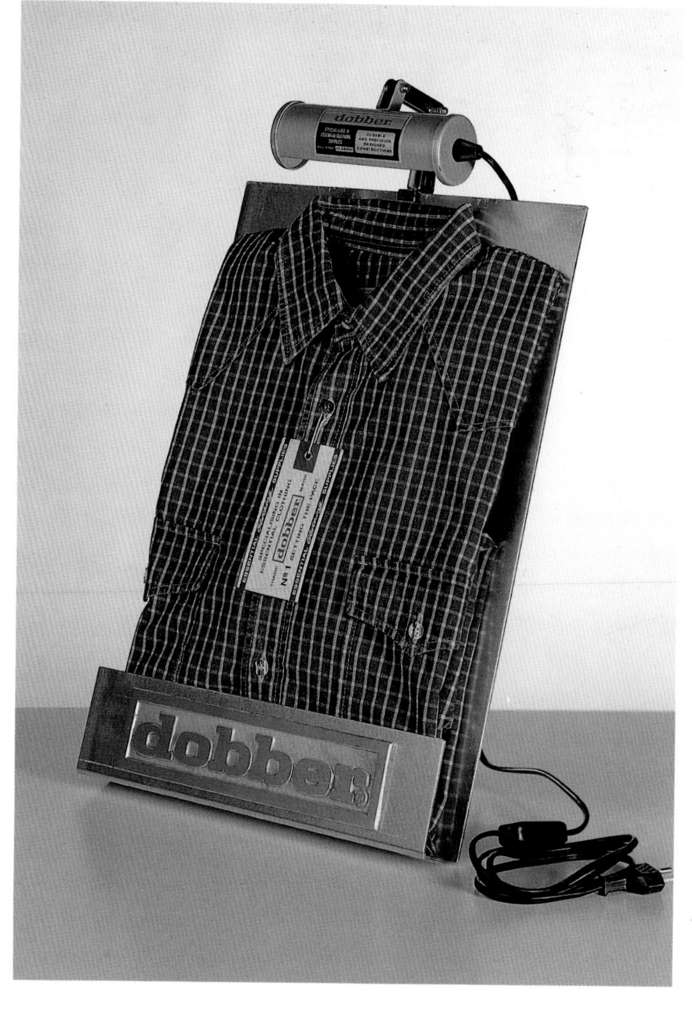
dobber
dobber

■ 1, 2 ART DIRECTOR/DESIGNER: JOSE SERRANO ILLUSTRATORS: WOODY WILSON, TONY DIPRETA, MORT WALKER, DEAN YOUNG, STAN DRAKE DESIGN FIRM: MIRES DESIGN CLIENT: UNION TRIBUNE COUNTRY: USA ■ 3 ART DIRECTOR/DESIGNER: JEFF WEITHMAN DESIGN FIRM/CLIENT: NIKE COUNTRY: USA

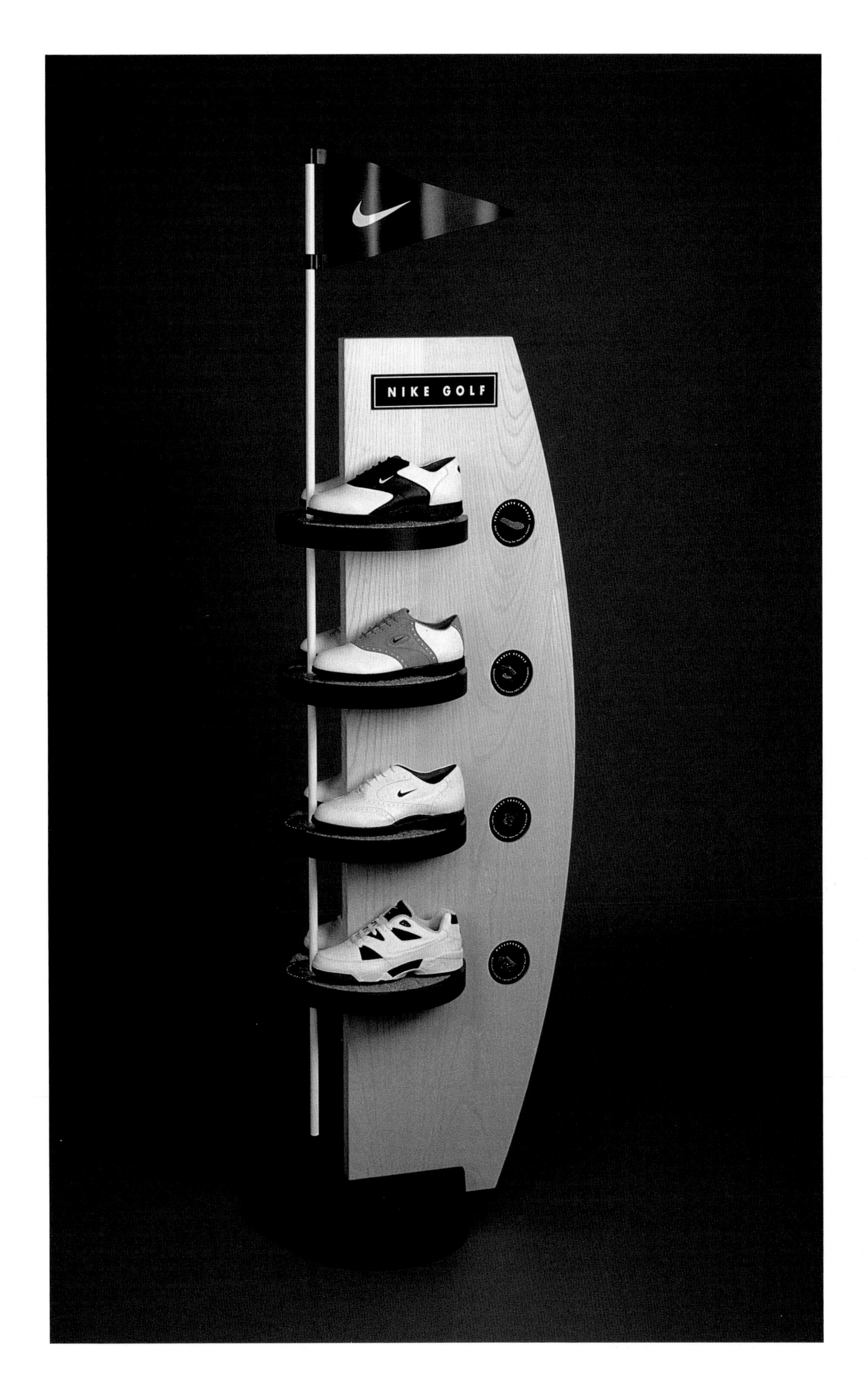
NIKE GOLF

EVELYN

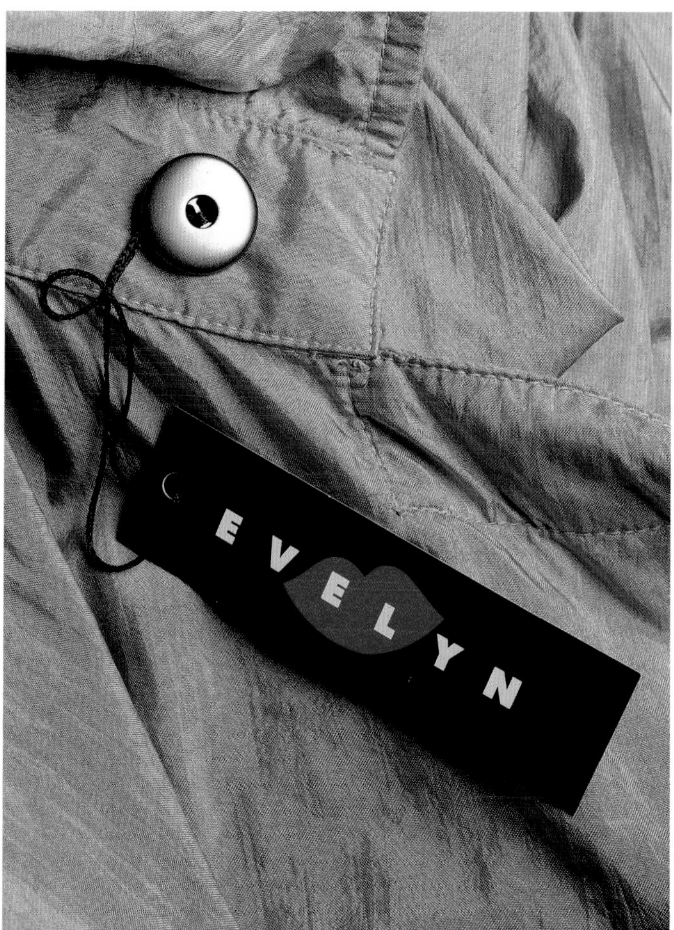
EVELYN

EVELYN

EVELYN
BALGEBRÜCKSTR. 14 BREMEN 0421-324221

■ 1–4 ART DIRECTOR/DESIGNER: SIBYLLE HAASE PHOTOGRAPHER: FRITZ HAASE DESIGN FIRM: HAASE & KNELS CLIENT: BOUTIQUE EVELYN COUNTRY: GERMANY ■ 5 ART DIRECTOR: JOAN DONNELLY DESIGNER: TIM A. FRAME PHOTOGRAPHER: PAM MONFORT DESIGN FIRM: SDI/HTI CLIENT: ACA JOE COUNTRY: MEXICO ■ (FOLLOWING SPREAD) 1–3 ART DIRECTOR/DESIGNER: JAN LORENC DESIGN FIRM: LORENC DESIGN

CLIENT: GEORGIA CENTER FOR CHILDREN COUNTRY: USA ■ 4 ART DIRECTOR/DESIGNER: KEVIN MCPHEE DESIGN FIRM: KEVIN MCPHEE + ASSOC. CLIENT: REVO SUNGLASSES COUNTRY: USA ■ 5, 6 ART DIRECTORS: TOM ANTISTA, THOMAS FAIRCLOUGH DESIGNERS: TOM ANTISTA, THOMAS FAIRCLOUGH DESIGN FIRM/CLIENT: ANTISTA FAIRCLOUGH DESIGN COUNTRY: USA ■ 7, 8 ART DIRECTOR: AKIO OKUMURA DESIGNER: EMI KAJIHARA DESIGN FIRM: PACKAGING CREATE INC. CLIENT: NEW OJI PAPER CO., LTD. COUNTRY: JAPAN

920
GEORGIA
CENTER
for
Children

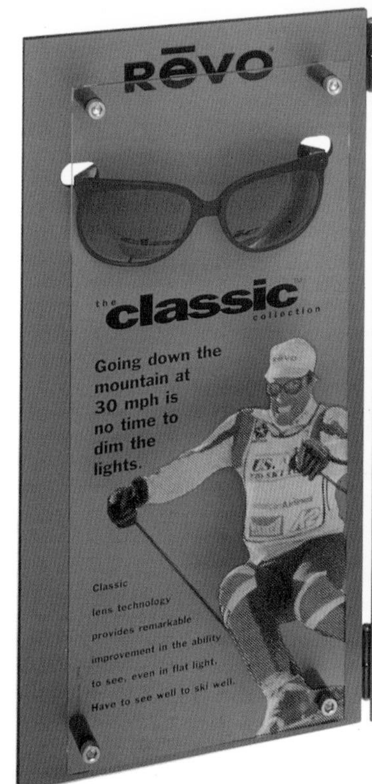
Rēvo
the classic collection
Going down the mountain at 30 mph is no time to dim the lights.
Classic lens technology provides remarkable improvement in the ability to see, even in flat light. Have to see well to ski well.

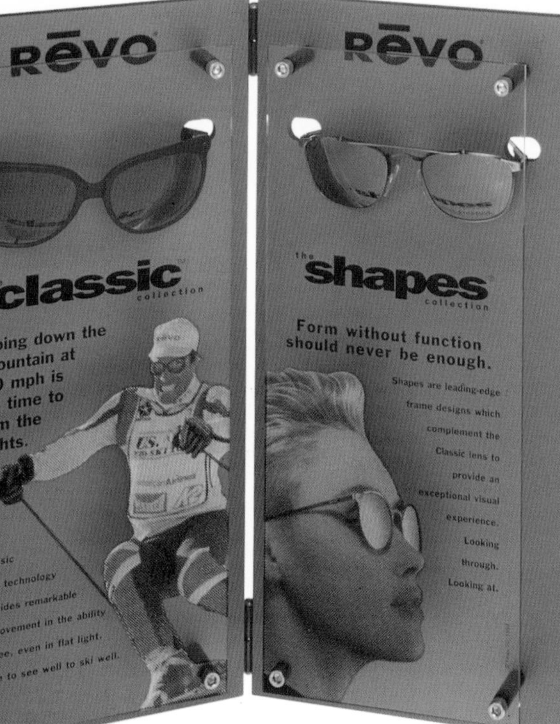
Rēvo
the shapes collection
Form without function should never be enough.
Shapes are leading-edge frame designs which complement the Classic lens to provide an exceptional visual experience. Looking through. Looking at.

Rēvo
the h2O collection
Go fish.
The H2O lens can provide 99% polarizing effectiveness, combined with Classic lens functionality to improve visual acuity. With remarkable ease, you see straight through the water's surface glare to the fish below. Now catch them.

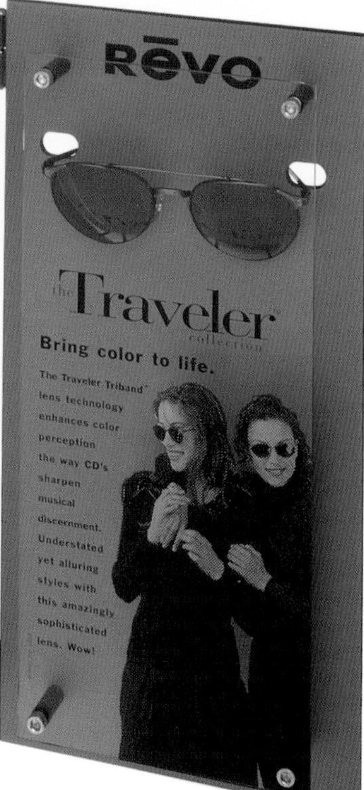
Rēvo
the Traveler collection
Bring color to life.
The Traveler Triband lens technology enhances color perception the way CD's sharpen musical discernment. Understated yet alluring styles with this amazingly sophisticated lens. Wow!

GREENS CORNER
K mart
UNITED ARTISTS Theatres
ROBOCOP THREE
LOOK WHO S TALKING NOW PG13
FATAL INSTINCT PG13
DEMOLITION MAN R
COOL RUNNINGS PG
ARMEN & JOSEPH JEWELERS

GINZA
GINZA

OJI PAPER GALLERY GINZA
OJI PAPER GALLERY GINZA

■ 1 ART DIRECTOR: CLIVE GAY DESIGNERS: CLIVE GAY, KOOS LE GRANGE DESIGN FIRMS: TRADEMARK DESIGN PTY, O'SULLIVAN CLIENT: BANK OF NAMIBIA COUNTRY: NAMIBIA ■ 2, 3 ART DIRECTOR/DESIGNER: JOOST VAN ROON CLIENT: BARCO GRAPHICS COUNTRY: BELGIUM

1000
Fortuna
1000
MILLE DUIZEND MIL THOUSAND TAUSEND

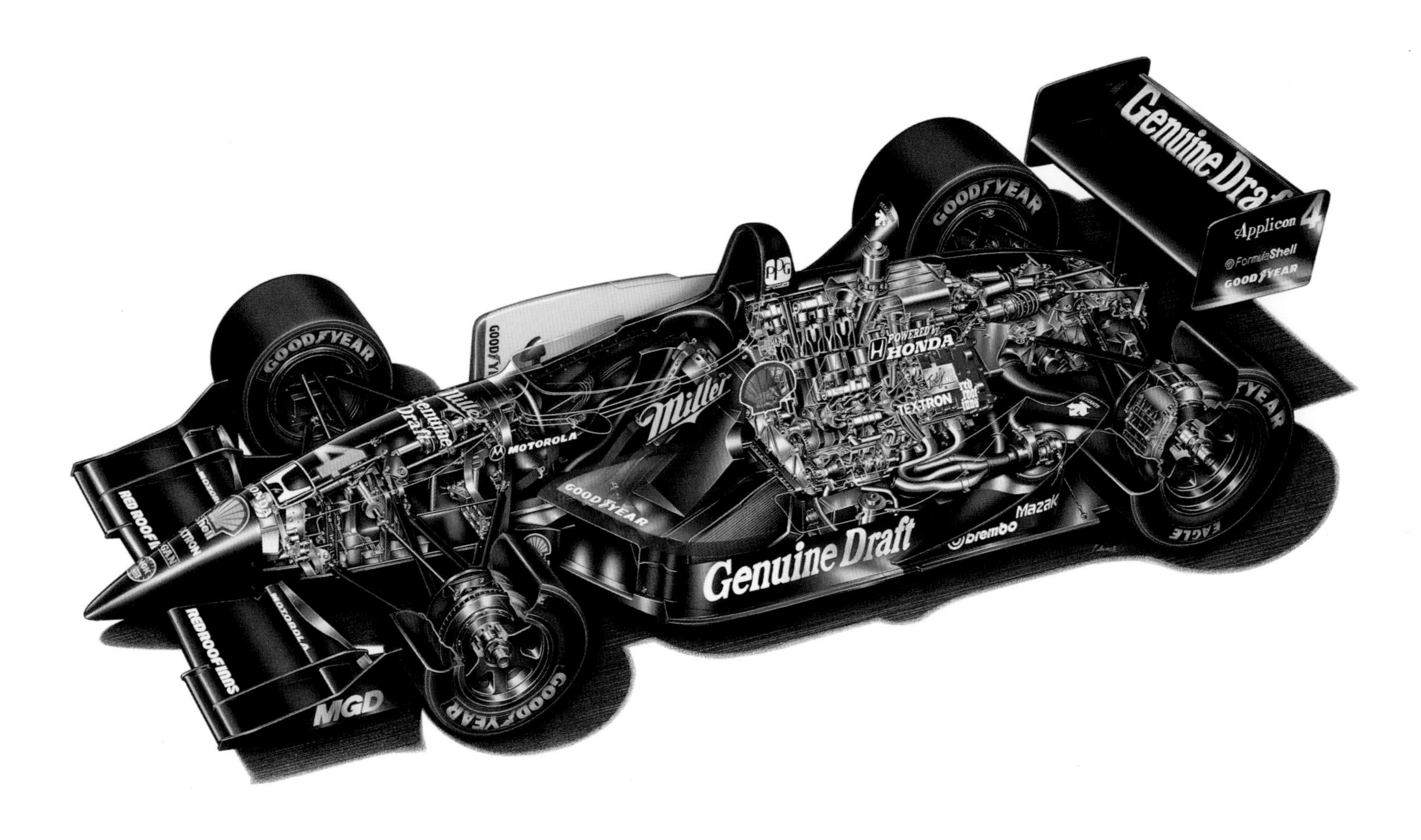

■ 1 Art Director: ALBERTO GARCIA-IZQUIERDO Illustrator: PETER KRÄMER Client: DEUTSCHE LUFTHANSA AG Country: GERMANY ■ 2 Illustrator: YOSHIHIRO INOMOTO Client: AMERICAN HONDA MOTOR CO., INC. Country: USA ■ 3 Art Director: ROSS WHITEHEAD Designer: ROSS WHITEHEAD Design Firm: HIMONT DESIGN CENTER Client: HIMONT USA INC. Country: USA

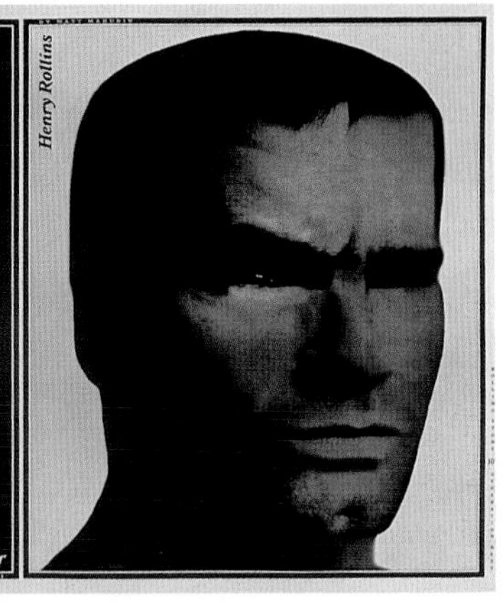

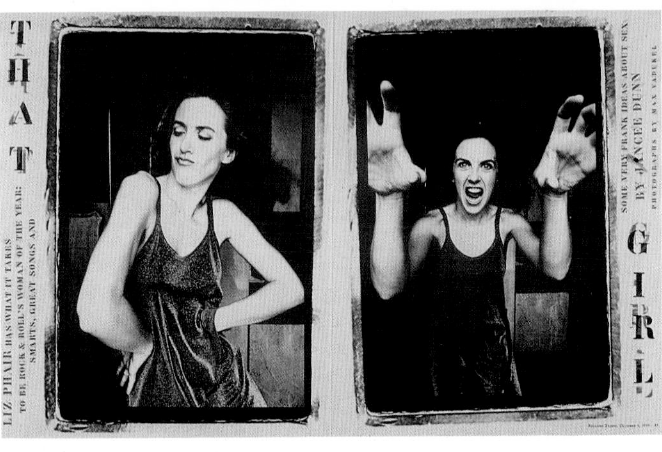

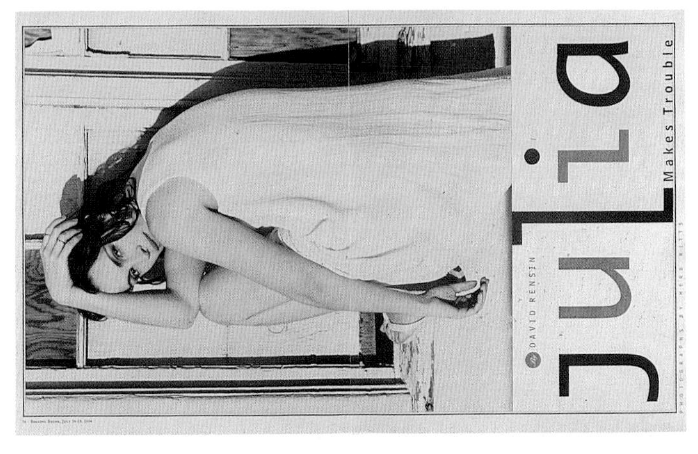

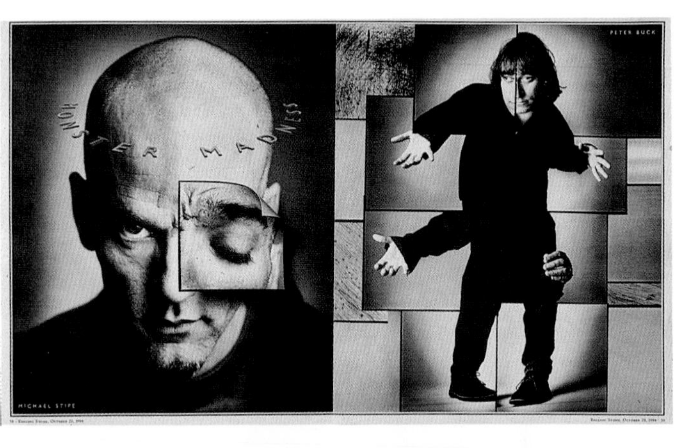

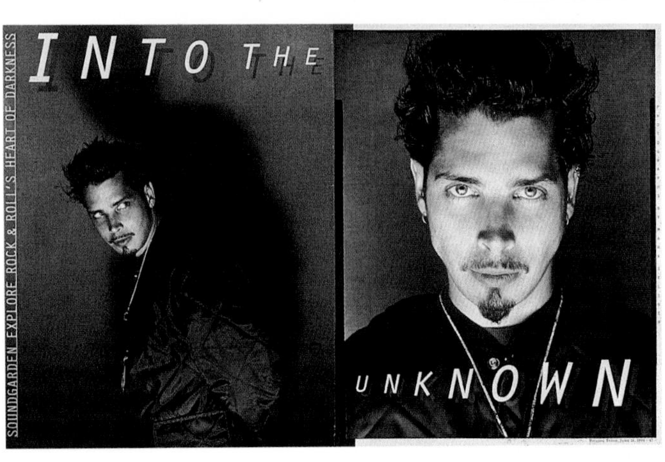

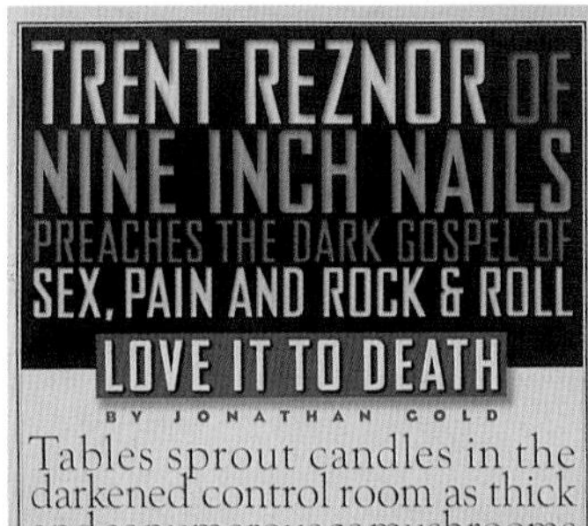
TRENT REZNOR OF
NINE INCH NAILS
PREACHES THE DARK GOSPEL OF
SEX, PAIN AND ROCK & ROLL
LOVE IT TO DEATH
BY JONATHAN GOLD
Tables sprout candles in the darkened control room as thick and as numerous as mushrooms on a dank forest floor, and miniskirted department-store mannequins are scattered about in various states of bon-

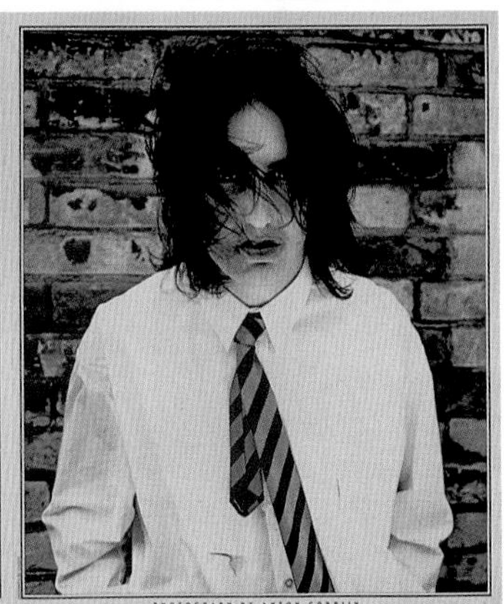

■ 1–10 ART DIRECTOR: FRED WOODWARD DESIGNERS: FRED WOODWARD, GAIL ANDERSON (1, 2, 10), GERALDINE HESSLER (1, 2, 10), LEE BEARSON (1, 2, 10) PHOTOGRAPHERS: MATT MAHURIN (1 LEFT, 2 RIGHT), MARK SELIGER (1 RIGHT, 6, 7), FRANK

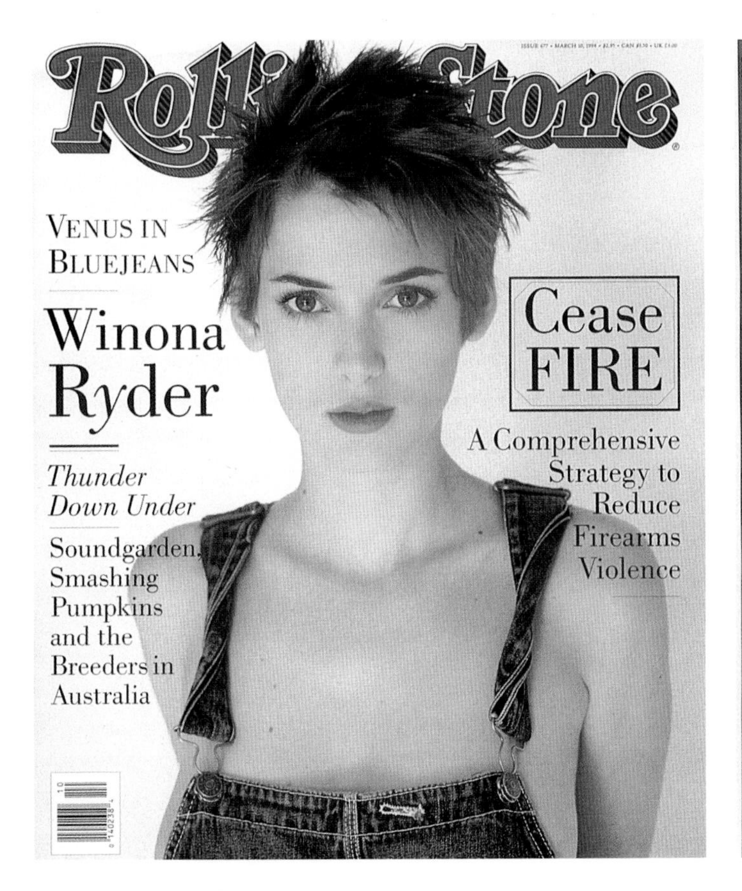

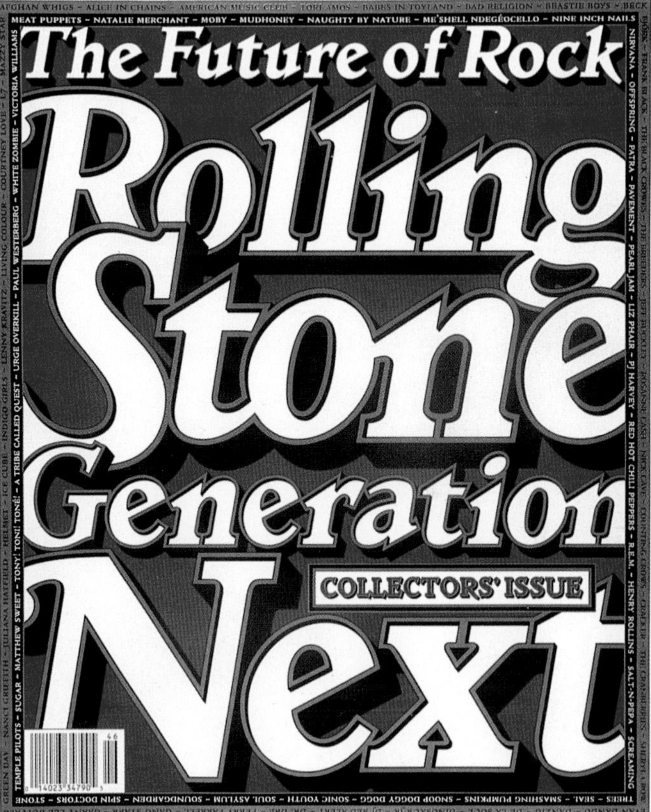

W. OCKENFELS 3 (2 LEFT), MAX VADUKUL (3), HERB RITTS (4, 9), GLEN LUCHFORD (5), ANTON CORBIJN (8) PHOTO EDITORS: JODI PECKMAN (1-8) LAURIE KRATOCHVIL (9) PUBLISHER: STRAIGHT ARROW PUBLISHERS/ROLLING STONE COUNTRY: USA

■ 1, 2 ART DIRECTOR: WAYNE FORD DESIGNER: WAYNE FORD PHOTOGRAPHERS: MATT MAHURIN (1), JASON BELL (2) PUBLISHER: HAYMARKET PUBLISHING LIMITED/XYZ MAGAZINE COUNTRY: GREAT BRITAIN ■ 3-6 (FROM TOP LEFT TO BOTTOM RIGHT) ART DIRECTOR:

HANS WOLF DESIGNER: BAS VAN DER PAARDT EDITOR: RONALD KRAAYEVELD PHOTOGRAPHERS: JEROEN KROOS (3), ZOLTAN (4) ILLUSTRATOR: MAKOTO SAITO (5) DESIGN FIRM: WIEDEN & KENNEDY (6) PUBLISHER: VNU-ADMEDIA/BLAD COUNTRY: NETHERLANDS

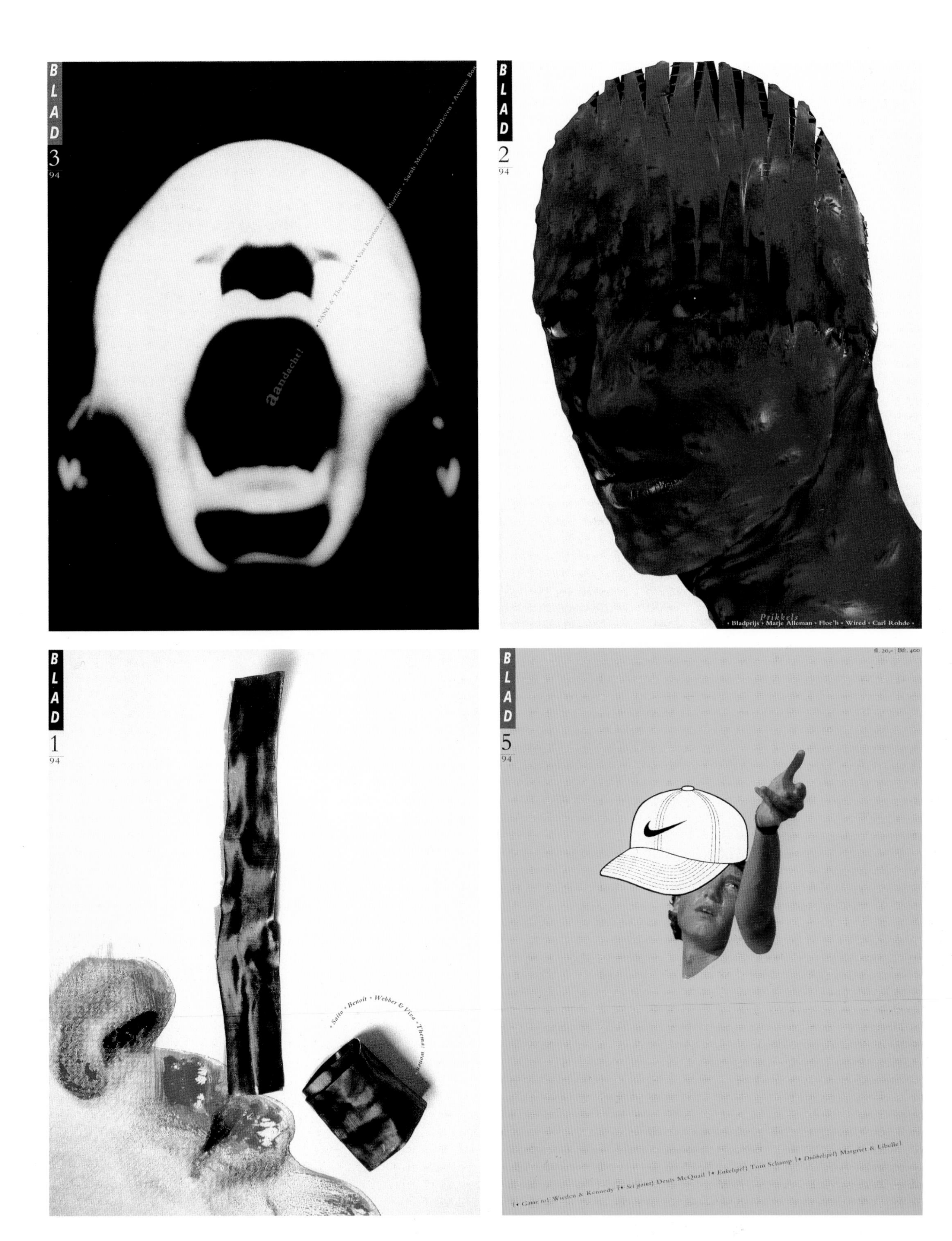
BLAD
3
94
aandacht!
• PANL & The Awards • Van Kooten ove Mortier • Sarah Moon • Zwitserleven • Avenue Box
BLAD
2
94
Prikkels
• Bladprijs • Marje Alleman • Floc'h • Wired • Carl Rohde •
BLAD
1
94
• Saito • Benoît • Webber & Viva • Thema:
fl. 20,- | Bfr. 400
BLAD
5
94
[• Game to] Wieden & Kennedy [• Set point] Denis McQuail [• Enkelspel] Tom Schamp [• Dubbelspel] Margriet & Libelle]

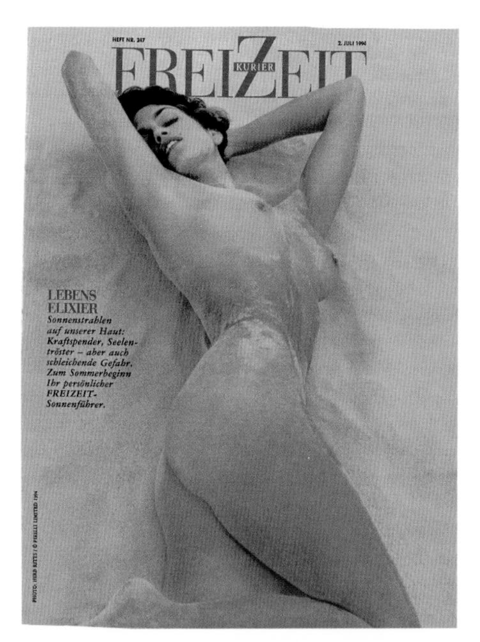

■ 1–6 (FROM TOP LEFT TO BOTTOM RIGHT) ART DIRECTOR: ANDREA SCHRAML DESIGNER: IRMGARD GABRIEL PHOTOGRAPHER: HERB RITTS (1), AGENTUR VIENNAREPORT (2), GIANNI VERSACE (4), NICK KNIGHT (5), WILLIAM WEGMAN (6) ILLUSTRATOR: PETER

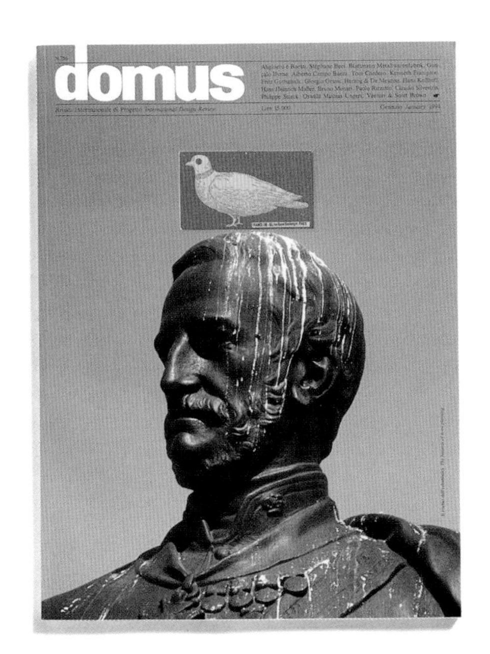

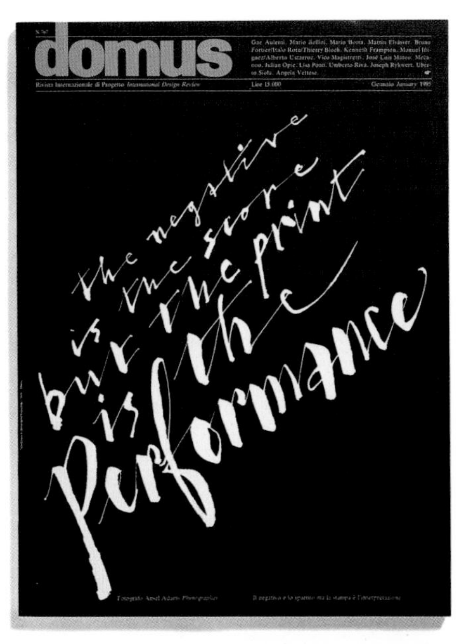

SENGL (3) PUBLISHER: KURIER REDAKTIONSGESMBH/FREIZEIT COUNTRY: AUSTRIA ■ **7–12** (FROM TOP LEFT TO BOTTOM RIGHT) DESIGNER: ALAN FLETCHER (7, 10–12) PHOTOGRAPHER: BOB MAUDE (7) PUBLISHER: EDITORIALE DOMUS/DOMUS COUNTRY: ITALY

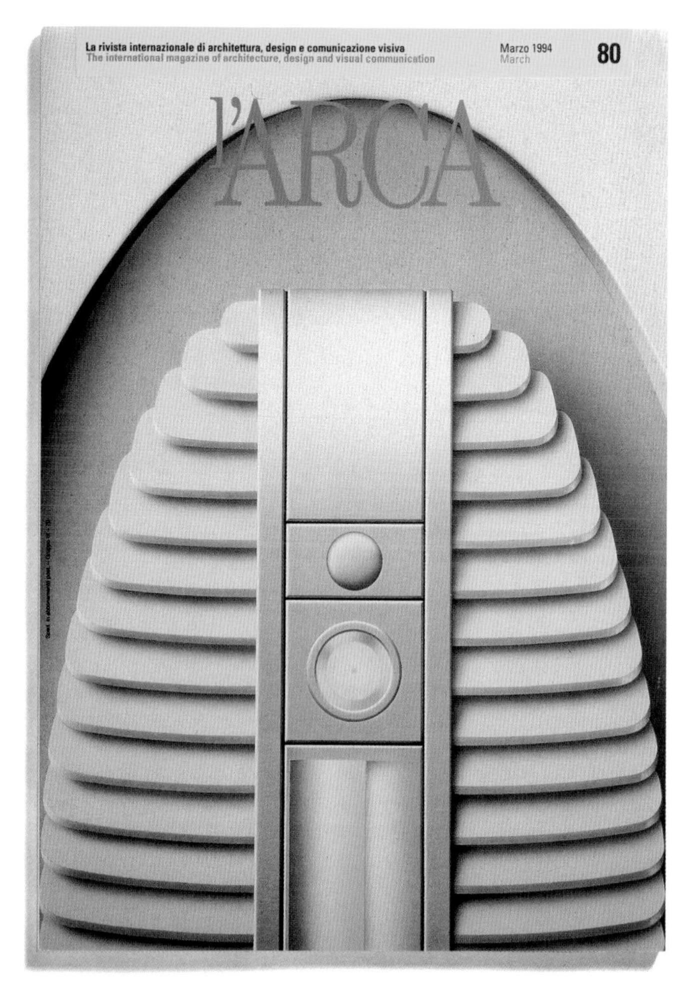
La rivista internazionale di architettura, design e comunicazione visiva
The international magazine of architecture, design and visual communication
Marzo 1994
March
80
l'ARCA

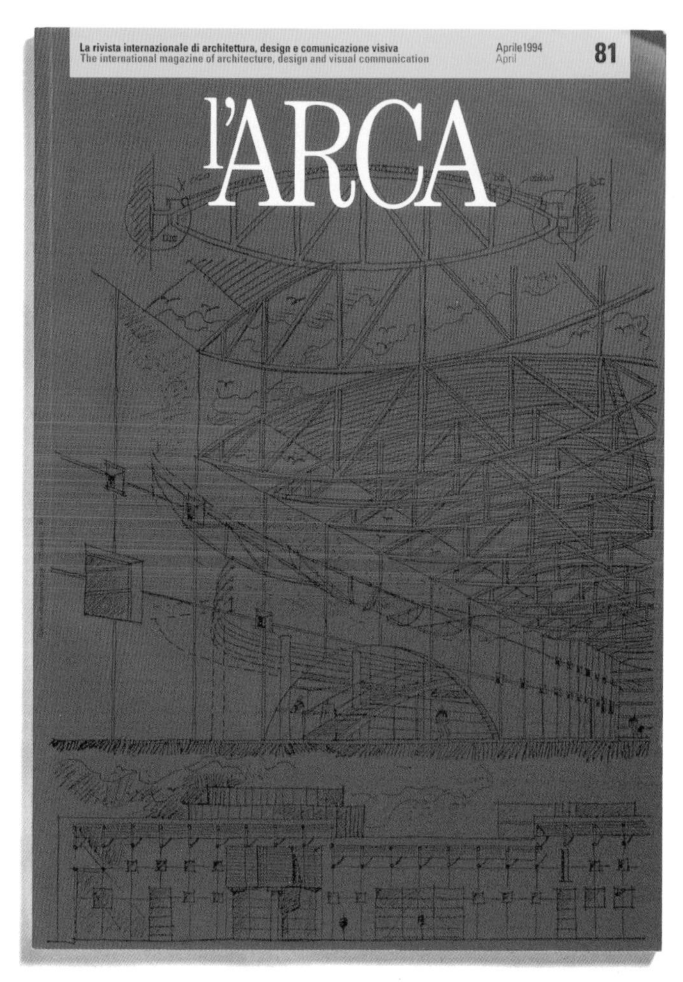
La rivista internazionale di architettura, design e comunicazione visiva
The international magazine of architecture, design and visual communication
Aprile1994
April
81
l'ARCA

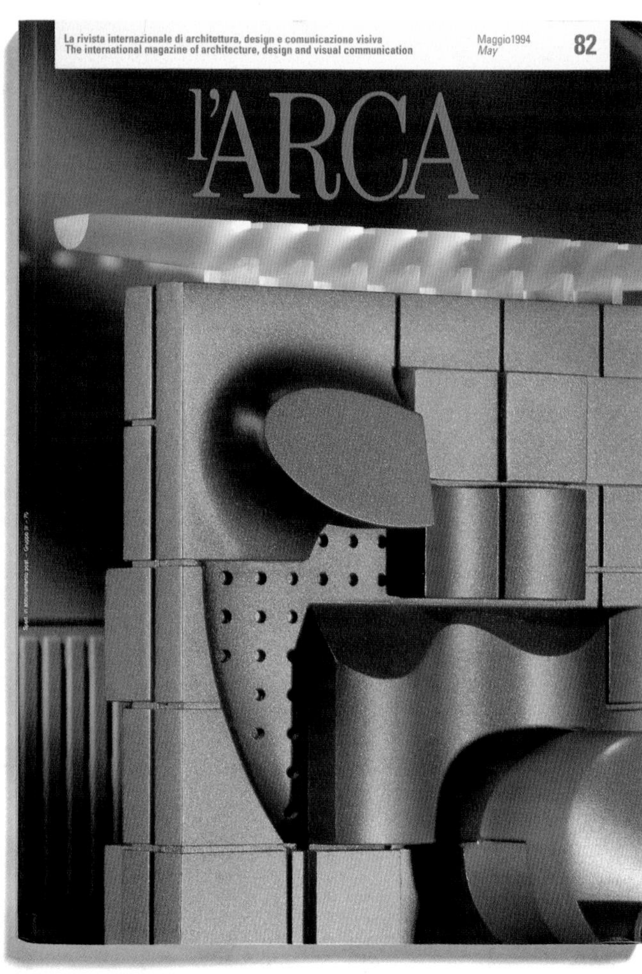
La rivista internazionale di architettura, design e comunicazione visiva
The international magazine of architecture, design and visual communication
Maggio1994
May
82
l'ARCA

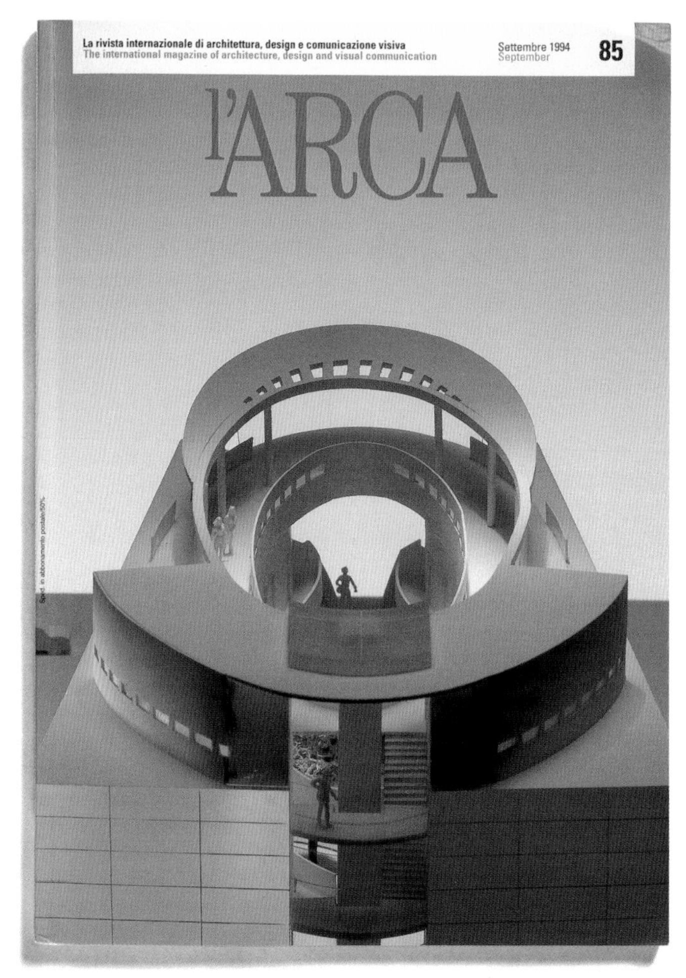
La rivista internazionale di architettura, design e comunicazione visiva
The international magazine of architecture, design and visual communication
Settembre 1994
September
85
l'ARCA

■ 1-4 ART DIRECTOR: BOB NOORDA PUBLISHER: L'ARCA EDIZIONI SPA/L'ARCA COUNTRY: ITALY ■ 5-10 EDITOR: MARCELO JÜNEMANN ART DIRECTOR/DESIGNER: VINCE FROST PHOTOGRAPHER: THE DOUGLAS BROTHERS (5), ANGELA HILL (6), JOHNATHON ABRIELLE (7), JOHN HUET (8), JAMES CANT (9) PUBLISHER: MARCELO JÜNEMANN/LOCATION PRINTING BIG, S.L./ BIG MAGAZINE COUNTRIES: SPAIN, USA

■ 1 ART DIRECTOR/DESIGNER: OSWALDO MIRANDA PHOTOGRAPHER: LOUIS FAURER (1) DESIGN FIRM: CASA DE IDE'IAS PUBLISHER: GRAFICA COUNTRY: BRASIL ■ 2–6 ART DIRECTOR/DESIGNER: OSWALDO MIRANDA PHOTOGRAPHERS: MAMORU HORIGUSHI (2), MARK LAITA (3), ERWIN BLUMENFELD (4), STEVEN KLEIN (5), SERGE LUTENS (6) DESIGN FIRM: CASA DE IDE'IAS PUBLISHER: ADD COUNTRY: BRASIL

A D.
Tim, Tim! Beverage's Campaign/ Paschoal Fabra Neto/
Anúncios do mês/ Retroactive/ A Fotografia Editorial, etc.
Anúncios do mês/
O Golden Boy dos Anos '90/ Os melhores
A D.
Alex Liberman e Erwin Blumenteld (Vogue)/
Leagas Delaney/ Agência: Talent/ ADC Show
Anúncio Brasileiros/
Jean Paul Goude, etc.
A D.
A D.
Serge Lutens Fantasy / Agência: W/Brasil/ In and Out
Art Director's Shows/
The Best in Editorial/ Anúncio
Ingleses, etc.

■ 1, 2 ART DIRECTORS/DESIGNERS: CARL BARTEL, SIMONE HÜETLIN (2) PHOTOGRAPHERS: CARL BARTEL, SIMONE HÜETLIN COPYWRITER: TIBOR BORBÉLY (1) PUBLISHER: JETZT, DAS JUGENDMAGAZIN DER SÜDDEUTSCHEN ZEITUNG COUNTRY: GERMANY ■ 3 ART DIRECTORS: TREVOR FLETT, RICHARD HENDERSON DESIGNERS: MEGAN STONE, KEITH SMITH ILLUSTRATOR: NAOMI HEWITT PHOTOGRAPHER/DESIGN

FIRM: FHA IMAGE DESIGN PUBLISHER: WKD MAGAZINE COUNTRY: AUSTRALIA ■ 4–6 ART DIRECTOR: TAMAS KOLTAI DESIGNER: GYÖRGY KEMÉNY PHOTOGRAPHER: ZSUZSA SZKAROSSY (5) PUBLISHER: SZINHAZ COUNTRY: HUNGARY ■ 7–9 ART DIRECTOR: YUTAKA SASAKI DESIGNER: YUTAKA SASAKI DESIGN FIRM: NIPPON DESIGN CENTER, INC. CLIENT: TAISEI CORP. COUNTRY: JAPAN ■ 10–12 ART DIRECTOR: KAZUMASA NAGAI DESIGNER: KAZUMASA NAGAI DESIGN FIRM: NIPPON DESIGN CENTER, INC. CLIENT: TAKEO CO., LTD. COUNTRY: JAPAN

SZÍNHÁZ
XXVII. ÉVF. 10. SZÁM 1994. OKTÓBER

NĀDASPĀR

MELEG
SZÍNHÁZ
XXVII. ÉVF. 1. SZÁM 1994. JANUÁR

SZÍNHÁZ
XXVII. ÉVF. 11. SZÁM 1994. NOVEMBER
F E S Z T I V Á L
K Ö R K É P

TQ
TAISEI QUARTERLY 88
1994 SPRING
特集：エントランスと、その奥にあるもの。

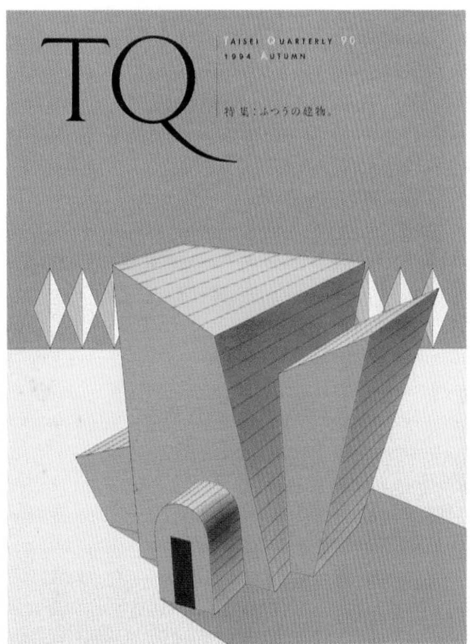
TQ
TAISEI QUARTERLY 90
1994 AUTUMN
特集：ふつうの建物。

TQ
TAISEI QUARTERLY 89
1994 SUMMER
特集：橋を渡る。

竹尾

マーメイド
竹尾

オーディス
竹尾

■ 1–6 ART DIRECTORS: CARL LEHMANN-HAUPT, NANCY KRUGER COHEN DESIGNERS: CARL LEHMANN-HAUPT, NANCY KRUGER COHEN EDITOR: SUSAN SZENASY PHOTOGRAPHERS: ANDREW WILLIAMSON (1), BILL STEELE (2), RICK ALBERT (4), COURTESY CENTRO STUDIO ALLESSI (5, BACKGROUND), COURTESY MARKUSE CORP. (5, BRUSH), PHILIP MEUSER (6, RED IMAGE), COURTESY THE BETTMANN ARCHIVE (6, BLUE IMAGE) SPECIAL PHOTOGRAPHY CONSULTANT: KEVIN SLAVIN (6) PUBLISHER: BELLEROPHON PUBLICATIONS/

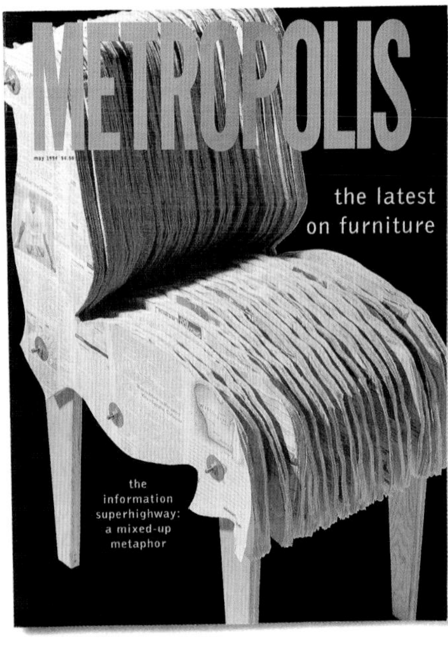

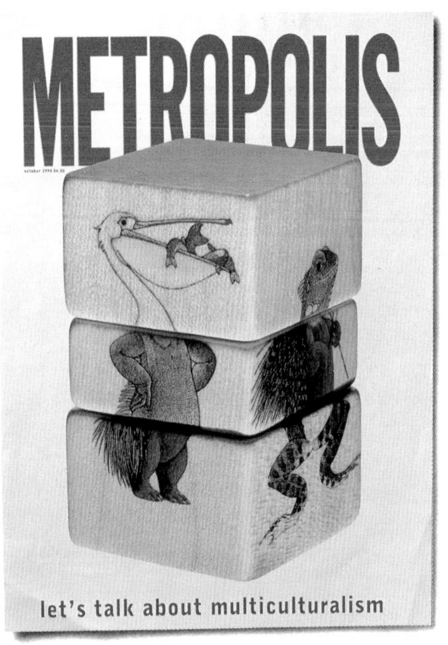

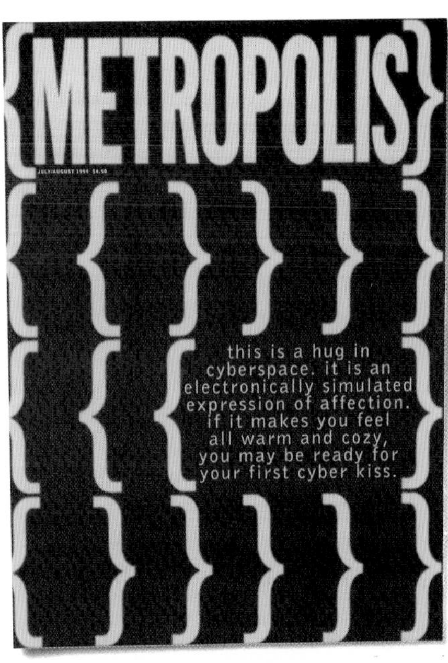

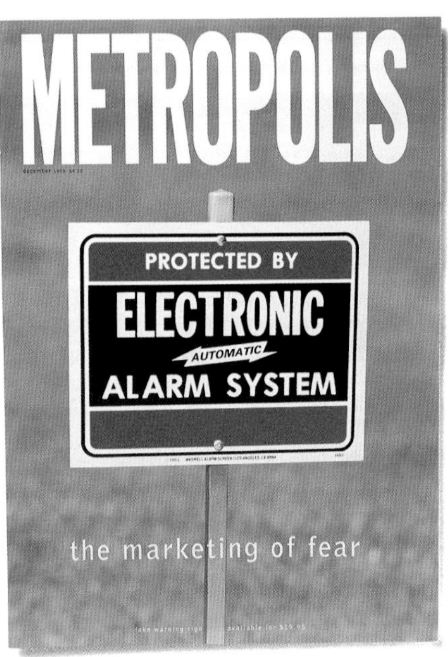

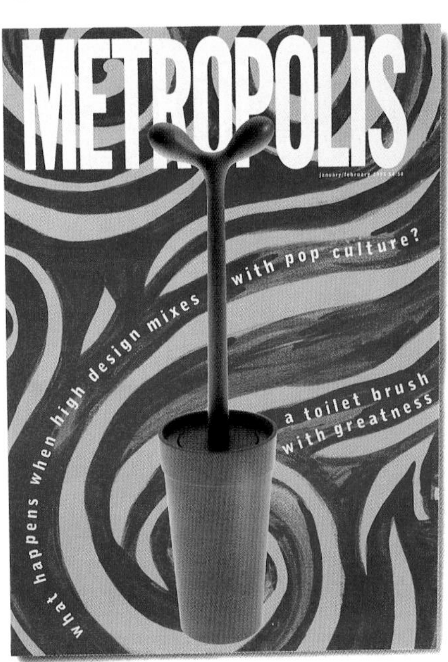

METROPOLIS COUNTRY: USA ■ 7 ART DIRECTOR: BOB SHELL DESIGNER: AILSA MCWHINNIE PHOTOGRAPHER: HIROSHI NONAMI PUBLISHER: PIC MAGAZINE COUNTRY: USA ■ 8 ART DIRECTOR: PAULA SCHER DESIGNERS: PAULA SCHER, RON LOUIE PHOTOGRAPHER: JOHN PAUL ENDRESS DESIGN FIRM: PENTAGRAM DESIGN PUBLISHER: MICHELE S. MAGAZINE & ASSOCIATES, INC./NYCHRISTMAS COUNTRY: USA ■ 9, 10 ART DIRECTORS: KEN MCGUIRE (9), NOAH TOM (10) DESIGNER: NOAH TOM PHOTOGRAPHERS: MIKE WAGGONER (9), STUART SAKOEKI (9), HANK (9), MICHAEL PAZ (9), GORDINHO (10) PHOTO EDITOR: BERNIE BAKER PUBLISHER: REID FUJITA/H30 MAGAZINE COUNTRY: USA

THE INTERNATIONAL SHOWCASE FOR PHOTOGRAPHERS
pic
IN THE STUDIO...
THE WORLD OF
HIROSHI NONAMI
ABSOLUTELY
FABULOUS
THE ART OF
SELLING VODKA
AUGUST 1994 £2.45
9 770956 228018

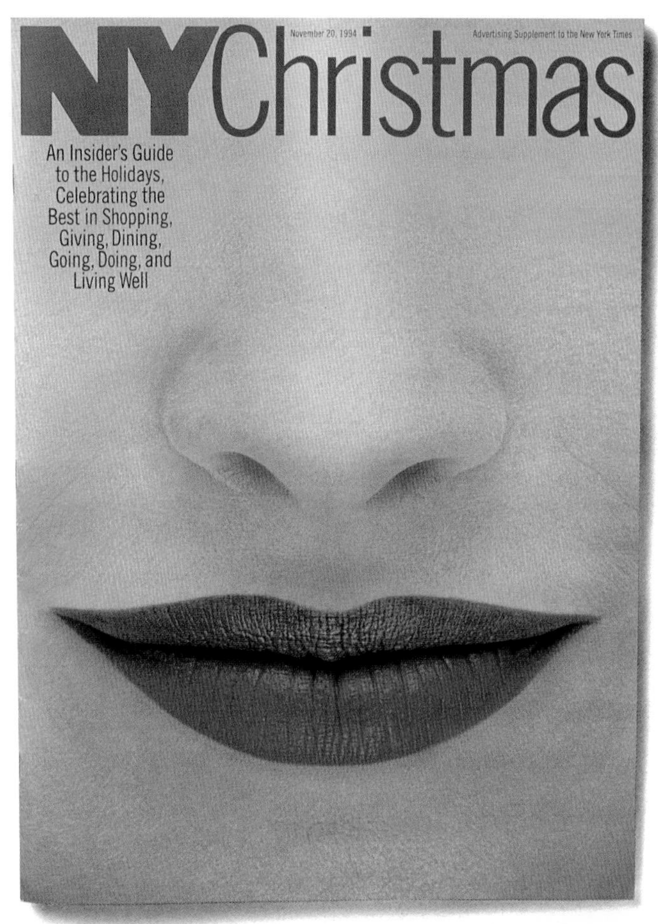
NYChristmas
November 20, 1994
Advertising Supplement to the New York Times
An Insider's Guide
to the Holidays,
Celebrating the
Best in Shopping,
Giving, Dining,
Going, Doing, and
Living Well

BU LA'IA
FREE
SEPTEMBER 1994
New & Improved
WILD WILD WET • BIG MELE 2 • BU KNOWS • US OPEN • JON-KELLY • JADE LUCAS

FEBRUARY 1994
ALL HAWAII, ALL THE TIME.
YEAR OF THE HAWAIIAN
FULL WINTER CONTEST COVERAGE.
EXCLUSIVE INTERVIEWS.
MEANEST PHOTOS EVER.

■ 1 ART DIRECTORS: HAL WOLVERTON, ALICIA JOHNSON DESIGNERS: HAL WOLVERTON, ALICIA JOHNSON, PAMELA RACS, KELLI KLEIN DESIGN FIRM: JOHNSON & WOLVERTON PUBLISHER: PLAZM COUNTRY: USA ■ 2–8 ART DIRECTORS: ANTHON BEEKE, LIDEWIJ EDELKOORT

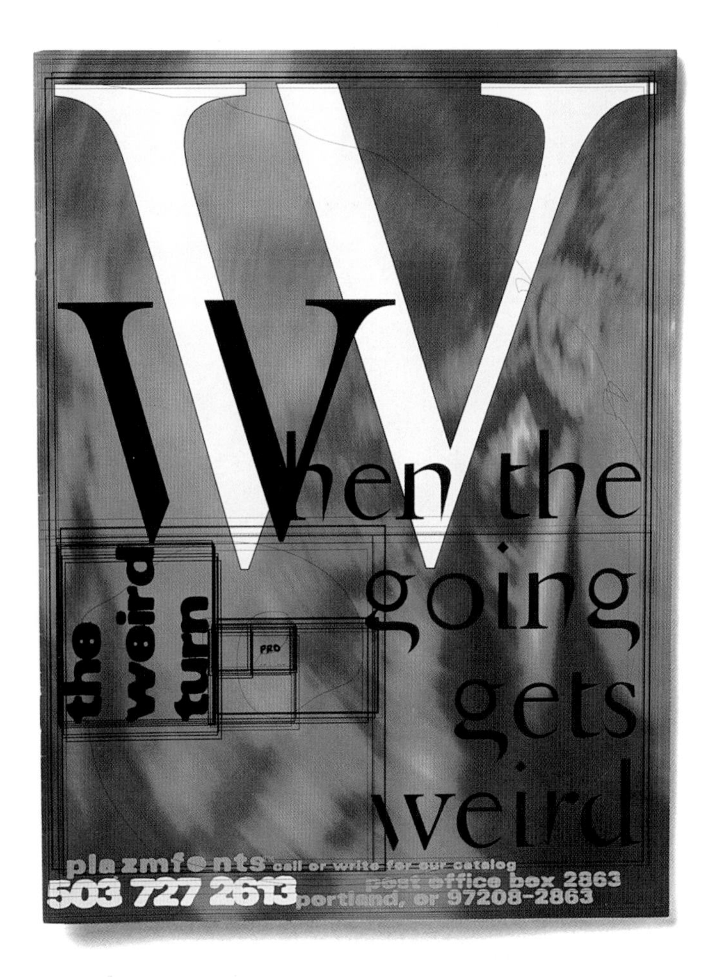

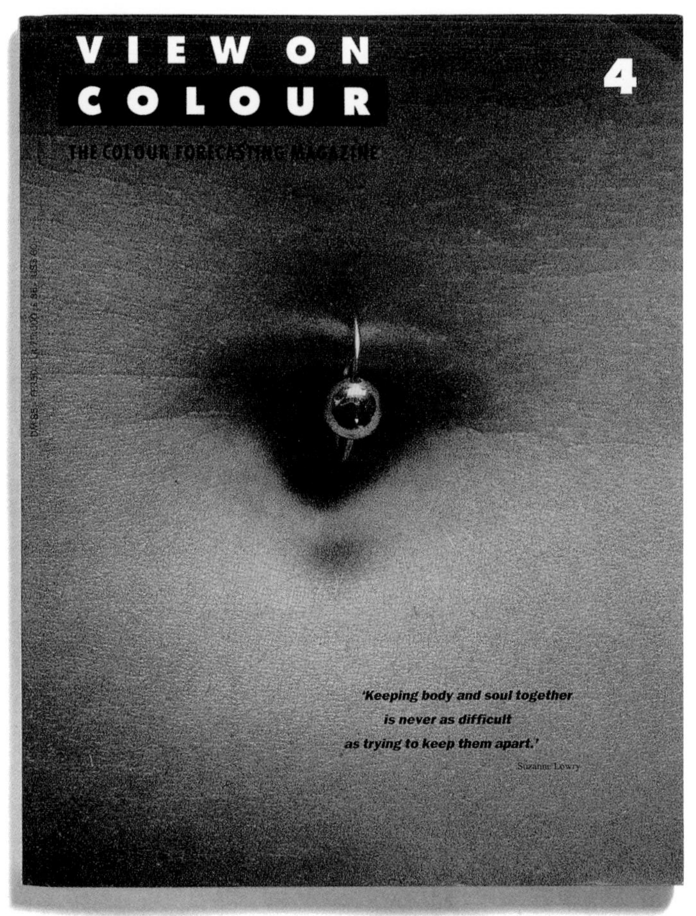

DESIGNER: ANTHON BEEKE PHOTOGRAPHERS: ANTHON BEEKE (2), MARCEL VAN DER VLUGT (3, 4), ANNA BEEKE (6), JOHAN VIGEVENO (7), PAOLO ROVERSI (8) DESIGN FIRM: STUDIO ANTHON BEEKE BV PUBLISHER: UNITED PUBLISHERS/VIEW ON COLOUR COUNTRY: FRANCE

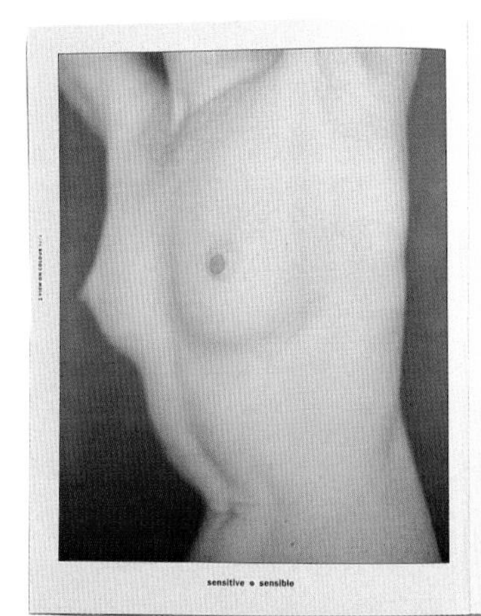

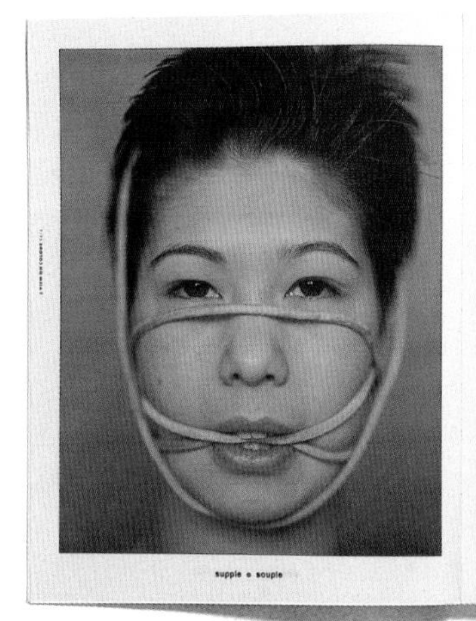

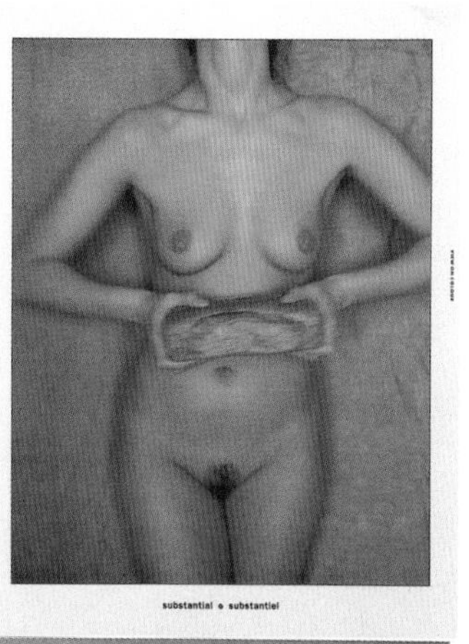

THE BODY OF LIGHT

From the most ancient evidence of the sacred to the cybernetic, synthetic visions of the New Age, light and colour have been metaphors for knowledge, wisdom, and the godhead throughout the millennia. Where words lead off, colour rushes in. Islam is no exception. The Qur'an is literally riddled with references to light; consequently, the language and texts of Sufi orders frequently refer to light, enlightenment and personal illumination. ■ In Persia, medieval Sufis elaborated a system of light and colour, to the exclusion of other symbols and metaphor networks. One of their basic ideas is that human beings are exiled from the world of light. Trapped in a material world of darkness, we are forgetful of our luminous origins until the moment when our supercelestial guides contact us and help us find our ways back to the realm of light. ■ The supercelestial guide is a polychromic, angelic being who appears to select Sufi adepts in a culminating vision of kaleidoscopic ecstasy. The angel is a light-being which awakens the light-being in the Sufi, and the two merge in a kind of awesome fireworks display. If there is a 'goal' to the mystic path of Iranian Sufism, it is exactly this vision. To paraphrase Islamic scholar Henri Corbin: In Christianity, God becomes man; in Sufism, man becomes God. ■ The Persian texts go to great lengths to explain how, where and why the angelic vision occurs. Some Sufi adepts were intrigued by mapping the spiritual world; their work resulted in detailed visionary landscapes complete with colour-coded geographic features. According to one version, the visionary sky is green, the sun luminous black and the stars fiery red. Other Sufis were interested in the development of parapsychological senses; these mystics left behind elaborate descriptions of a 'subtle' physiology, complete with colour-coded super-sensory organs. The heart, for example, is a deep emerald green, while the 'lower' soul is aqua blue. And still others measured their spiritual progress through coloured flashes of light, a kind of chromatic Morse code which leads the adept up the emerald mountain of Qaf and into the arms of the angel.

THE SUPER-CELESTIAL COLOUR CODE

The master of the visionary colour code was one Najmoddin Kobrâ, who was born in Central Asia in 1145 and died a heroic death in 1220. He left behind a diary of his spiritual journey which succeeding generations of followers have continued to comment on, clarify and disagree with. ■ A kind of experimental method of mystic control, the notion of coloured lights was introduced by Kobrâ as a spiritual rating system. Called 'photisms' by contemporary scholars (who also study them in functionally 'blind' patients), these coloured lights communicate to the adept what he or she is encountering on the mystical plane and allow his or her teacher to monitor progress on the spiritual path. Coloured photisms gauge the adept's enlightenment, warn of danger, and reward the spiritual work or **dhikr**. They are not 'hallucinations,' which imply psychological pathology; nor are they 'allegories,' which refer to some kind of made-up or imaginary phenomena. On the contrary: the testimony of Kobrâ and his followers suggests that photisms are actual physical perceptions which occur in 'normal' consciousness as well as in the hypnagogic state between waking and sleeping, in meditation and in dreams. ■ If a pale green flash occurs, in the vicinity of a flesh-and-blood being, it can 'tell' the adept where this person is on the spiritual path; if a sunny yellow light sparks during reading, it can draw attention to the spiritual merit of a particular idea or passage; if a sprinkle of silver photisms occurs in the domestic domain it can signal to the adept that a particular thought is worth noting. ■ Not only the colour, but the size, number and duration of the flashes add finesse to the language. Gradually the adept increases his or her spiritual capacity and the photisms become more frequent, taking on a greater range of saturation, tone and hue. Sometimes the incremental photisms solidify in coloured rays, or suns, or formless glows. As spiritual development progresses, parapsychological activity becomes more pronounced. In Sufism, telepathy, clairvoyance, telekinesis and levitation are viewed as divine gifts, never as 'powers' used for material gain. ■ Unfortunately, different Sufi documents have different scales of colour, from the murky hues of fledgling insights to the bright, crisp colours – cobalt, crimson, emerald–which reward considerable spiritual achievement. Correspondences between different colour sequences, let alone their significations, are difficult to sort out. Every writer has a personalized technicolor vision and produces a slight variation on the scale, sometimes assigning different meanings to different hues, though they all eventually arrive at the kaleidoscopic, multicolor vision which coincides with the ecstatic experience of meeting with the angel. For purposes of illustration, I'll draw primarily form Semnâni's scale here. ■ At the lowest end is simple darkness, a sort of dirty darkness, sometimes brownish or greyish, which signifies the material world that clouds or obscures the world of light. At the next level is blue–a robin's egg blue indicates spiritual naïvete, but if the photism appears as ultramarine, it's a message from the vital soul that spiritual development is well underway. A navy blue is a benevolent sign, a kind of angelic encouragement, while azure is an enthusiastic confirmation of spiritual progress. The red light follows, signifying theological wisdom–the more it resembles pure fire, the more it has to do with spiritual vitality, but if it's sienna or brick coloured, watch out ! It may be diabolic, though a dim fire suggests nothing more than fatigue. Next in line is white, the brighter, the better. The whites have to do with the super-consciousness according to some commentators, the light of Islam according to others. A smoky white is a warning sign that the lower soul is gaining ground. Yellow comes next. Ochre may indicate a lessening in a parapsychological activity, while lemony yellows, even limes, stand for fidelity and faith. ■ The next stage is crucial. It is the stage of a difficult trial for the erstwhile adept, when the 'luminous black light' of the 'midnight sun' shines and the ecstasy is about to be attained. At this step those who lack spiritual moxie and psychological maturity risk losing their minds, while those who are prepared for the thrilling experience bask in the black light of passionate love. Finally the climax occurs – the emerald green light of ecstasy. This is the light of the pacified soul, the heart's knowledge, of the guardian angel. It is accompanied by a polychromy, or what Kobrâ has called 'the field of colours,' when the adept is liberated from matter and glimpses his or her supercelestial origins in the world of fluorescent light. ■ In keeping with their colour-coded spiritual adventure, Sufis who have attained the polychromic ecstasy wear colourful patchwork caftans or robes of bright emerald green, while those who aspire from the lower ranks wear pale blue and grey. Some Sufi orders use colours as an aid to concentration–one of the holy names of Allah, for example, is written in gold ink on a fuchsia background and stared at during meditation. Colour codes are also inscribed in Sufi parables, poems, and stories. Sounds have colours, as do tastes, feelings, ideas, and so on. Some Sufis apparently experience a synesthesia of colour, a veritable spectral fantasia which transforms normal consciousness into a shimmering, variegated reality, as different from our perception of the world as vibrant colour is to plain old black and white.

PHILOSUFI

COLOUR CORRESPONDENCES

Although possibly no other mystic or spiritual group has devised a colour code as elaborate as the Iranian Sufis, the concept of spiritual colour codes has been around from the beginning of civilization. ■ In Pharaonic Egypt, different colours stood for different gods. Osiris, for example, was represented by the colour green which, in turn, stood for fertility, the annual inundation of the Nile, and so on. In Asia, colour codes play a central role in Buddhist and Tantric art, and in Europe colour codes literally infuse the stained glass windows of the great cathedrals. During the Renaissance, colour was an important part of alchemy, a fact which was of interest to the Hermetic magic groups which flourished throughout Europe and in America at the turn of the last century. Madame Blavatsky's Theosophists went so far as to publish a compendium of colour-coded shapes, known as 'thought forms,' each accompanied by their precise theosophical meaning. Not unlike the Iranian Sufis and their offshoots, the theosophists are trained to 'see' colour forms or photisms floating near people's heads, around objects and in the landscape. ■ Why does colour play such an ascendant role in religious and spiritual traditions? Henri Corbin, the scholar who has done the most to bring the colour code of the Iranian Sufis to the Western world, drew from Goethe's **Farbenlehre** to answer that question. ■ In Goethe's much-disputed treatise on colour, he describes a simple experiment in which, say, a bright blue disk is placed on a white piece of paper. The subject stares at the disk, noting a reddish-yellow light at the periphery which eventually turns into an orb that 'detaches' from the blue. If the blue disk is snatched away at this point, the red-yellow orb lingers, which suggested to Goethe that colour is not simply a passive impression received from the material world, but that it has a psychological quality irrespective of its material data. ■ Much to the chagrin of scientific minds, Goethe discusses elsewhere the mystical and spiritual dimension of colour, arguing, not unlike the Iranian Sufis, that colour is as much inside man as it is outside in the world. Or, as Corbin would interpret it, 'Colour is not a passive impression, but the language of the soul.' Certainly our Sufi mystics would heartily agree.

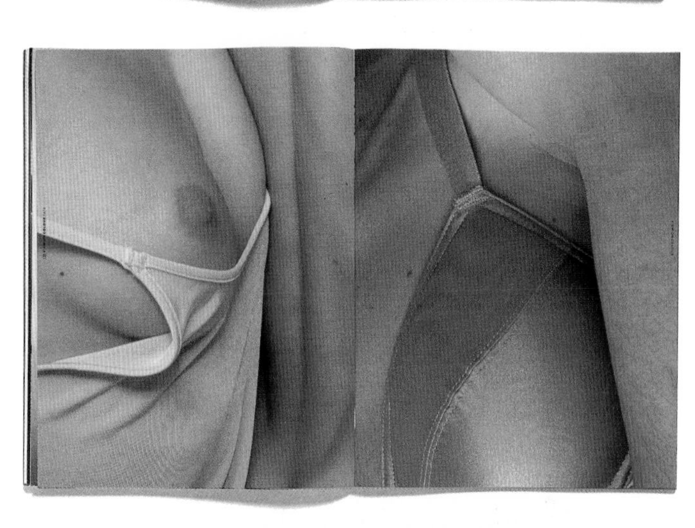

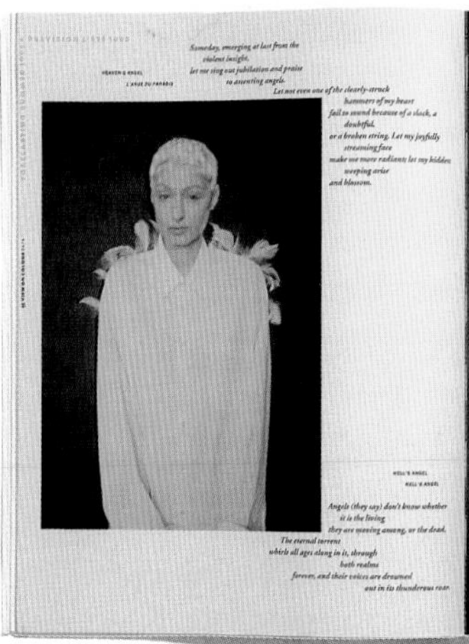

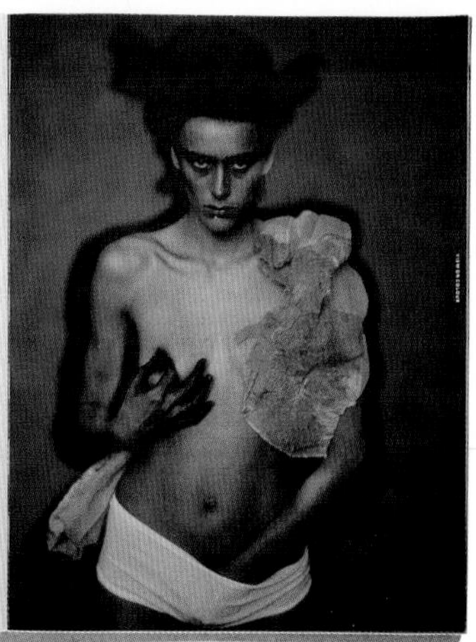

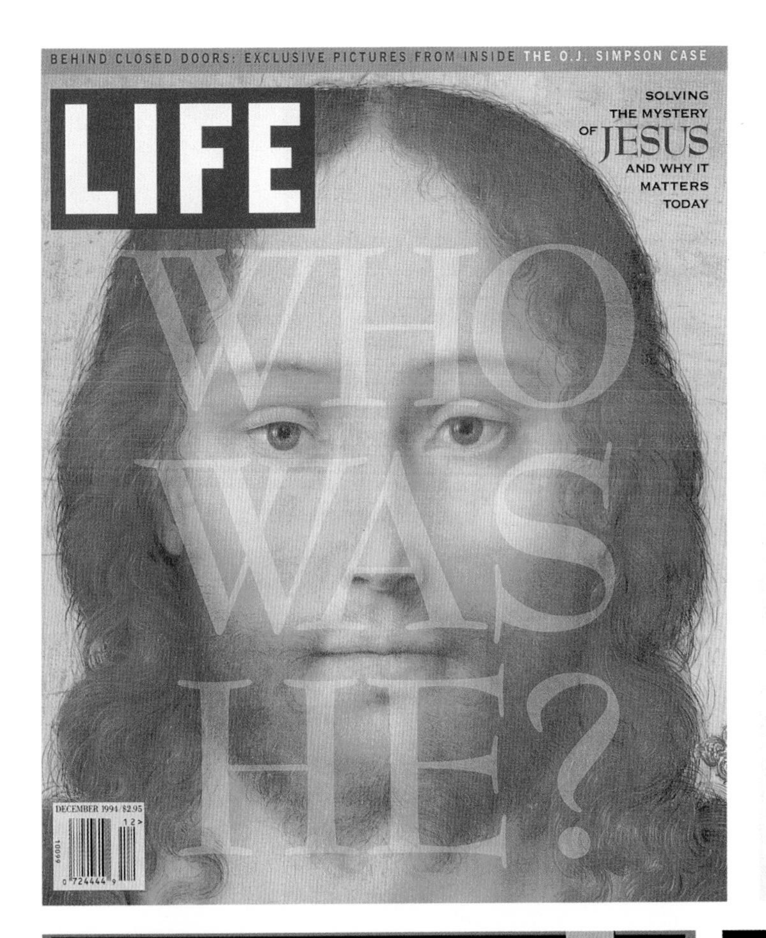
BEHIND CLOSED DOORS: EXCLUSIVE PICTURES FROM INSIDE THE O.J. SIMPSON CASE
LIFE
SOLVING THE MYSTERY OF JESUS AND WHY IT MATTERS TODAY
WHO WAS HE?
DECEMBER 1994/$2.95

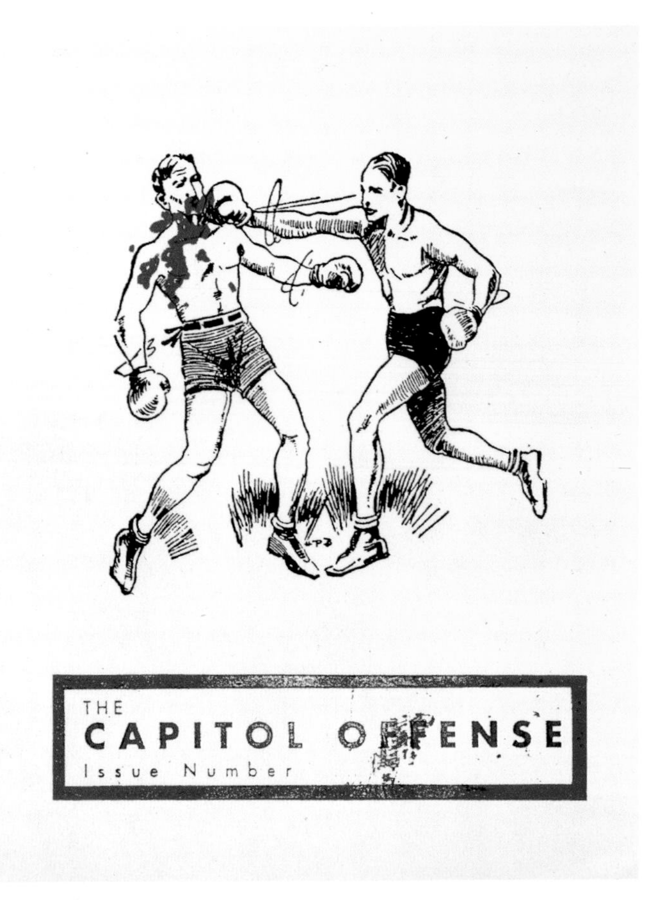
THE
CAPITOL OFFENSE
Issue Number

PETER LYNCH Picks Four Turnaround Stocks
OCTOBER 1994
worth
FINANCIAL INTELLIGENCE
60
AMERICA'S BEST FINANCIAL ADVISORS
PLUS Market Timing vs. Buy and Hold • The True Cost of Discount Brokers • Hidden Conflicts in Bank Funds • The Billion-Dollar Tax Break

SWING
PREMIERE ISSUE
NOVEMBER '94 $2
CYNICAL DREAMER
SKEPTICAL IDEALIST
POLITICAL SLACKER
PROMISCUOUS AIDS ACTIVISTS
INTERNET SEX PHAT INTERNET
HEROIC APATHY HEROIC
THE PARADOX
GENERATION
INFLUENTIAL
SEGREGATION
REAL WORLD HYPE REAL
ALTERNATIVE TRENDS
BEAVIS BUNCH
LOLLAPALOOZA
AMERICA'S MOST POWERFUL 20-SOMETHINGS
WHO'S GOING TO RUN OUR COUNTRY NEXT?

■ 1 ART DIRECTOR: TOM BENTKOWSKI DESIGNERS: TOM BENTKOWSKI, STEVE WALKOWIAK PUBLISHER: TIME & LIFE, INC./LIFE MAGAZINE COUNTRY: USA ■ 2 CREATIVE DIRECTOR: JEFF FEY DESIGNERS: MICHAEL STRASSBURGER, ROBYNNE RAYE, VITTORIO COSTARELLA, GEORGE ESTRADA ILLUSTRATORS: MICHAEL STRASSBURGER, ROBYNNE RAYE, VITTORIO COSTARELLA, GEORGE ESTRADA DESIGN FIRM:

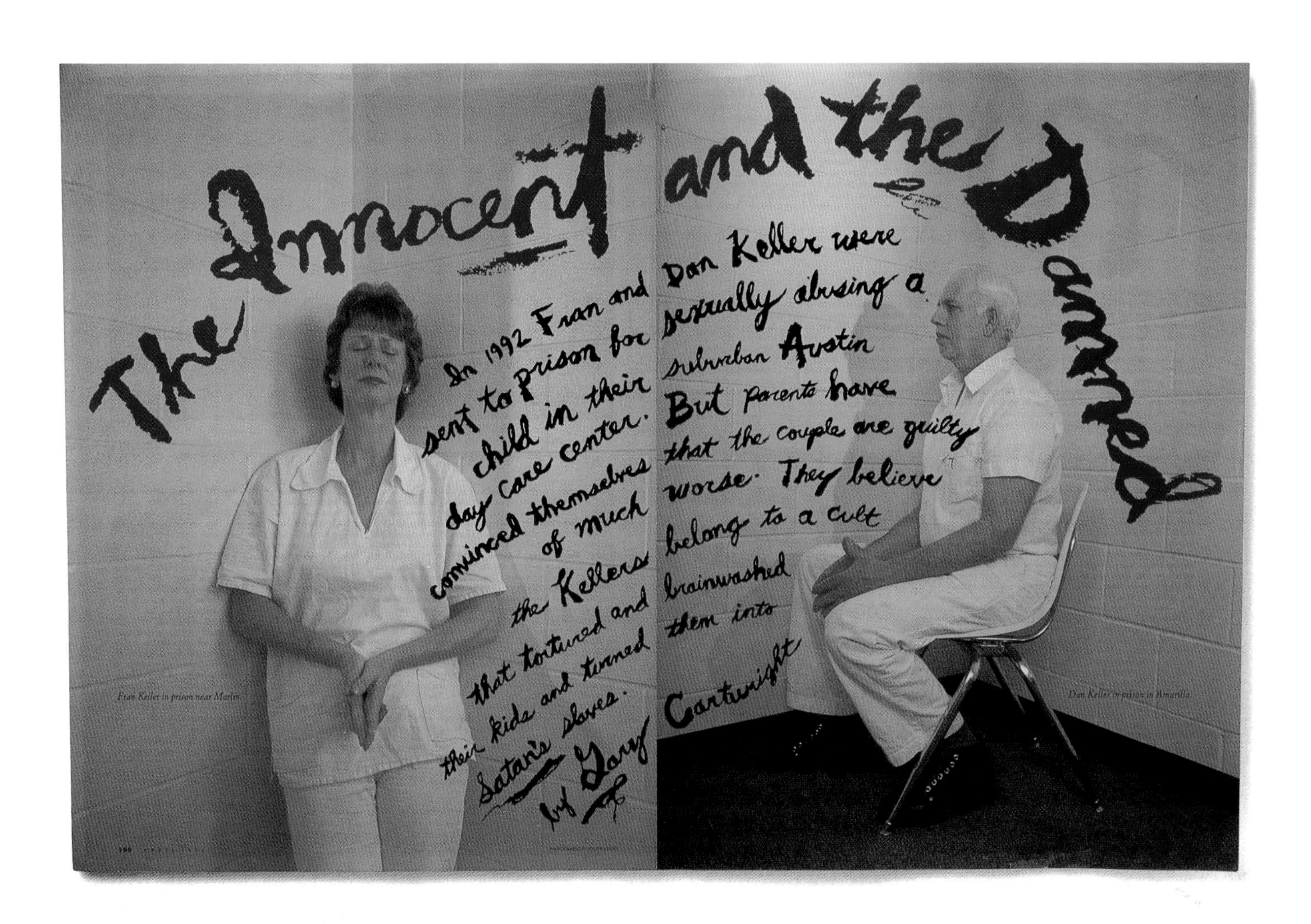

MODERN DOG CLIENT: CAPITOL RECORDS COUNTRY: USA ■ 3 ART DIRECTOR: INA SALTZ DESIGNER: PHILLIP BRATTER PUBLISHER: WORTH MAGAZINE COUNTRY: USA ■ 4 ART DIRECTOR/DESIGNER: ADAM Z. SMITH PUBLISHER: SWING MAGAZINE COUNTRY: USA ■ 5 ART DIRECTOR: D.J. STOUT DESIGNERS: D.J. STOUT, NANCY E. MCMILLEN PHOTOGRAPHER: JOSEPH VENTO PUBLISHER: TEXAS MONTHLY COUNTRY: USA

■ 1, 2 EDITOR-IN-CHIEF: TIBOR KALMAN ART DIRECTOR: MARK PORTER PHOTOGRAPHER: COURTESY BIJAN (1), SERGIO MERLI (2) PUBLISHER: BENETTON/COLORS COUNTRIES: ITALY, USA ■ 3, 4 ART DIRECTOR: D.J. STOUT DESIGNERS: D.J. STOUT, NANCY E. MCMILLEN PHOTOGRAPHER: DAN WINTERS (3), RICK PATRICK & ANALISA (4) PUBLISHER: TEXAS MONTHLY COUNTRY: USA ■ 5–10 ART DIRECTOR: RENÉ ABBÜHL PHOTOGRAPHERS: INEZ VAN LAMSWEERDE (5, 6), JOHAN DE BOER (7), PIET BROER (8 LEFT), ROBERT BENSCHOP (8 RIGHT), THOMAS SCHENK (10) PUBLISHER: DE GEÏLLUSTREERDE PERS BV/AVENUE COUNTRY: NETHERLANDS

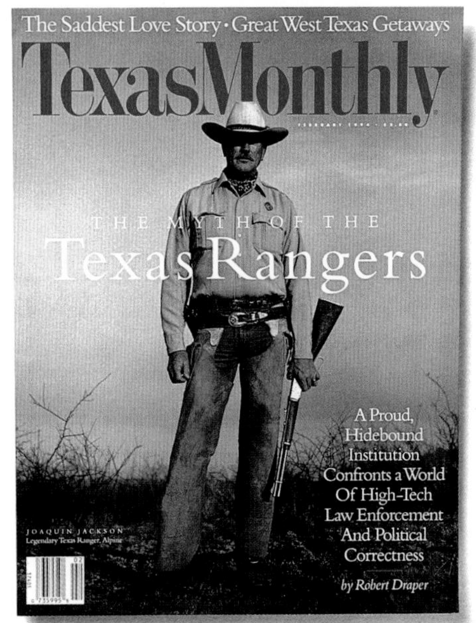

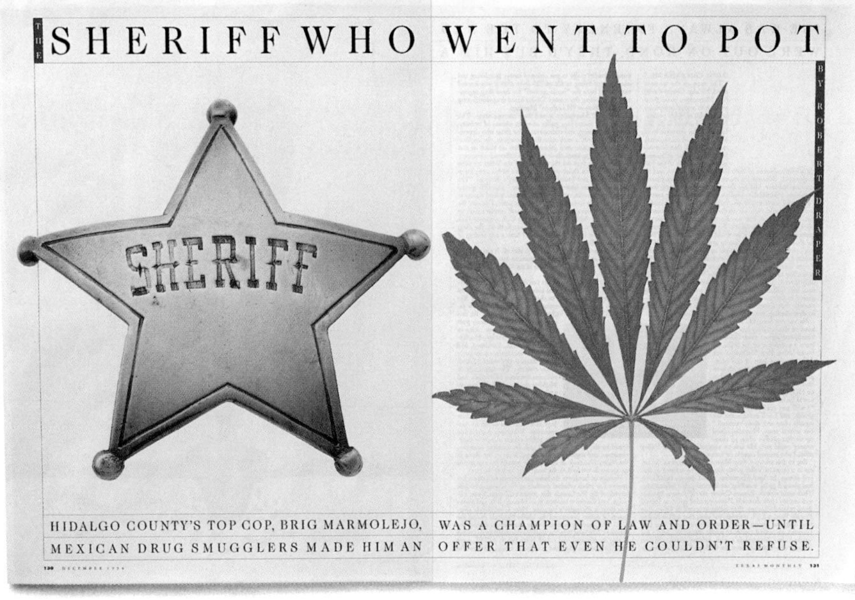

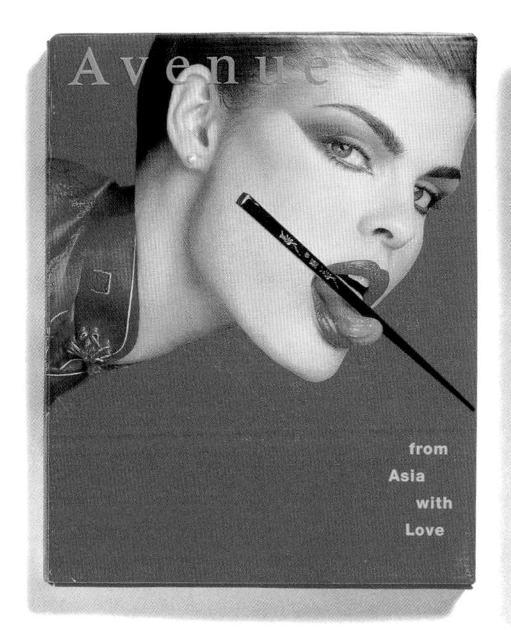
Avenue
from
Asia
with
Love

Avenue

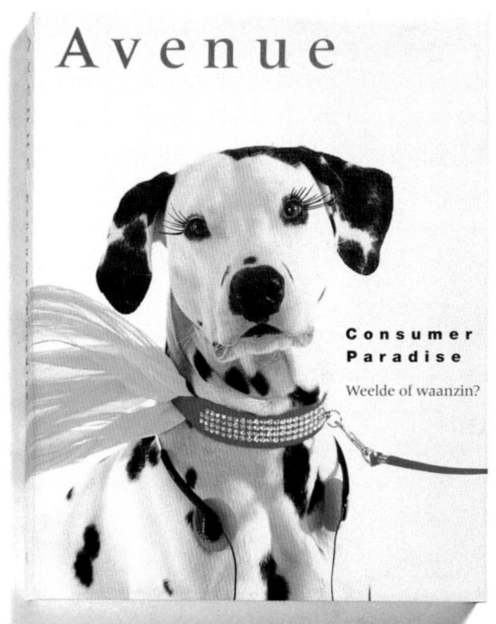
Avenue
Consumer
Paradise
Weelde of waanzin?

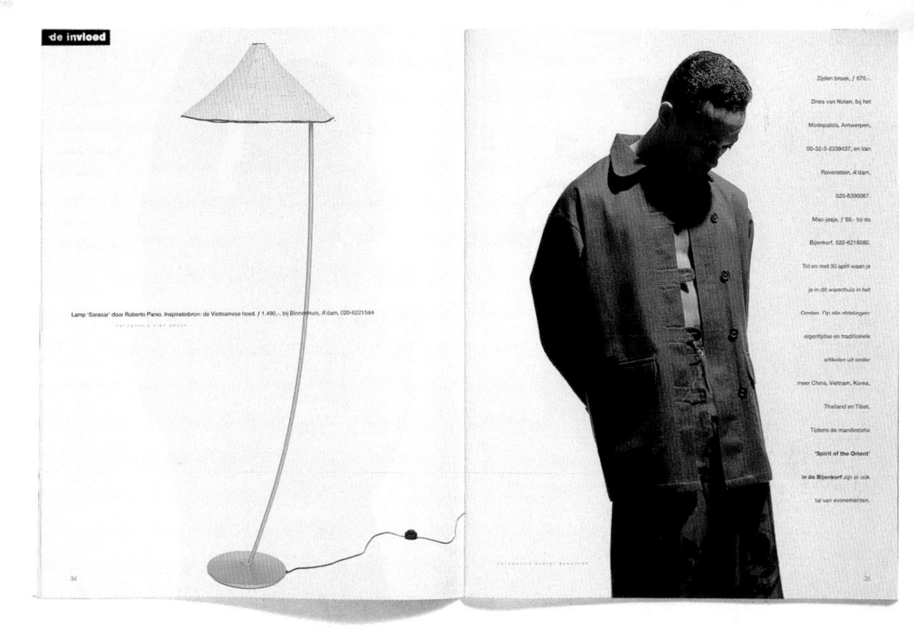
de invloed

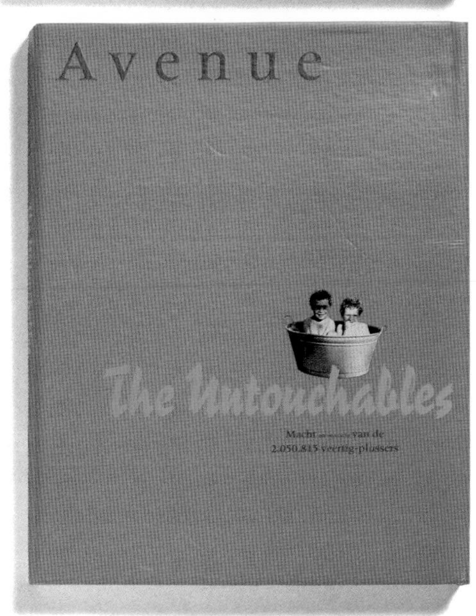
Avenue
The Untouchables

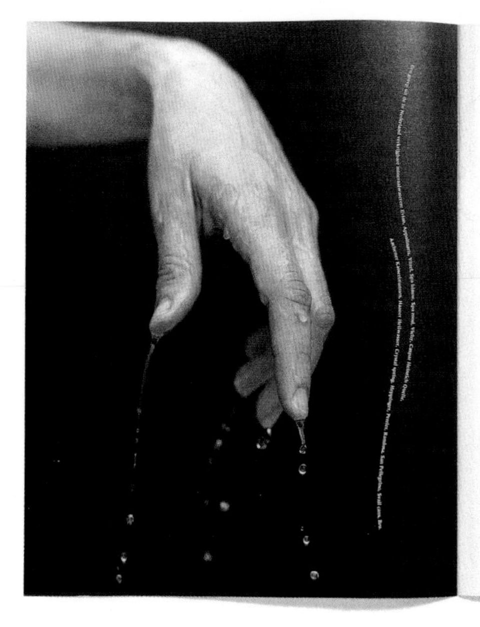

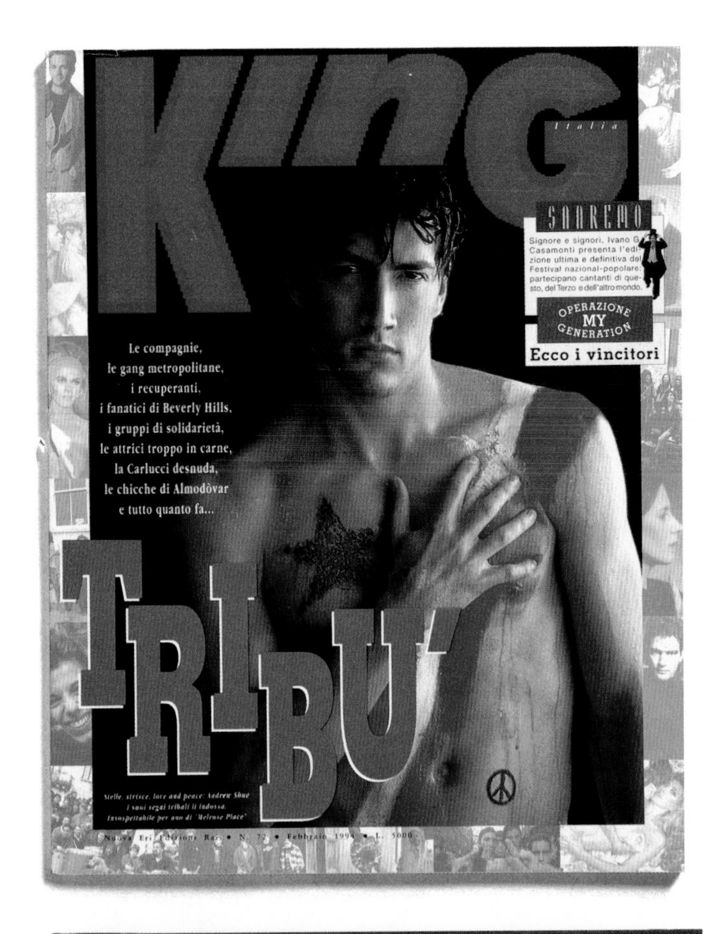
KING
Italia
SANREMO
Signore e signori, Ivano G. Casamonti presenta l'edizione ultima e definitiva del Festival nazional-popolare.
OPERAZIONE MY GENERATION
Ecco i vincitori
Le compagnie,
le gang metropolitane,
i recuperanti,
i fanatici di Beverly Hills,
i gruppi di solidarietà,
le attrici troppo in carne,
la Carlucci desnuda,
le chicche di Almodòvar
e tutto quanto fa...
TRIBÙ

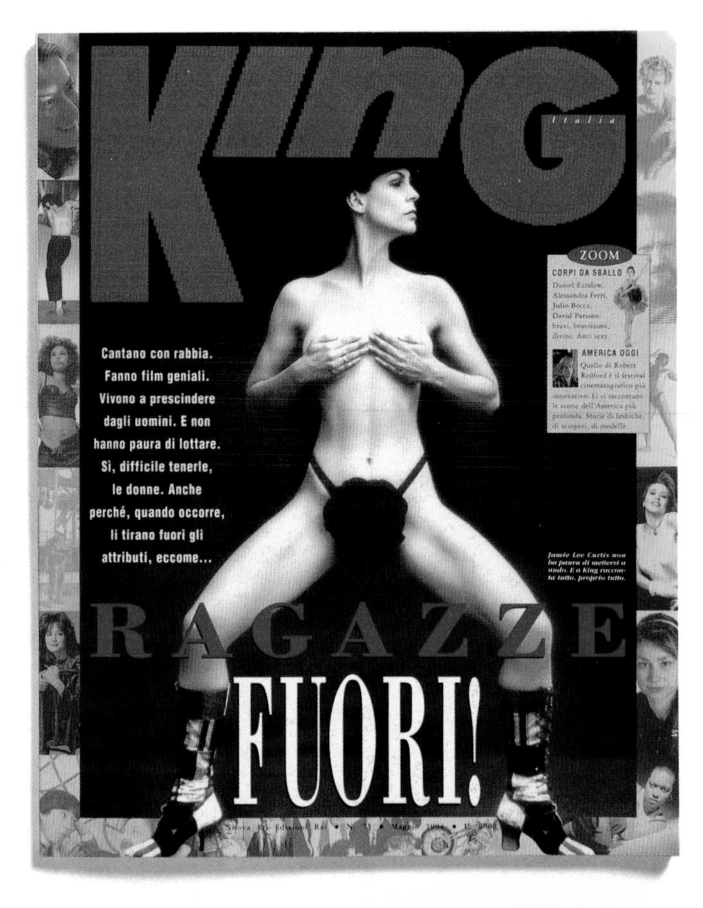
KING
Italia
ZOOM
CORPI DA SBALLO
AMERICA OGGI
Cantano con rabbia.
Fanno film geniali.
Vivono a prescindere
dagli uomini. E non
hanno paura di lottare.
Sì, difficile tenerle,
le donne. Anche
perché, quando occorre,
li tirano fuori gli
attributi, eccome...
RAGAZZE
FUORI!

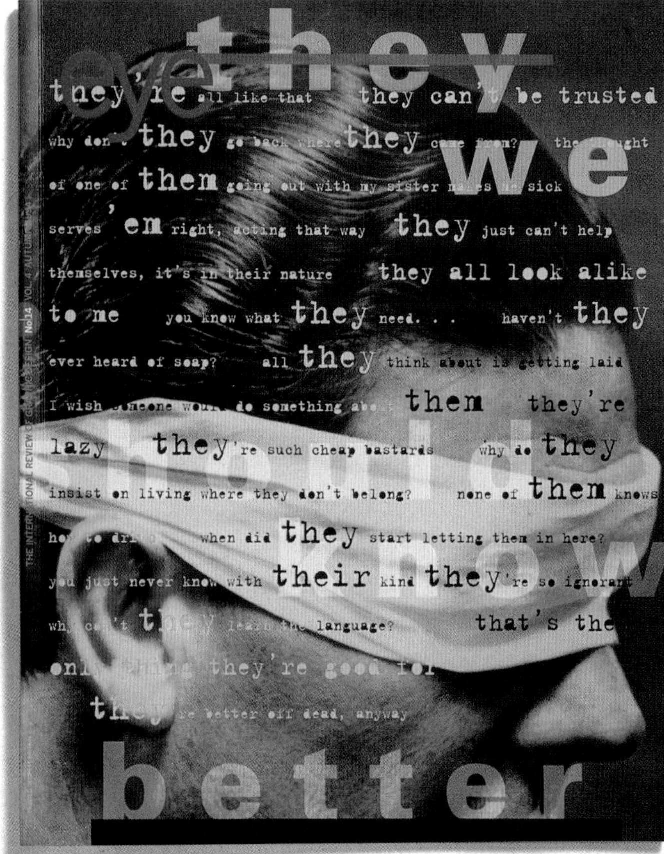
eye
they
they're all like that they can't be trusted
we
they all look alike
to me you know what they need... haven't they
ever heard of soap?
they're such cheap bastards
they just never know with their kind
that's the
they're better off dead, anyway
better
THE INTERNATIONAL REVIEW OF GRAPHIC DESIGN No14 VOL 4 AUTUMN 1994

eye
[type]
TYPOGRAPHY SPECIAL ISSUE
THE INTERNATIONAL REVIEW OF GRAPHIC DESIGN No15 VOL. 4 WINTER 1994
PRINTED IN GREAT BRITAIN

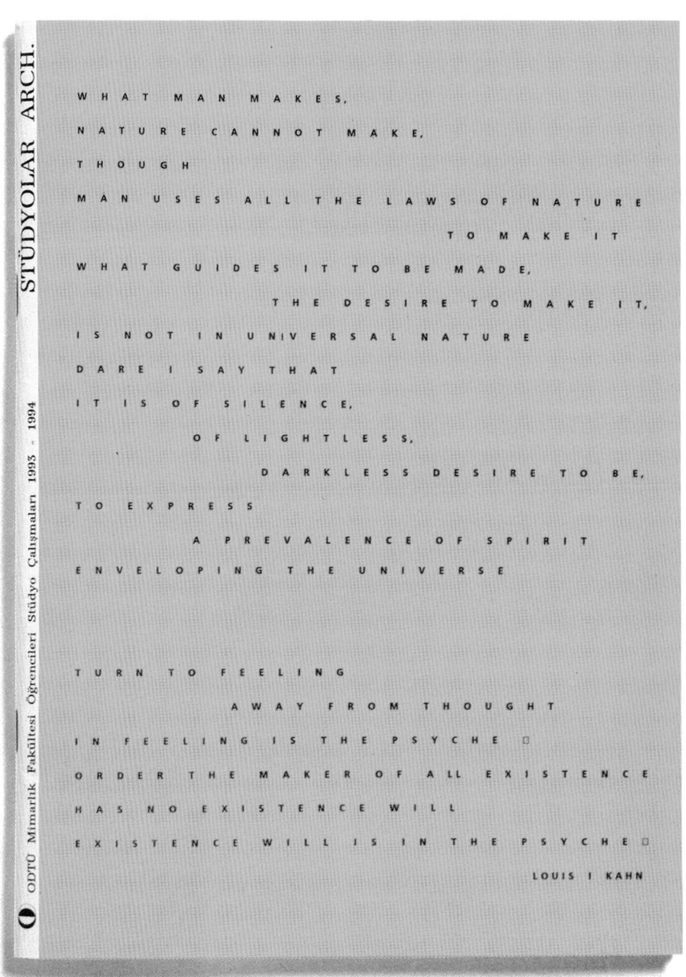

■ 1, 2 ART DIRECTOR: MARIAPIA COPPIN PHOTOGRAPHER: BOB FRAME (1), DAVIS FACTOR (2) PHOTO EDITOR: RITA CROTTI PUBLISHER: NUOVA ERI-EDIZIONI RAI/KING COUNTRY: ITALY ■ 3, 4 ART DIRECTOR/DESIGNER: STEPHEN COATES PUBLISHER: EMAP ARCHITECTURE/ EYE COUNTRY: GREAT BRITAIN ■ 5 ART DIRECTOR: DOMENIC LIPPA DESIGNERS: MARK DIAPER, DOMENIC LIPPA, RACHAEL DINNIS, MICHAEL DAVIES, MARCUS DOLING DESIGN FIRM: LIPPA PEARCE DESIGN LIMITED PUBLISHER: THE DOWNLOW COUNTRY: GREAT BRITAIN ■ 6 ART DIRECTOR/CLIENT: MIDDLE EAST TECHNICAL UNIVERSITY, FACULTY OF ARCHITECTURE DESIGNER: KEMAL ARAN COUNTRY: TURKEY

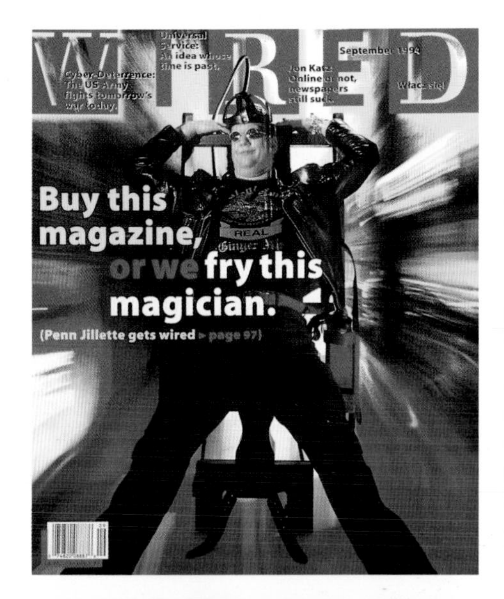

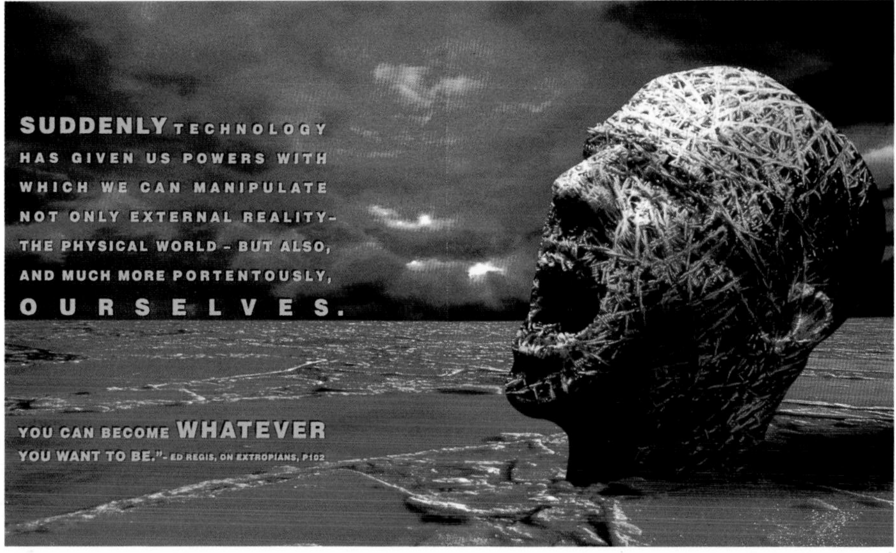

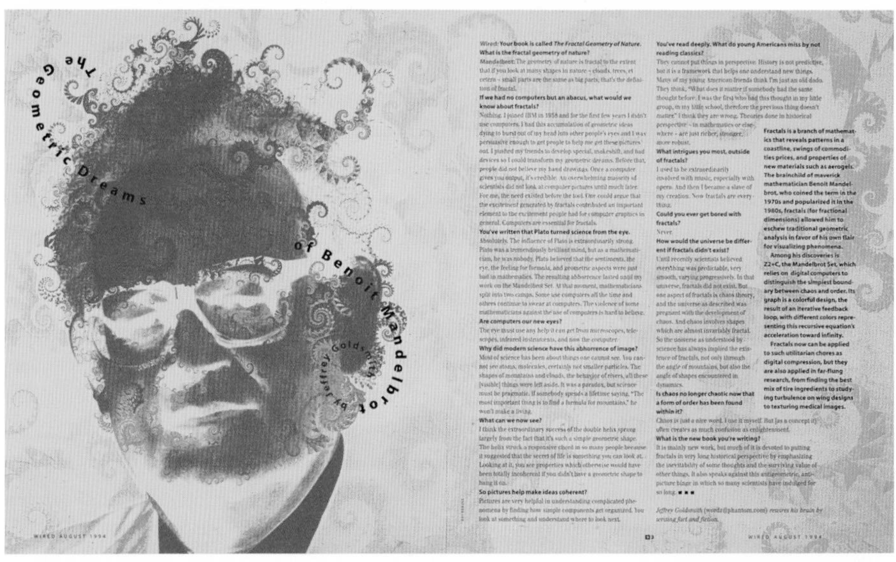

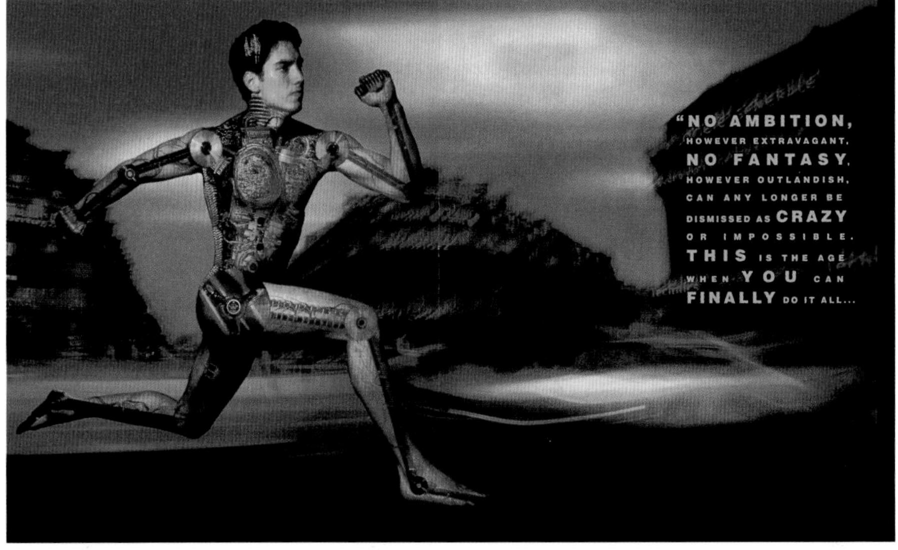

■ **1-6** ART DIRECTORS: JOHN PLUNKETT, BARBARA KUHR (1, 3, 5) DESIGNERS: THOMAS SCHNEIDER (2, 6), TRICIA MCGILLIS (4) PHOTOGRAPHERS: JIM PORTO (1, 2, 6), NEIL SELKIRK (3), KAREN MOSKOWITZ (5) ILLUSTRATOR: KAI KRAUSE (4) DESIGN FIRM: PLUNKETT + KUHR PUBLISHER: WIRED MAGAZINE COUNTRY: USA ■ **7-12** (FROM TOP LEFT TO BOTTOM RIGHT) CREATIVE DIRECTOR: ULI

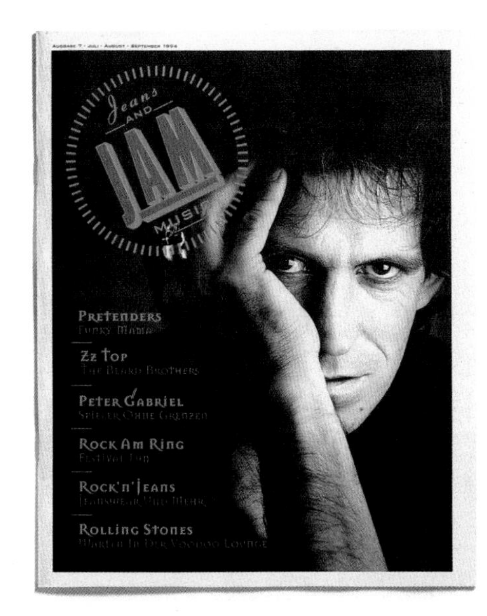

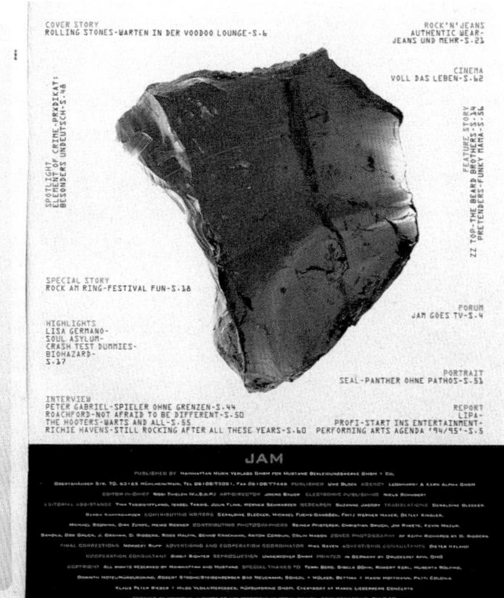

WEBER ART DIRECTOR/DESIGNER: JOERG BAUER PHOTOGRAPHERS: D. RIDGERS (7), BAUER & SCHUBERT (8), SHEILA ROCK (9, 10), ANDY DELUXE/ALEXANDER VON FÄCKL (11), GLEN ERLER (12) DESIGN FIRM: LEONHARDT + KERN ALPHA GMBH CLIENT: MUSTANG BEKLEIDUNGSWERKE GMBH + CO. PUBLISHER: MAINHATTAN MEDIA MUSIK UND KOMMUNIKATIONS GMBH COUNTRY: GERMANY

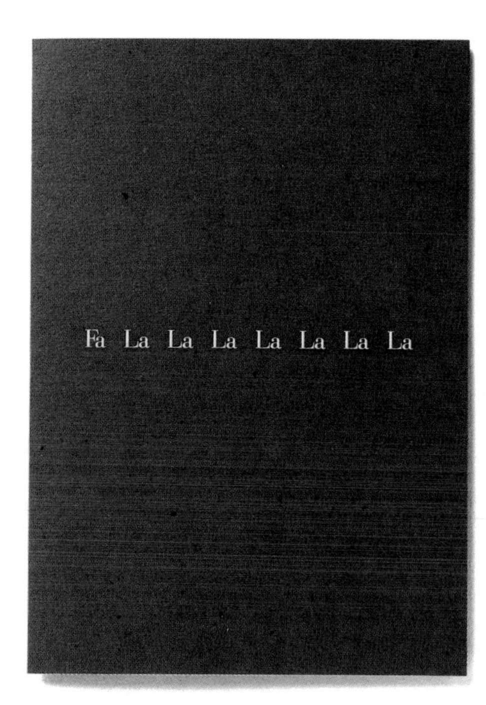

Fa La La La La La La La

■ 1, 2 ART DIRECTOR: MICHAEL BROCK DESIGNERS: MICHAEL BROCK, HOLLY CAPORALE PHOTOGRAPHER: TOM KELLER DESIGN FIRM: MICHAEL BROCK DESIGN CLIENT: WARNER HOME VIDEO COUNTRY: USA ■ 3 ART DIRECTOR: DICK MITCHELL DESIGNER: DICK MITCHELL ILLUSTRATOR: WAYNE JOHNSON DESIGN FIRM/CLIENT: RBMM/THE RICHARDS GROUP COUNTRY: USA ■ 4 ART DIRECTOR: VOLKMAR PÖTSCH DESIGNER: MARTINA KOTHGASSER DESIGN FIRM: HARTINGER CONSULTING CLIENT: HARTINGER CONSULTING COUNTRY: AUSTRIA

Wer gut
schmiert,
fährt gut!
Was man in die-
sem Jahr von der
Welt nicht behaup-
ten kann, hat für
uns durchaus
seine Richtigkeit.
"1992 lief wie ge-
schmiert". Viel
Teamgeist, viel neu-
es Interesse. Viel
Verständnis für un-
SCHWARZES
GOLD
Hartinger
CONSULTING

■ 1, 3, 4 ART DIRECTOR: BARRY SHEPARD DESIGNER: NATHAN JOSEPH DESIGN FIRM/CLIENT: SHR PERCEPTUAL MANAGEMENT COUNTRY: USA ■ 2 ART DIRECTOR/DESIGNER: CAROL BURKE DESIGN FIRM/CLIENT: EDS MARKETING COMMUNICATIONS COUNTRY: USA ■ 5, 6, 8, 9 ART

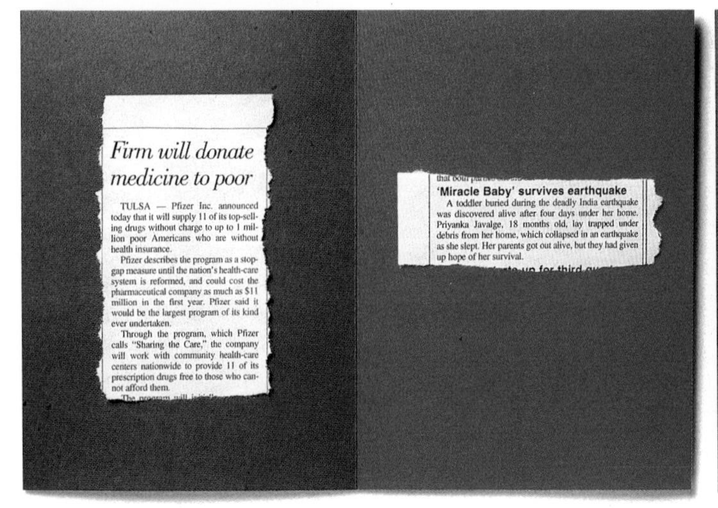

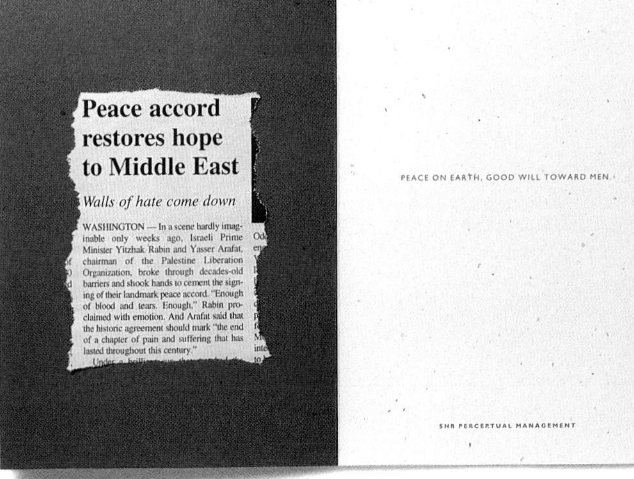

DIRECTORS: RON SULLIVAN, DAN RICHARDS DESIGNER/ILLUSTRATOR: DAN RICHARDS DESIGN FIRM: SULLIVAN PERKINS COUNTRY: USA ■ 7 ART DIRECTOR/DESIGNER/ILLUSTRATOR: YUTAKA K. SASAKI DESIGN FIRM: SAINTLIGHT INC. CLIENT: INNOV DESIGN COUNTRY: USA

Will she be the first woman to walk on Mars?

Will she grow up to be President?

©YUTAKA SASAKI

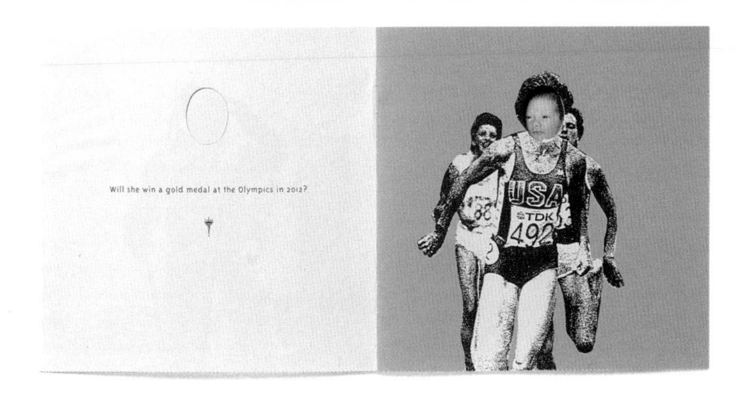
Will she win a gold medal at the Olympics in 2012?
USA
TDK
492

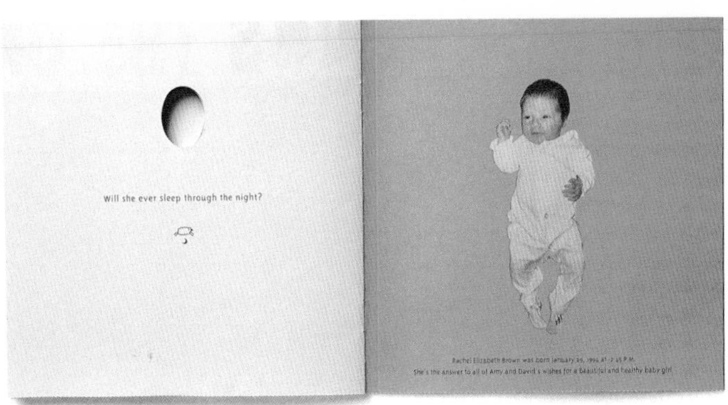
Will she ever sleep through the night?
She's the answer to all of Amy and David's wishes for a beautiful and healthy baby girl

Unity
A HISTORY OF HOSPITALITY
Please go away and let me sleep
DES MOINES

■ 1 DESIGNER: JAMES F. SUNDSTAD COUNTRY: USA ■ 2 ART DIRECTOR/DESIGNER: JOHN SAYLES ILLUSTRATOR: JOHN SAYLES DESIGN FIRM: SAYLES GRAPHIC DESIGN CLIENT: HOTEL FORT DES MOINES COUNTRY: USA ■ 3 ART DIRECTOR/DESIGNER: WOLFGANG HASLINGER ILLUSTRATOR: WOLFGANG HASLINGER CLIENT: BZW-WERBEAGENTUR COUNTRY: AUSTRIA ■ 4–6 ART DIRECTOR/DESIGNER: WOLFGANG

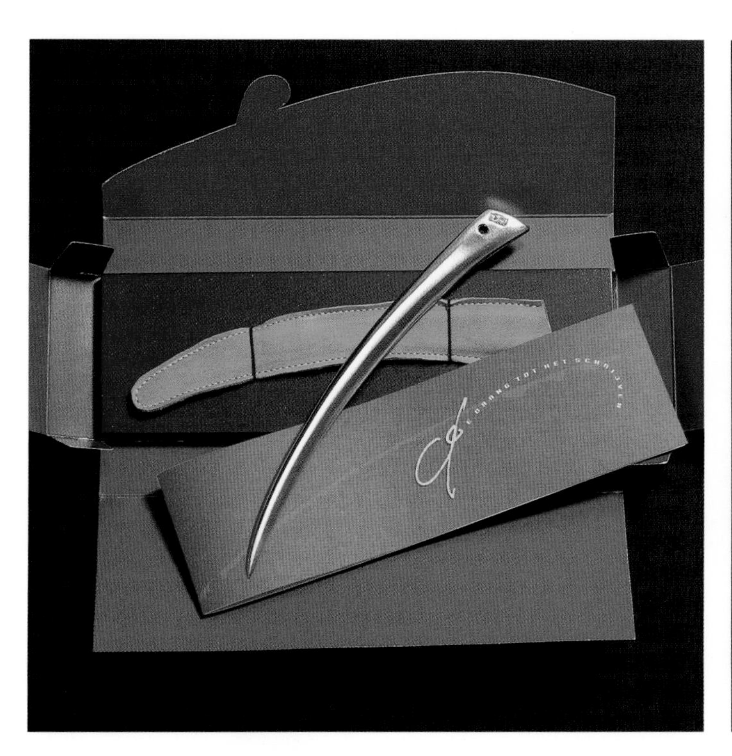

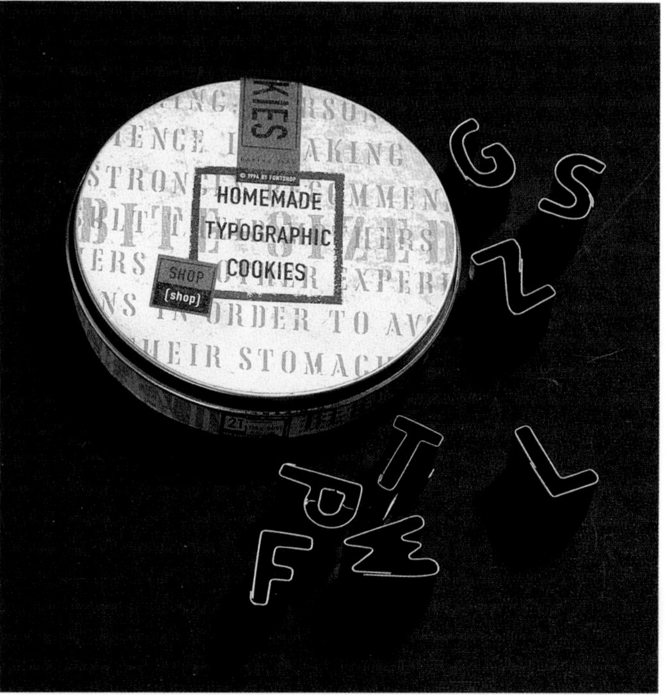

HASLINGER COUNTRY: AUSTRIA ■ 7 ART DIRECTOR: HUGO PUTTAERT DESIGNERS: HUGO PUTTAERT, JOHAN JACOBS, POL QUADENS DESIGN FIRM: VISION & FACTORY CLIENT: VISION & FACTORY COUNTRY: BELGIUM ■ 8 ART DIRECTOR: RÜDIGER GÖTZ ILLUSTRATOR: RÜDIGER GÖTZ DESIGNERS: RÜDIGER GÖTZ, OLAF STEIN DESIGN FIRM: FACTOR DESIGN CLIENT: FONT SHOP GERMANY COUNTRY: GERMANY

■ 1 ART DIRECTOR/DESIGNER/PHOTOGRAPHER: TADASHI MORISAKI DESIGN FIRM/CLIENT: MANDARIN BOOKS COUNTRY: JAPAN ■ 2, 3 ART DIRECTOR/DESIGNER/ILLUSTRATOR: SCOTT THARES DESIGN FIRM/CLIENT: JOHN RYAN COMPANY COUNTRY: USA ■ 4 ART DIRECTOR/DESIGNER:

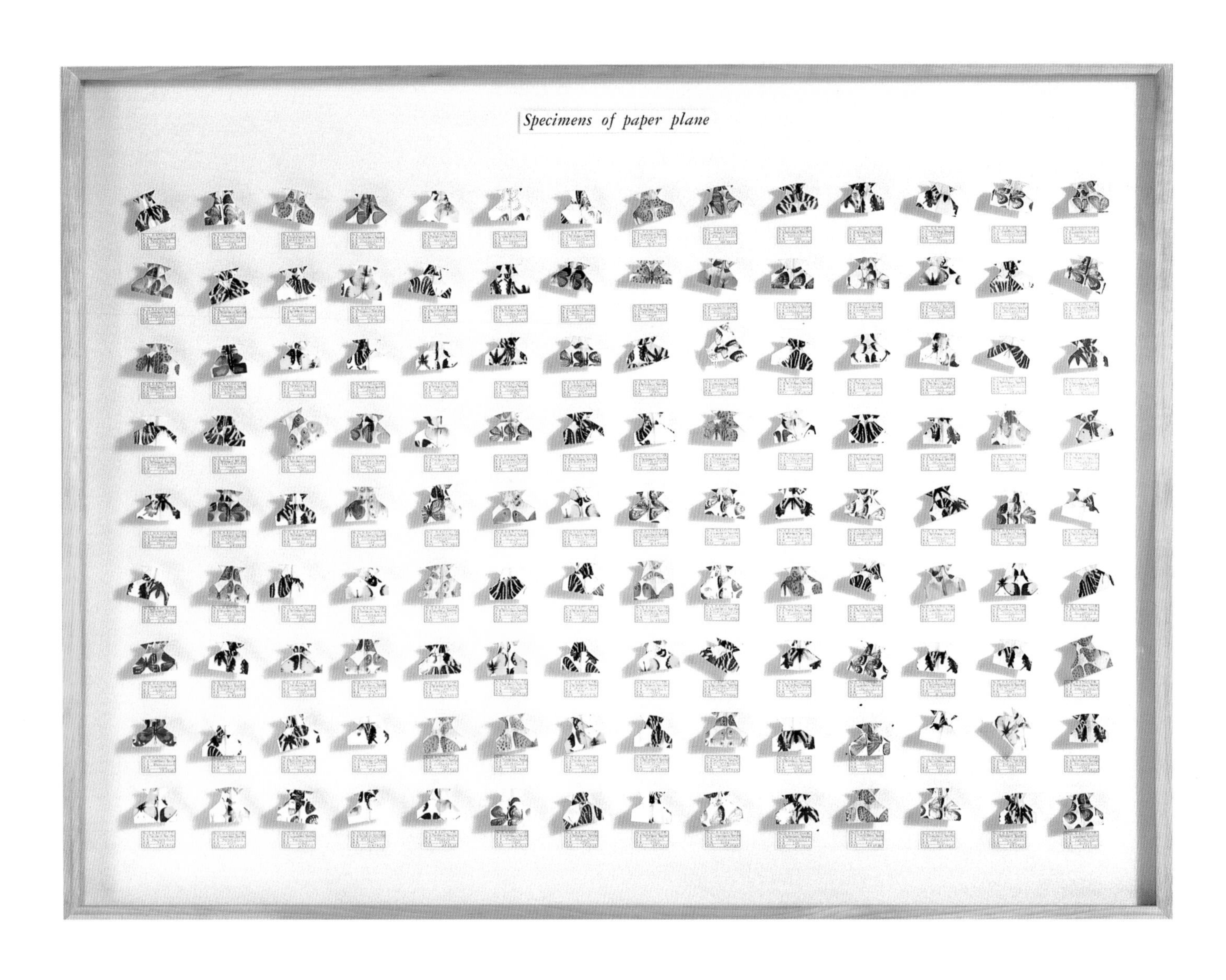

JOHN SAYLES ILLUSTRATOR: JOHN SAYLES DESIGN FIRM: SAYLES GRAPHIC DESIGN CLIENT: THE DES MOINES ART CENTER COUNTRY: USA ■ 5 ART DIRECTOR/DESIGNER: KEISUKE UNOSAWA DESIGN FIRM: KEISUKE UNOSAWA DESIGN CLIENT: DESIGN-M COUNTRY: JAPAN

U.S.POSTAGE
John Doe
JOHN RYAN
A Spicy Soiree

Festive Footsteps & Fancy Footwork
A Very Merry Mambo
It Takes Two To Tango
Get ready for a midwinter
be decked with Blackjack
tables where you can
double down for charity. So
prepare to be transported
from the icy chill of winter
to the throbbing tropics
Cuba and Jamaica,

ART
P·A·R·K
ART IN THE PARK
June
4-5
Iowa State Fairgrounds

design
MASAKI
MORITA
TOKYO

■ 1 ILLUSTRATOR: ROBERT GIUSTI COUNTRY: USA TITLE: JUNGLE CATS ■ 2 ILLUSTRATOR/ART DIRECTOR: SIEGMAR MÜNK COUNTRY: GERMANY TITLE: DO YOU LOVE ME? ■ (FOLLOWING SPREAD) 1–3 ILLUSTRATOR/ART DIRECTOR/DESIGNER: MILTON GLASER DESIGN FIRM: MILTON GLASER, INC. CLIENT: CRISTINA TAVERNA COUNTRY: ITALY ■ 4 ILLUSTRATOR: JEFF KOEGEL COUNTRY: USA ■ 5 ILLUSTRATOR: JEFF KOEGEL DESIGNER: MICHELLE ARANDA DESIGN FIRM: MIRIELLO GRAPHICA NOVAIDEA CLIENT: HEWLETT PACKARD COUNTRY: USA

Do you Love me?

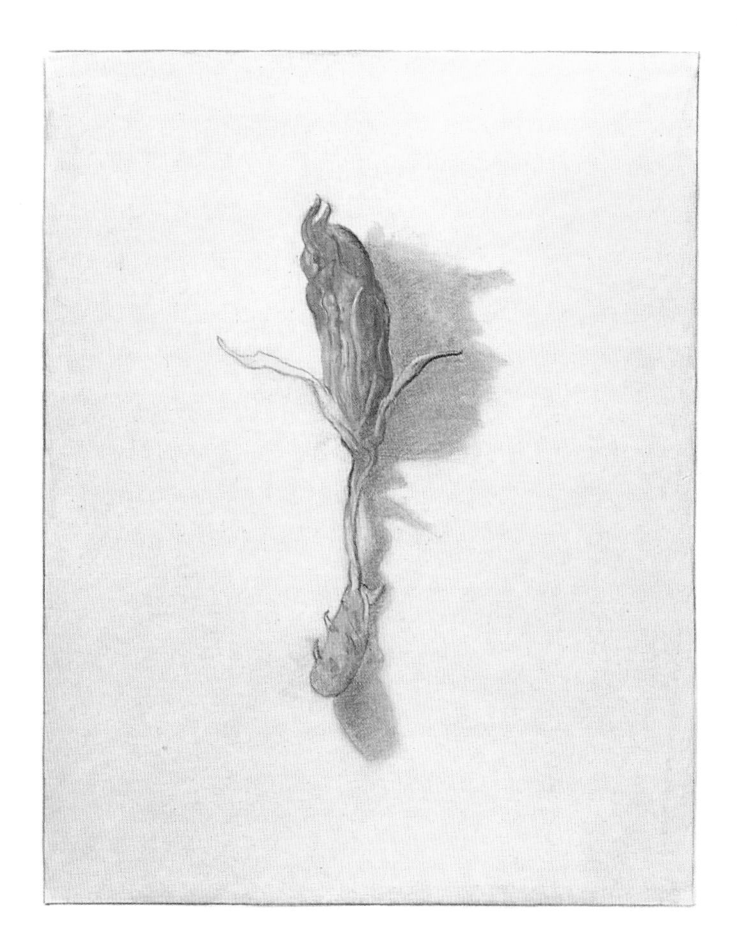

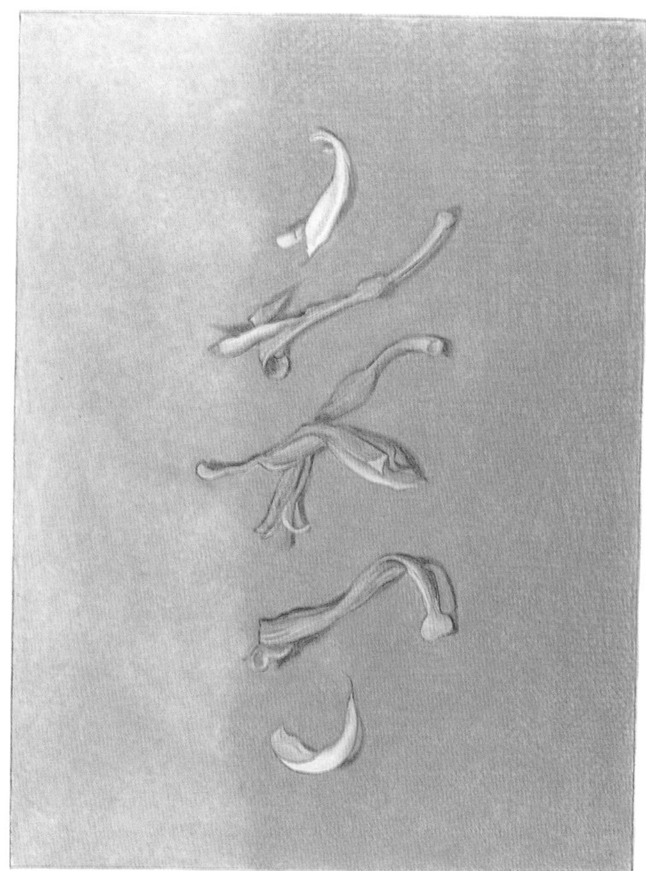

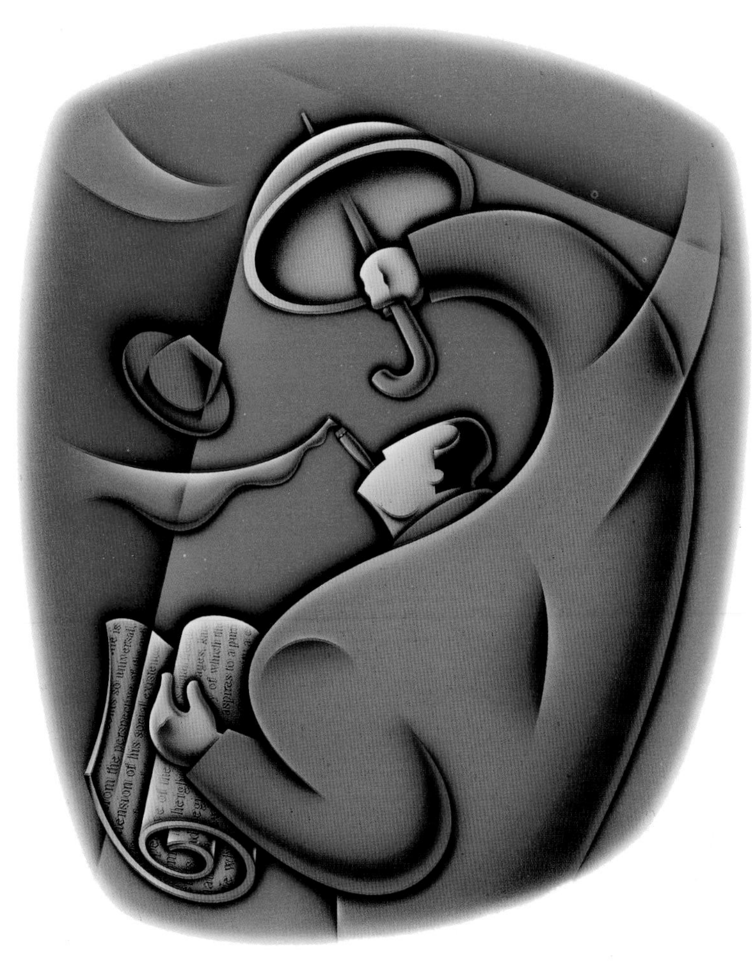

(THIS SPREAD)
ILLUSTRATOR: GEORG STELZNER
PUBLISHER/CLIENT: TETRA VERLAG,
TETRA WERKE DR. RER. NAT. ULRICH BAENSCH GMBH
COUNTRY: GERMANY

■ (THIS PAGE) 1 ILLUSTRATOR: JAMES LACEY ART DIRECTOR: BOB DENNARD DESIGNER: JAMES LACEY DESIGN FIRM: DENNARD CREATIVE, INC. CLIENT: DALLAS VISUAL ART CENTER COUNTRY: USA ■ (OPPOSITE) 2, 3 ILLUSTRATOR: REGAN DUNNICK COUNTRY: USA

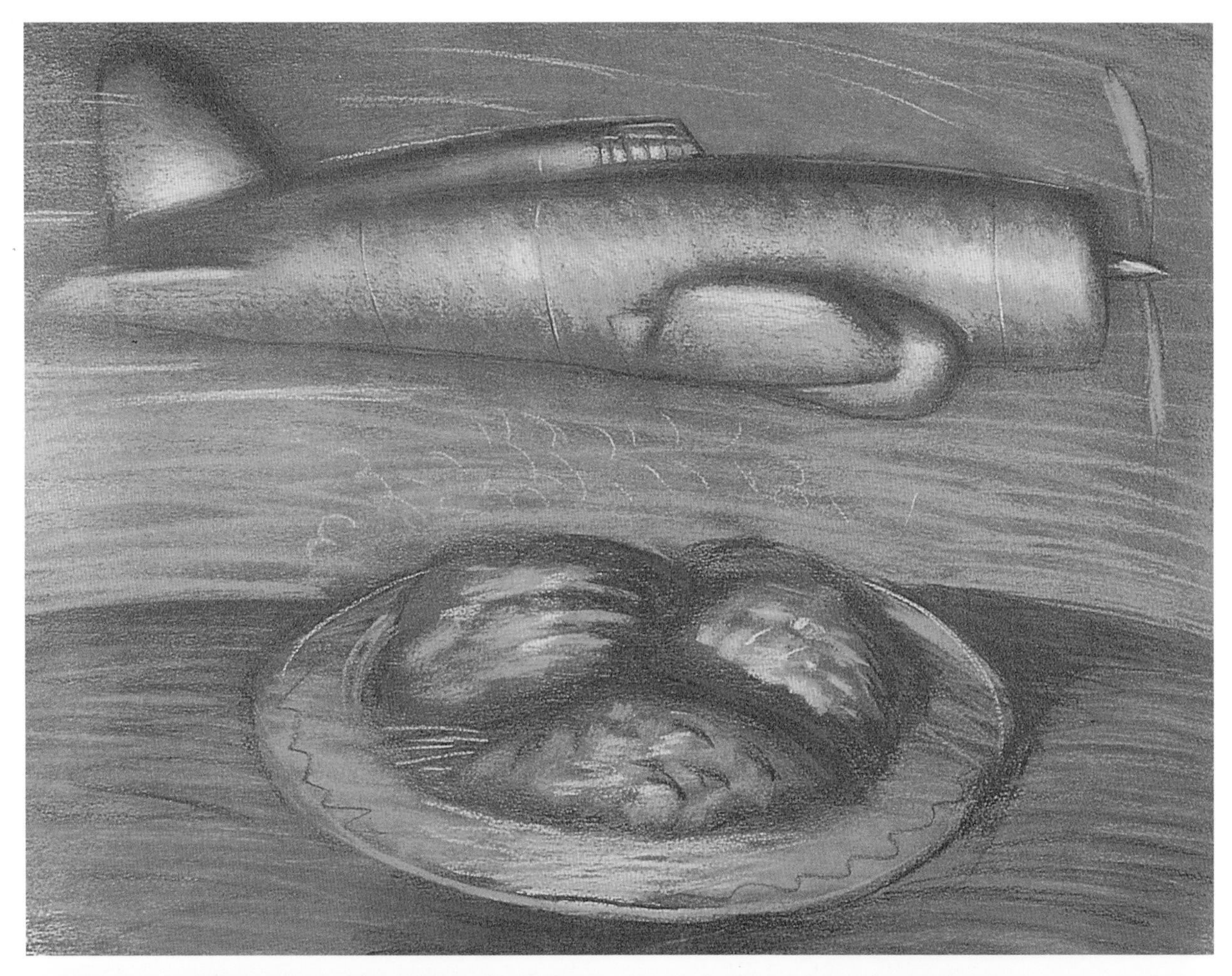

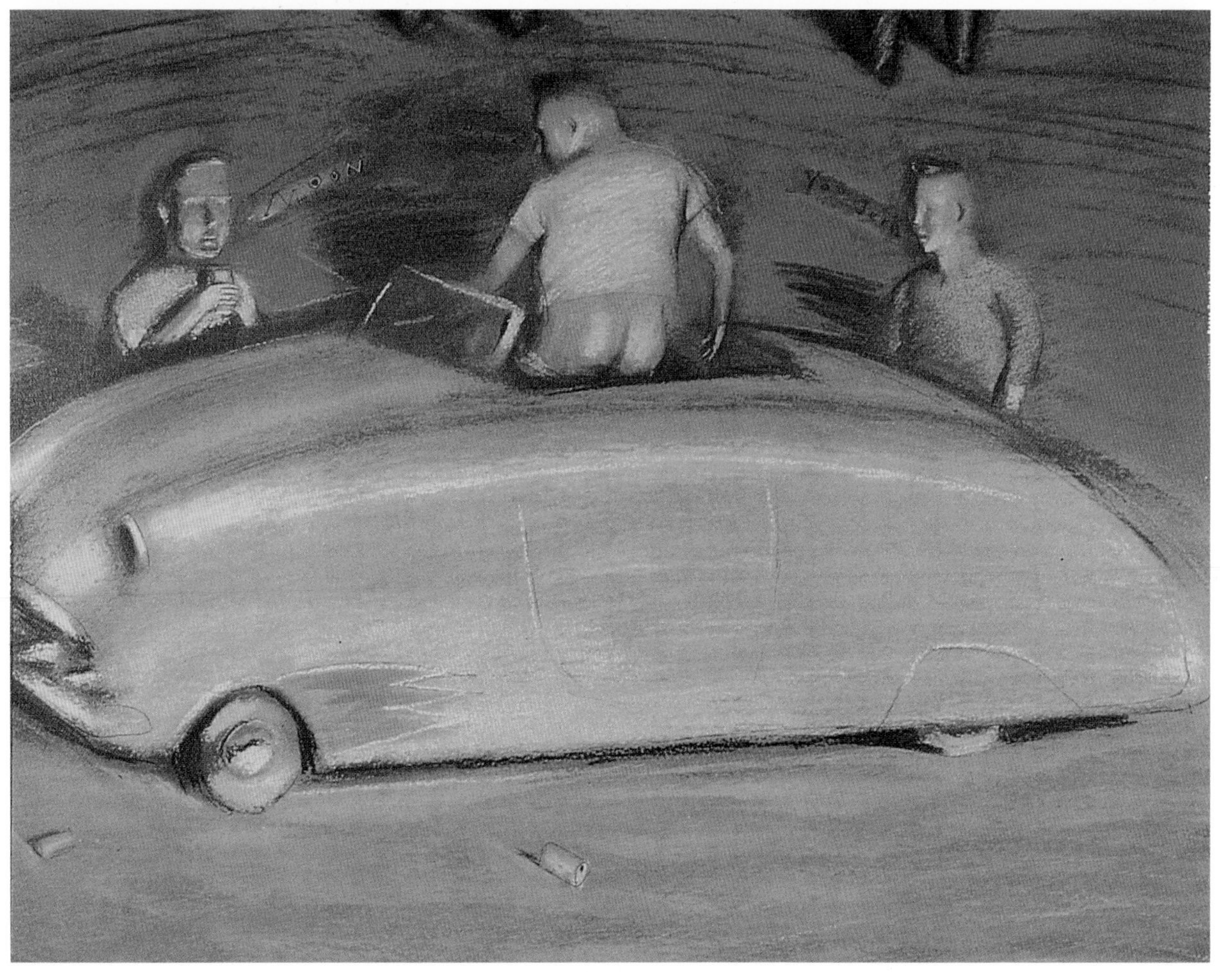

■ 1 ILLUSTRATOR: HANNAH GAL DESIGNER: HANNAH GAL COUNTRY: GREAT BRITAIN ■ 2 ILLUSTRATOR/DESIGNER: WIESLAW SMETEK ART DIRECTORS: WOLFGANG BEHNKEN, FRANZ EPPING PUBLISHER/CLIENT: *STERN*/GRUNER + JAHR COUNTRY: GERMANY ■ 3 ILLUSTRATOR:

CATHLEEN TOELKE ART DIRECTOR: WENDY BASS DESIGNER: WENDY BASS CLIENT: ATHENEUM COUNTRY: USA ■ (FOLLOWING SPREAD) 1 ILLUSTRATOR/ART DIRECTOR: GREG TUCKER COUNTRY: USA ■ 2 ILLUSTRATOR: ALLA CARTI COUNTRY: USA TITLE: CIRCUS OF MY LIFE

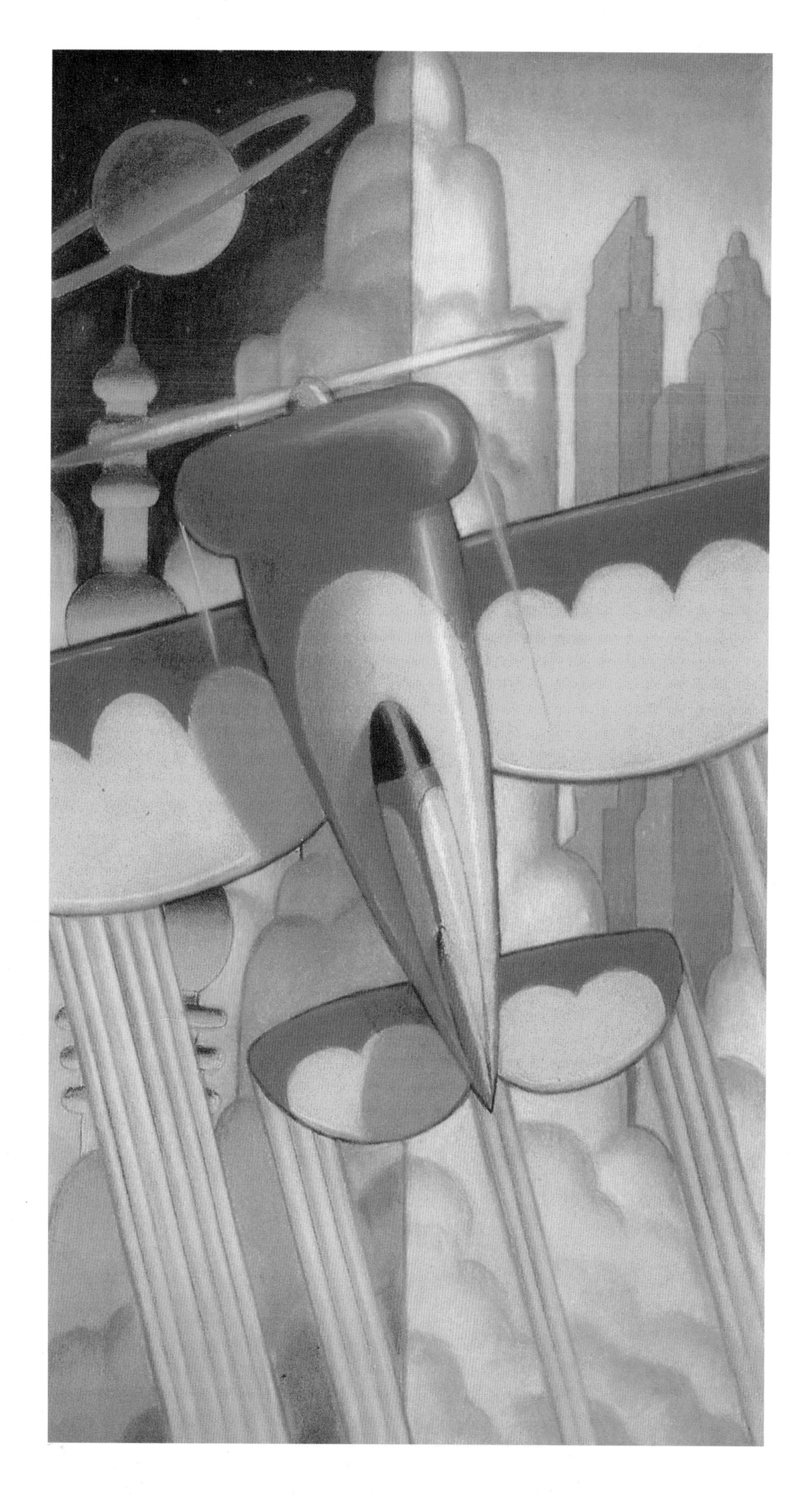

■ 1 ILLUSTRATOR/ART DIRECTOR/DESIGNER: OLE FLYV CHRISTENSEN CLIENT: AALBORG UNIVERSITY COUNTRY: DENMARK ■ 2 ILLUSTRATOR: REINHOLD HEROLD COUNTRY: GERMANY TITLE: ELFENBEINTURM ■ 3 ILLUSTRATOR: ANDREW CAWRSE ART DIRECTOR/DESIGNER: ANDREW CAWRSE DESIGN FIRM: CAWRSE & EFFECT COUNTRY: USA TITLE: DOG ■ 4 ILLUSTRATOR: ROY CARRUTHERS COUNTRY: USA TITLE: THE TYPIST

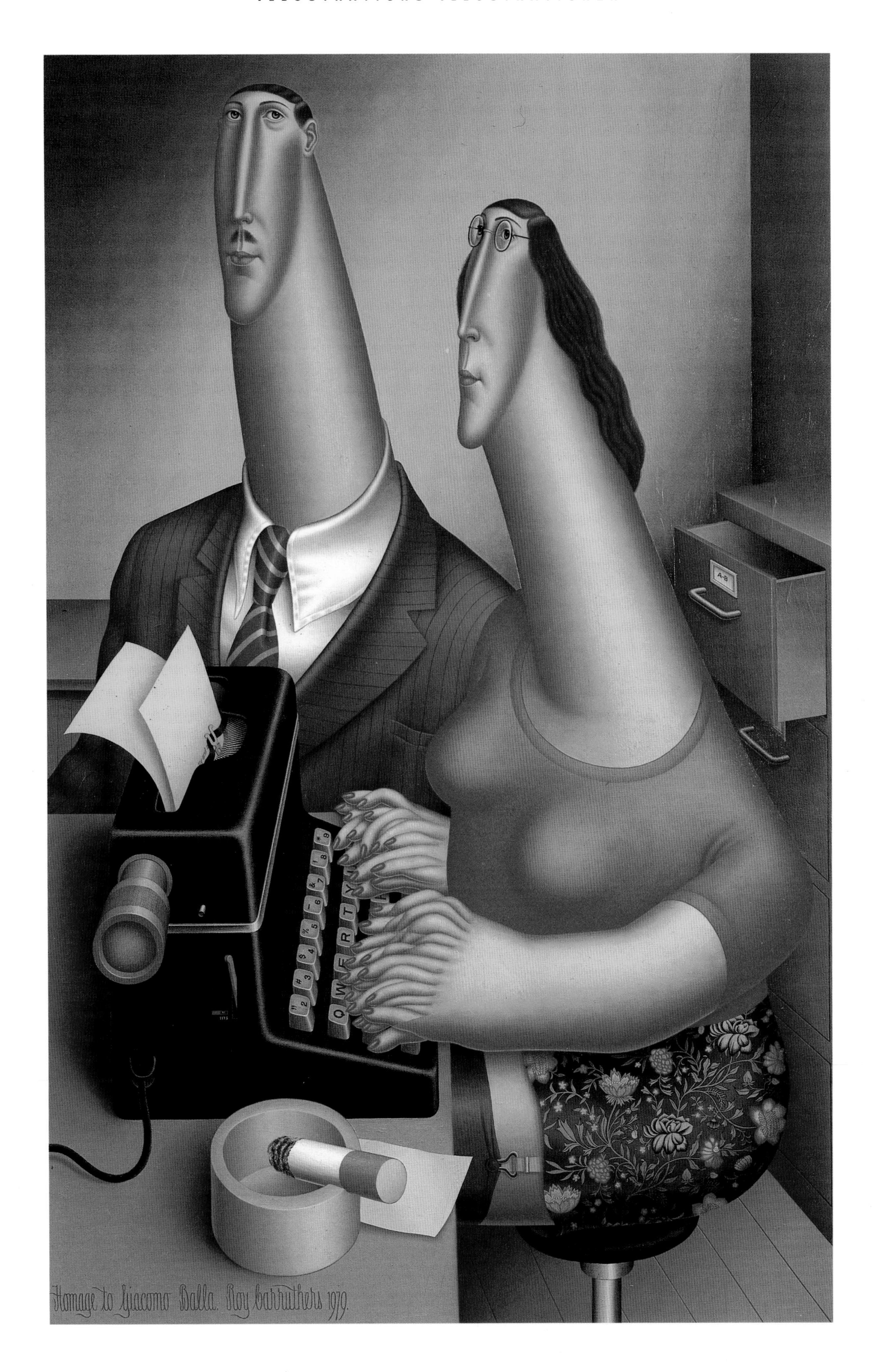
A-B
Homage to Giacomo Balla. Roy Carruthers 1979.

■ 1 ILLUSTRATOR: LISA MANNING COUNTRY: USA TITLE: WRITER'S BLOCK? ■ 2 ILLUSTRATOR: DENNIS CORRIGAN COUNTRY: USA TITLE: MAN WITH A SNICK ON HIS FACE ■ 3 ILLUSTRATOR: SEYMOUR CHWAST ART DIRECTOR: SEYMOUR CHWAST DESIGNER: SEYMOUR CHWAST COUNTRY: USA TITLE: THE FACTORY ■ 4, 5 ILLUSTRATOR: GREG TUCKER ART DIRECTOR: GREG TUCKER COUNTRY: USA

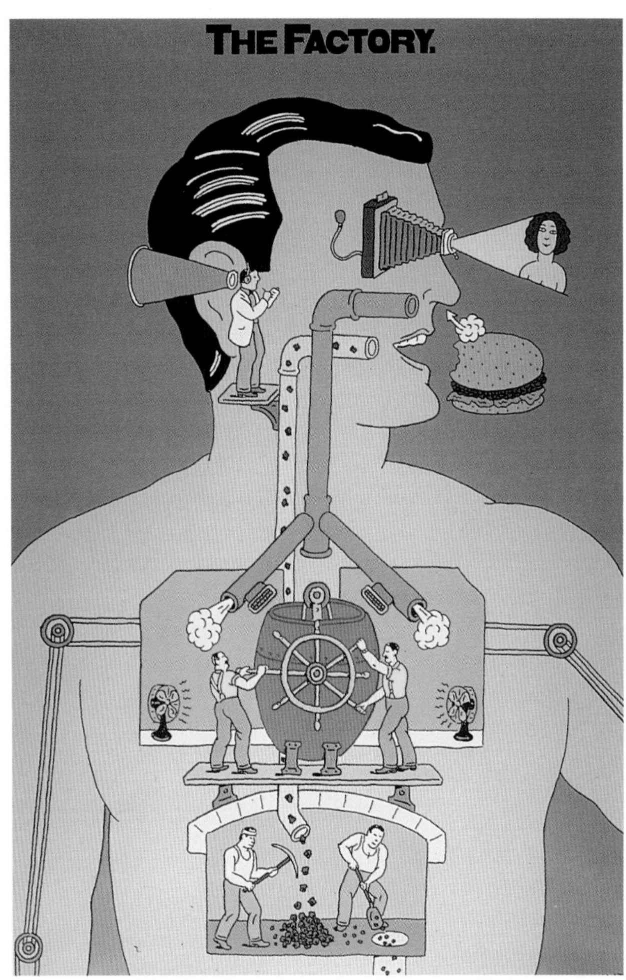
THE FACTORY.

■ 1 ILLUSTRATOR: PAUL ROGERS ART DIRECTOR: TIM A. FRAME DESIGN FIRM: SDI/HTI CLIENT: BORDERS, INC. COUNTRY: USA ■ 2 ILLUSTRATOR: PETER KRÄMER ART DIRECTOR: JORDAN BARRETT DESIGN FIRM: JORDAN BARRETT & ASSOCIATES, INC. CLIENT: PORT OF MIAMI COUNTRY: USA ■ 3 ILLUSTRATOR: RICHARD HESS COUNTRY: USA TITLE: MIKE'S NOSE

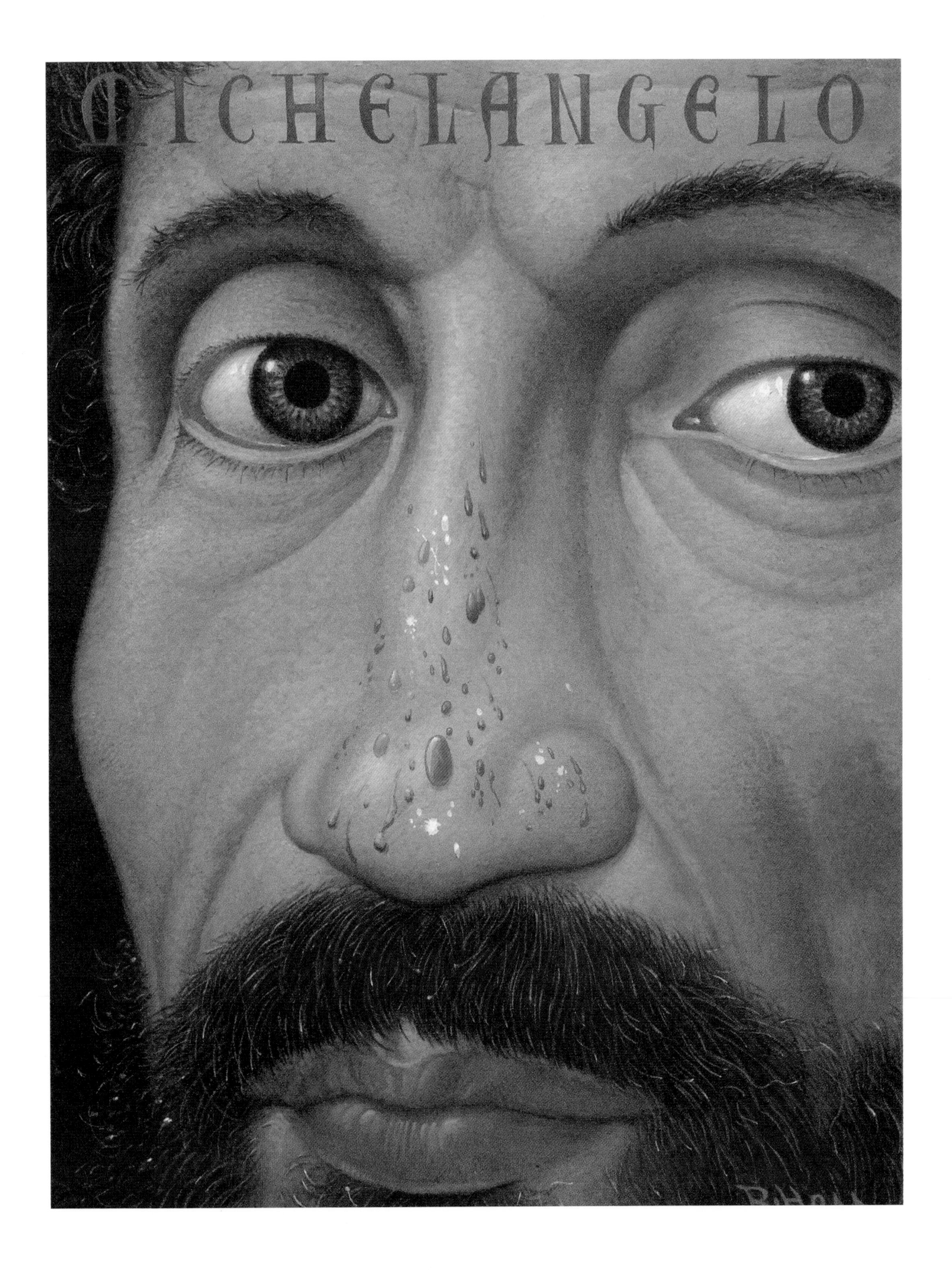
MICHELANGELO

Union
SPD

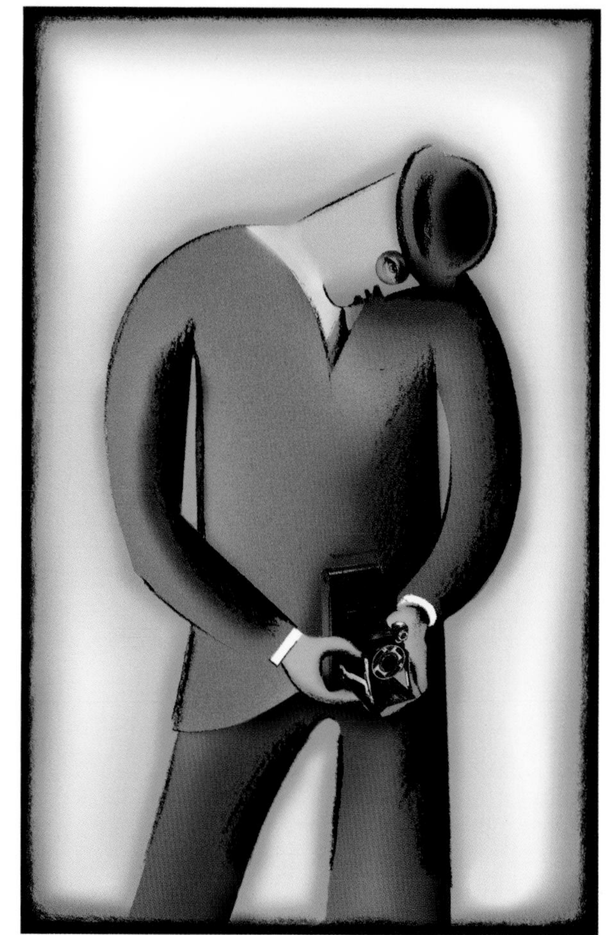

■ 1 ILLUSTRATOR: WIESLAW SMETEK ART DIRECTOR: FRANZ EPPING DESIGNER: WOLFGANG BEHNKEN PUBLISHER/CLIENT: *STERN*/GRUNER + JAHR COUNTRY: GERMANY ■ 2 ILLUSTRATOR: BARBARA NESSIM ART DIRECTORS: ARTHUR HOCHSTEIN, JANET WAEGEL DESIGNER: TOM MILLER PUBLISHER: *TIME* MAGAZINE CLIENT: TIME, INC. COUNTRY: USA ■ 3 ILLUSTRATOR: FRANK VIVA ART DIRECTOR: FRANK VIVA DESIGNERS: FRANK VIVA, KAREN SATAK DESIGN FIRM: VIVA DOLAN COMMUNICATIONS & DESIGN CLIENT: ARJO WIGGINS FINE PAPERS COUNTRY: USA ■ 4 ILLUSTRATOR: JOHN HOWARD COUNTRY: USA TITLE WILD PIANO

■ 1 ILLUSTRATOR: BRAD HOLLAND ART DIRECTOR: WAYNE FITZPATRICK PUBLISHER: *EMERGE* MAGAZINE COUNTRY: USA ■ 2 ILLUSTRATOR: CATHLEEN TOELKE ART DIRECTOR: DECK REEKS CLIENT: HOTEL MACKLOWE COUNTRY: USA ■ 3 ILLUSTRATOR: MARK ULRIKSEN ART DIRECTOR:

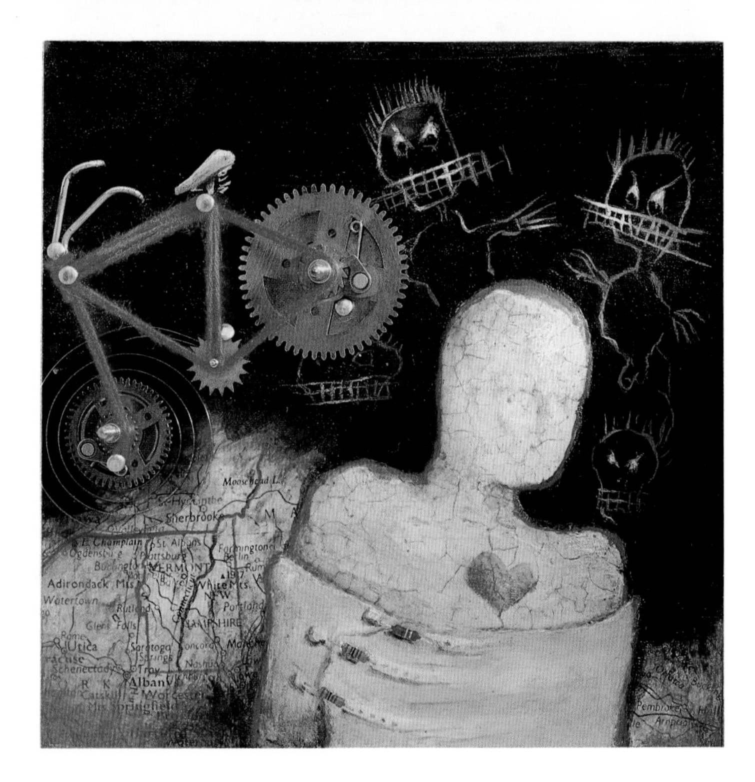

DEBORAH RUST PUBLISHER: *HARPERS* MAGAZINE COUNTRY: USA ■ 4 ILLUSTRATOR: STEIN LOKEN ART DIRECTOR: KARIN STOK PUBLISHER: TIDEN NORSK FORLAG COUNTRY: NORWAY ■ 5 ILLUSTRATOR: KINUKO KRAFT ART DIRECTOR: INA SALTZ PUBLISHER: *WORTH* MAGAZINE COUNTRY: USA

CHICAGO BOARD OF TRADE

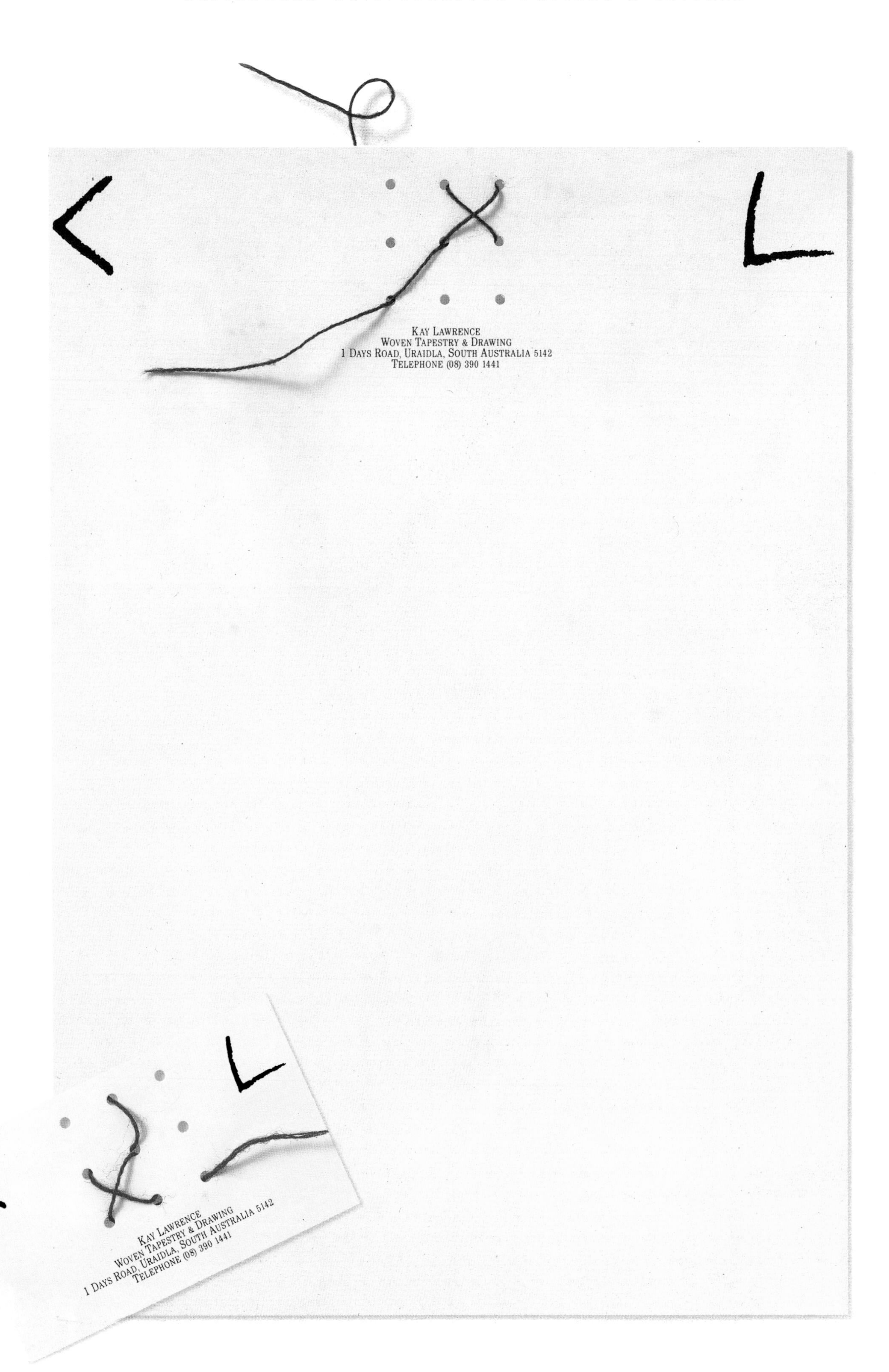
KAY LAWRENCE
WOVEN TAPESTRY & DRAWING
1 DAYS ROAD, URAIDLA, SOUTH AUSTRALIA 5142
TELEPHONE (08) 390 1441
KAY LAWRENCE
WOVEN TAPESTRY & DRAWING
1 DAYS ROAD, URAIDLA, SOUTH AUSTRALIA 5142
TELEPHONE (08) 390 1441

STEVE DAW
Photographer
DIRECTOR
STEVE DAW
Director

Kaisaniemen
DYNAMO
7008
3821
7 0 0 8 3 8 2 1
206078
TAAJARANTA, TARVONEN, KUJALA, KÄRKKÄINEN JA KUMPPANIT. KOLMAS KELPO MAINOSTOIMISTO SUOMESSA.

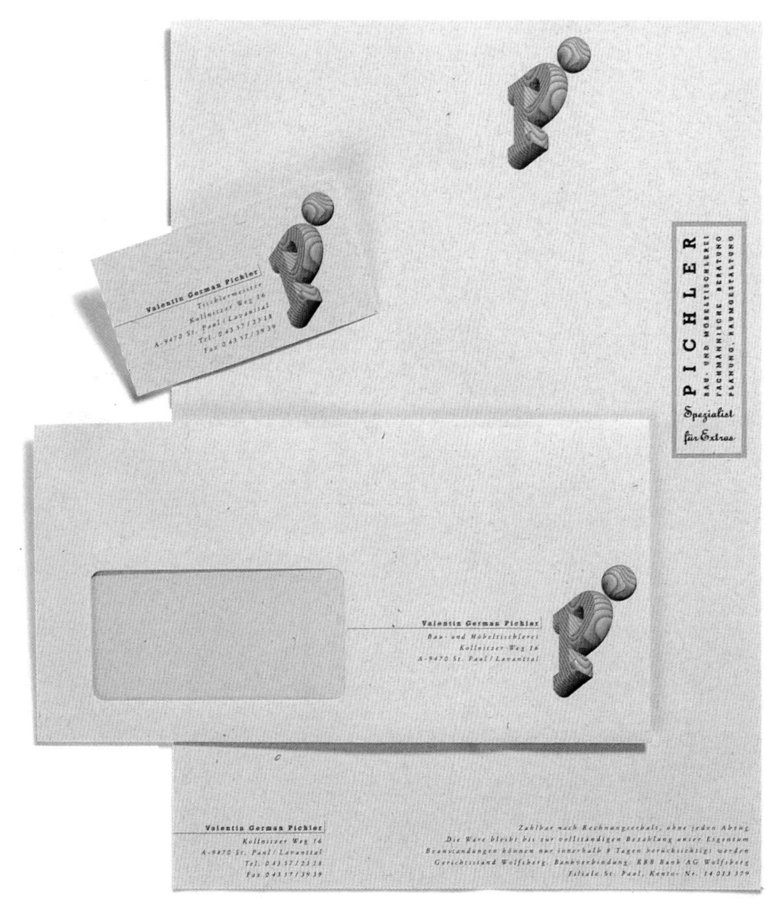
PICHLER
Spezialist
für Extras
Valentin German Pichler

■ (PRECEDING SPREAD) **1** ART DIRECTOR: JOHN NOWLAND DESIGNER: JOHN NOWLAND DESIGN FIRM: JOHN NOWLAND DESIGN CLIENT: WOVEN TAPESTRY & DRAWING COUNTRY: AUSTRALIA ■ **2** ART DIRECTOR: SHYAM MADIRAJU DESIGNER: SHYAM MADIRAJU ILLUSTRATOR: SHYAM MADIRAJU DESIGN FIRM: LEO BURNETT CLIENT: STEVE DAW COUNTRY: HONG KONG ■ (THIS SPREAD) **1** ART DIRECTOR: ILKKA KÄRKKÄINEN

DESIGNER: ILKKA KÄRKKÄINEN DESIGN FIRM/CLIENT: KAISANIEMEN DYNAMO COUNTRY: FINLAND ■ **2** ART DIRECTOR: ERWIN SCHMÖLZER DESIGNER: ERWIN SCHMÖLZER DESIGN FIRM: SCHMÖLZER, KONIAREK KUNST & DESIGN GMBH CLIENT: PICHLER COUNTRY: AUSTRIA ■ **3** ART DIRECTOR: HEINZ WILD DESIGNER: HEINZ WILD DESIGN FIRM: WILD & FREY CLIENT: KINOS AARAU COUNTRY: SWITZERLAND

PARADISE WILD

BREMER
STOLZ

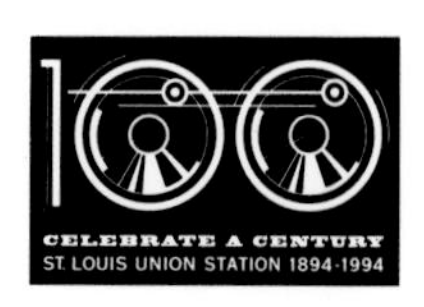
100
CELEBRATE A CENTURY
ST LOUIS UNION STATION 1894-1994

columbia
international

PIECES

LUNAISON

dobber

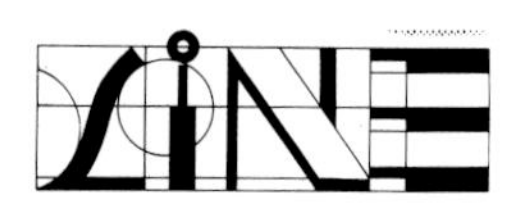
LINE

WARNER
ARCHIVES
WARNER BROS.
2-45456
WB

EDI MAGIC

SAYLES
GRAPHIC
DESIGN

■ 1 Art Director/Designer: ANDREW DOLAN Design Firm: SUPON DESIGN GROUP, INC. Client: PARADISE WILD Country: USA ■ 2 Art Director/Designer/Illustrator: KEITH HARRIS Design Firm: KEITH HARRIS PACKAGE DESIGN Client: KAFFEERÖSTEREI TEMPELMANN Country: GERMANY ■ 3 Art Director: RON SULLIVAN Designer: KELLY ALLEN Design Firm: SULLIVANPERKINS Client: THE ROUSE COMPANY Country: USA ■ 4 Art Director: TONY SELLARI Designers: KAREN GREENBERG, MARK KINGSLEY Design Firm: GREENBERG KINGSLEY Client: SONY MUSIC Country: USA ■ 5 Art Director: SUPON PHORNIRUNLIT Designer: DAVID CARROLL Design Firm: SUPON DESIGN GROUP, INC. Client: SUPON DESIGN GROUP, INT'L BOOK DIVISION Country: USA ■ 6 Art Director: JOHN COY Designers: JOHN COY, ALBERT CHOI, ROKHA SREY Photographer: DAVID JORDAN WILLIAMS Design Firm: COY Client: PIECES Country: USA ■ 7 Art Director/Designer/Illustrator: RÜDIGER GÖTZ Design Firm: FACTOR DESIGN Client: LUNAISON Country: GERMANY ■ 8 Art Director: NIKKO AMANDONICO Designer: PAUL BARRY Design Firm: ENERGY PROJECT Client: DOBBER Country: ITALY ■ 9 Art Director: SERGEI KUZHAVSKY Client: LINE Country: RUSSIA ■ 10 Art Directors: JERI HEIDEN, MICHAEL G. REY Designer: GREG LINDY Client: WARNER BROS. RECORDS INC. Country: USA ■ 11 Art Director: ZACHARIAS Designer: LUCAS BUCHHOLZ Design Firm: *) MEDIAWERK Client: FELIX HELLENKAMP STAHLDESIGN Country: GERMANY ■ 12 Art Director/Designer: SHIGEO KATSUOKA Design Firm: SHIGEO KATSUOKA DESIGN STUDIO Client: THE MEIJI MUTUAL LIFE INSURANCE COMPANY Country: JAPAN ■ 13 Art Director:

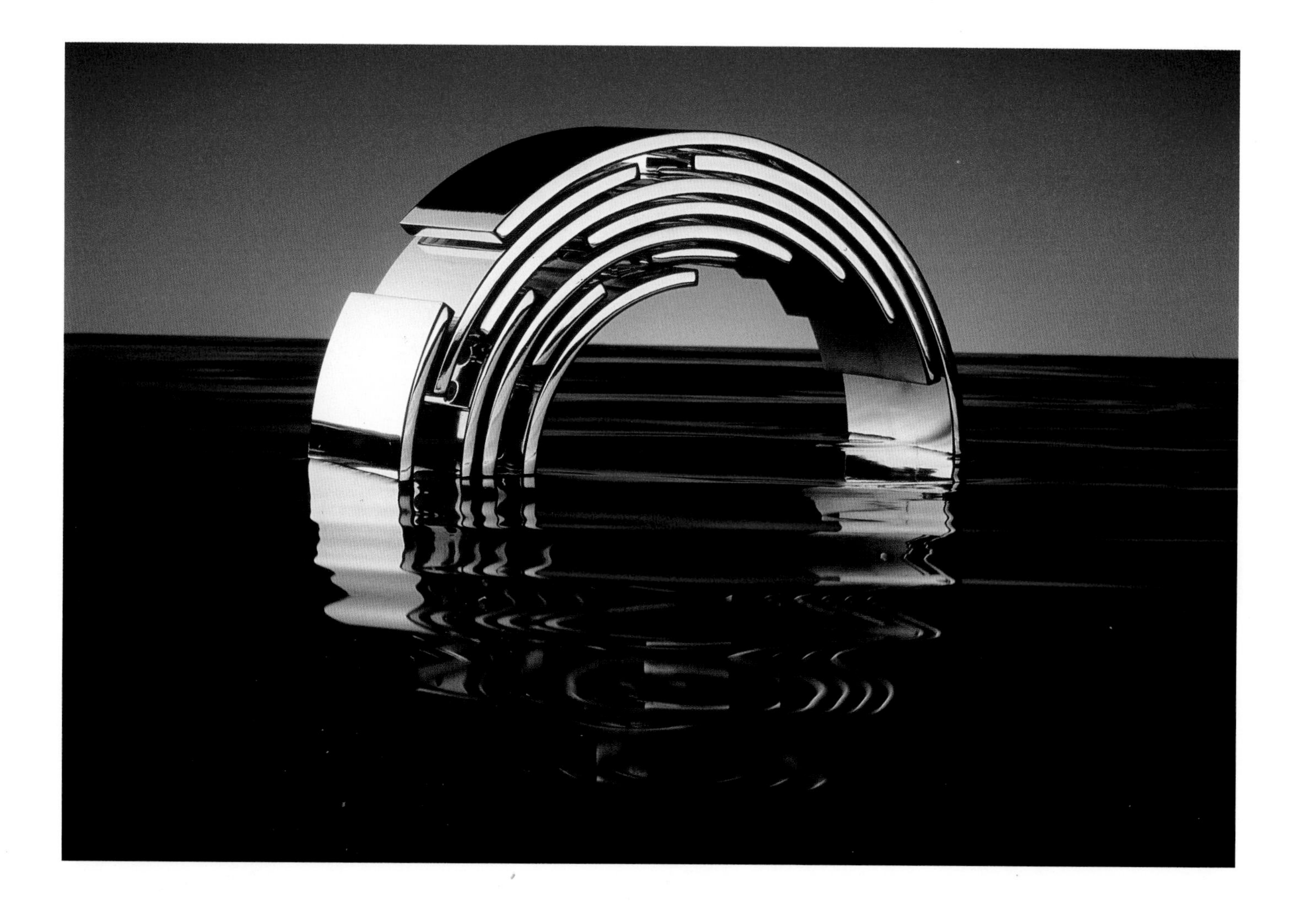

HUDSON HILL Designer/Illustrator: MICHAEL SCHWAB Design Firm: GREENSTONE ROBERTS Client: EDI MAGIC Country: USA ■ 14 Art Director/DesignerLUIS ACEVEDO Illustrator: LUIS ACEVEDO Design Firm: RBMM/THE RICHARDS GROUP Client: BLITZ SOFTWARE INC. Country: USA ■ 15 Art Director/Designer: JOHN SAYLES Illustrator: JOHN SAYLES Design Firm/ Client: SAYLES GRAPHIC DESIGN Country: USA ■ 16 Art Director: TOR PETTERSEN Designers: TOR PETTERSEN, CRAIG JOHNSON, JOANNA PETTERSEN Design Firm: TOR PETTERSEN & PARTNERS LTD. Client: ENTERPRISE OIL PLC Country: GREAT BRITAIN ■ (FOLLOWING SPREAD) 1 Art Director: MICHAEL DENNY Designers: JOHN BATESON, DEBORAH OSBORNE, ANDREW ROSS, JONATHAN SIMPSON, RACHAEL DINNIS Design Firm: ROUNDEL DESIGN GROUP Client: THE CZECH TECHNOLOGY PARK, BRNO A.S. Country: CZECH REPUBLIC ■ 2 Art Director: NICHOLAS THIRKELL Designers: NICHOLAS THIRKELL, NEIL WALKER, IAIN CROCKART Design Firm: CDT DESIGN LIMITED Client: OUR PRICE MUSIC Country: GREAT BRITAIN ■ 3 Art Director: JACK ANDERSON Designers: JACK ANDERSON, DAVID BATES, CLIFF CHUNG Design Firm: HORNALL ANDERSON DESIGN WORKS Client: CF2GS Country: USA ■ 4 Art Director: JOSEPH RATTAN Designers: GREG MORGAN, JOSEPH RATTAN Illustrator: DIANA MCKNIGHT Design Firm: JOSEPH RATTAN DESIGN Client: GROUP GALLAGHER Country: USA ■ 5 Art Director: JOSEPH RATTAN Designer: DIANA MCKNIGHT Design Firm: JOSEPH RATTAN DESIGN Client: PRIME RETAIL (INDIANA FACTORY SHOPS) Country: USA ■ 6 Art Director: JOSEPH RATTAN Designer: GREG MORGAN Design Firm: JOSEPH RATTAN

cf2GS

DESIGN CLIENT: PRIME RETAIL (FLORIDA KEYS FACTORY SHOPS) COUNTRY: USA ■ 7 ART DIRECTOR: JOSEPH RATTAN DESIGNER: DIANA MCKNIGHT DESIGN FIRM: JOSEPH RATTAN DESIGN CLIENT: PRIME RETAIL (GULFPORT FACTORY SHOPS) COUNTRY: USA ■ 8 ART DIRECTOR: JOSEPH RATTAN DESIGNER: DIANA MCKNIGHT DESIGN FIRM: JOSEPH RATTAN DESIGN CLIENT: MARKETING VISION COUNTRY: USA ■ 9 ART DIRECTOR: JAMIE KOVAL DESIGNER/ILLUSTRATOR: MICHAEL SCHWAB DESIGN FIRM: VSA PARTNERS, INC. CLIENT: HYATT GRAND VICTORIA CASINO COUNTRY: USA ■ 10 ART DIRECTOR: BILL HIGGINS DESIGNER/ILLUSTRATOR: MICHAEL SCHWAB STUDIO: MICHAEL SCHWAB DESIGN CLIENT: BUCKHEAD ROADHOUSE COUNTRY: USA ■ 11 ART DIRECTORS: JAMI SPITTLER, RICH SILVERSTEIN DESIGNER/ ILLUSTRATOR:

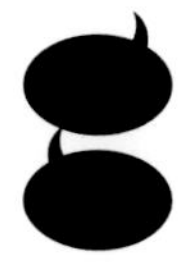

MICHAEL SCHWAB STUDIO: MICHAEL SCHWAB DESIGN CLIENT: GOLDEN GATE NATIONAL PARK ASSOC. COUNTRY: USA ■ 12 ART DIRECTOR: DOUG GILMOUR DESIGNER/ILLUSTRATOR: MICHAEL SCHWAB CLIENT: AQUACUISINE COUNTRY: USA ■ 13 ART DIRECTORS: DAVID PAYNE, DARREN BRIGGS DESIGNER: MICHAEL SCHWAB ILLUSTRATOR: MICHAEL SCHWAB STUDIO: MICHAEL SCHWAB DESIGN CLIENT: CANNONBALL GRAPHICS COUNTRY: USA ■ 14–18 DESIGNER: JOHANN TERRETTAZ ILLUSTRATOR: JOHANN TERRETTAZ DESIGN FIRM: TINGUELY CONCEPT CLIENT: NIDECKER COUNTRY: SWITZERLAND ■ 19–23 DESIGNER: JEFF POLLARD ILLUSTRATOR: JEFF POLLARD DESIGN FIRM: POLLARD DESIGN CLIENTS: BAUDELAIRE INC. (19, 20, 22), SUNDOG PRODUCTIONS (21) GROVE INVESTMENT (23) COUNTRY: USA

■ 1 Art Director: ALBERT SHU SUNG WAN Designer/Illustrator: PATRICK TAM KWOK KEE Design Firm: A. STUDIO & ASSOCIATES CO. LTD. Client: LINGNAN OLD BOY ASSOCIATION Country: HONG KONG ■ 2 Art Director/Designer/Client: HAT NGUYEN Design Firm: HAT NGUYEN DESIGN Country: USA ■ 3 Art Director/Designer: KAZUMASA NAGAI Design Firm: NIPPON DESIGN CENTER, INC. Client: CHIBA CITY MUSEUM OF ART Country: JAPAN ■ 4 Art Director: TDC BOARD OF DIRECTORS Designer: GERARD HUERTA Illustrators: GERARD HUERTA, BARBARA GIBB Design Firm: GERARD HUERTA DESIGN, INC. Client: TYPE DIRECTORS CLUB Country: USA ■ 5 Art Director: DAN REISINGER Designer: AVITAL KELLNER-GAZIT Design Firm: STUDIO REISINGER Client: TAMBOUR Country: ISRAEL ■ 6 Art Director/Illustrator: KOBE Designers: KOBE, ALAN LEUSINK Design Firm: DUFFY DESIGN Client: HONEY BAKED HAM COMPANY Country: USA ■ 7 Art Director/Designer: ANDREW DOLAN Design Firm: SUPON DESIGN GROUP, INC. Client: CREATIVE STRATEGY, INC. FOR AXENT TECHNOLOGIES, INC. Country: USA ■ 8 Art Director/Designer: TOM ANTISTA Design Firm: ANTISTA FAIRCLOUGH DESIGN Client: ATLANTA STARZ Country: USA ■ 9 Art Director: RAY DOTZLER Designer: TIM GRUTSCH Design Firm/Client: DOTZLER CREATIVE ARTS Country: USA ■ 10 Art Director/Designer: DON WELLER Design Firm: THE WELLER INSTITUTE FOR THE CURE OF DESIGN Client: THE PRAXIS INSTITUTE Country: USA ■ 11 Designer/Illustrator: MARK FOX Design Firm: BLACKDOG Client: BACKBONE Country: USA ■ 12 Art Director: JIM BERTE Designer: JIM GUERARD Design Firm: RUNYAN HINSCHE ASSOCIATES Client: BANCENTRO Country: MEXICO ■ 13 Art Director/Designer/Illustrator: DAVID ZAUHAR Design Firm: ZAUHAR DESIGN Client: GREATER MINNEAPOLIS COUNCIL OF CHURCHES Country: USA ■ 14 Art Director/Designer: MARKUS HEINBACH Client: HISTORISCHE BAUERNSCHAFT BLECHE Country: GERMANY ■ 15 Art Director/Designer: PAMELA CHANG Design Firm: RBMM/THE RICHARDS GROUP Client: TALKTECH Country: USA ■ 16 Art Director/Designer: ART GARCIA Design Firm: SULLIVANPERKINS Client: METROWEST LANDSCAPE COMPANY Country: USA ■ 17 Art Director: IRAJ MIRZA-ALIKHANI Designer/Illustrator: LADAN REZAEI Design Firm: ASHENA ADVERTISING Client:

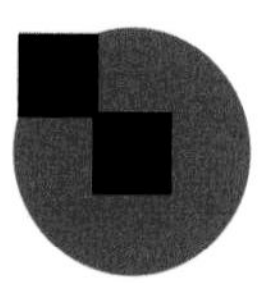

NOORI TEX. LTD. Country: IRAN ■ 18 Art Director/Designer: DAVID LERCH Design Firm: PENNEBAKER DESIGN Client: GUNTHER CONCEPTS Country: SWITZERLAND ■ 19 Art Director: MIKE HICKS Designer: MATT HECK Design Firm: HIXO Client: TRAVEL FEST Country: USA ■ 20 Art Director: CHRISTIE LAMBERT Designer/Illustrator: JOY CATHEY Design Firm: LAMBERT DESIGN STUDIO Client: ANITA MISRA PAULUS, DDS Country: USA ■ 21 Art Directors: DANA LYTLE, KEVIN WADE Designer: KEVIN WADE Design Firm: PLANET DESIGN COMPANY Client: CANDINAS CHOCOLATIER Country: USA ■ 22 Art Director/Designer: SCOTT ARROWOOD Design Firm: ARROWOOD DESIGN Client: THE INSIGHT GROUP Country: USA ■ 23 Art Director/Designer: SANG YOON Design Firm: SERAN DESIGN Client: JAMES MADISON UNIVERSITY/COLLEGE OF EDUCATION & PSYCHOLOGY Country: USA ■ 24 Designer/Illustrator: MICHAEL CONNORS Design Firm: SPANGLER ASSOCIATES INC. Client: GROUP HEALTH COOPERATIVE Country: USA ■ 25 Art Director/Designer: DIMITRI KAPELNIKOV Design Firm: ADF CREATIVE CLUB Client: MIDWEST LTD. Country: UKRAINE ■ 26 Art Director/Designer/Illustrator: HORACIO COBOS Design Firm: RBMM/THE RICHARDS GROUP Client: AMERIFEST DALLAS Country: USA ■ 27 Art Director/Designer: BRIAN LARSON Client: TWIN CITY SCHOOL OF DANCE & BALLET Country: USA ■ 28 Art Director/Designer: JOSE SERRANO Illustrator: TRACY SABIN Design Firm: MIRES DESIGN, INC. Client: BOY SCOUTS PACK 260 Country: USA ■ 29 Art Director: JOHN SWIETER Designers: JOHN SWIETER, MARK FORD Design Firm: SWIETER DESIGN UNITED STATES Client: STREET SAVAGE SPORTSWEAR Country: USA ■ 30 Art Director/Designer: GARY DANIELS Design Firm: EDS MARKETING COMMUNICATIONS Client: EDS LEADERSHIP DEVELOPMENT Country: USA

THE HONEYBAKED HAM COMPANY

STAR

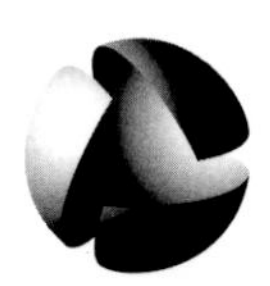

1394
1994

METROWEST

PINE WOOD
Derby '94

■ 1, 2 RECORD COMPANY: WARNER BROS. RECORDS ART DIRECTOR: JERI MCMANUS PHOTOGRAPHER: AARON RAPOPORT PERFORMING ARTIST: VAN HALEN ALBUM TITLE: 5150 ■ 3, 4 RECORD COMPANY: MCA RECORDS ART DIRECTOR: TIM STEDMAN DESIGNER: DAVID HIGH ILLUSTRATOR: MARK DURHAM DESIGN FIRM: HIGH DESIGN PERFORMING ARTIST: VARIOUS ALBUM TITLE: MCA MUSCLE ALTERRAIN ■ 5, 6 RECORD COMPANY: FLYING NUN RECORDS DESIGNERS: ALEC BATHGATE, CHRIS KNOX PERFORMING ARTIST: TALL DWARFS ALBUM TITLE: 3 EPS ■ 7, 8 RECORD

COMPANY: KITTY ENTER PRISES INC. ART DIRECTOR/DESIGNER: YOSHIRO NAKAMURA DESIGN FIRM: YEN INC. PERFORMING ARTIST: VARIOUS ALBUM TITLE: SOUNDTRACK ■ 9, 10 RECORD COMPANY: CECI-CÈLA/VIRGIN FRANCE DESIGNER (METAL BOX)/ILLUSTRATOR: GÉRARD LO MONACO PERFORMING ARTIST: RENAUD ALBUM TITLE: A LA BELLE DE MAI ■ 11, 12 RECORD COMPANY: VIRGIN RECORDS ART DIRECTOR/ DESIGNER: PETER CORRISTON ILLUSTRATOR: CHRISTIAN PIPER PERFORMING ARTIST: THE ROLLING STONES ALBUM TITLE: TATTOO YOU

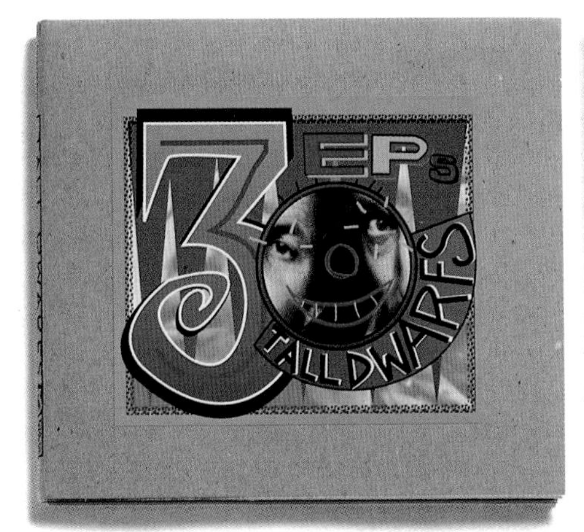
3 EPs
TALL DWARFS

3 EPs
3 EPs
TALL DWARFS
Made in the U.K.
FNCD296 D31156
FLYING NUN RECORDS
COMPACT
disc
DIGITAL AUDIO

一、オートバイ少女のテーマ
三、黄昏波止場は茜色
四、火星日報第一面の大見出し
五、月影のCINE C'ITTA
六、まぶたと胸とで憶えてる
七、海辺のメモリー
八、道草のラプソディ
九、港ヶ丘教会のある風景
十、夏だけの陽炎
十一、オートバイと私
十二、さらばオルガンの鳴る夜
十三、CINE C'ITTAの月影
十四、まぶたと胸とで憶えてる
十五、少年の胸のボタン

オートバイ少女
KTCR-1268
あがた森魚
イメージサウンドトラック盤
制作・鈴木惣一朗
SAMPLE

RENAUD
10
Les 3 Tirs
A LA BELLE DE MAI

RENAUD
À LA BELLE DE MAI
RENAUD
10
Les 3 Tirs
A LA BELLE DE MAI

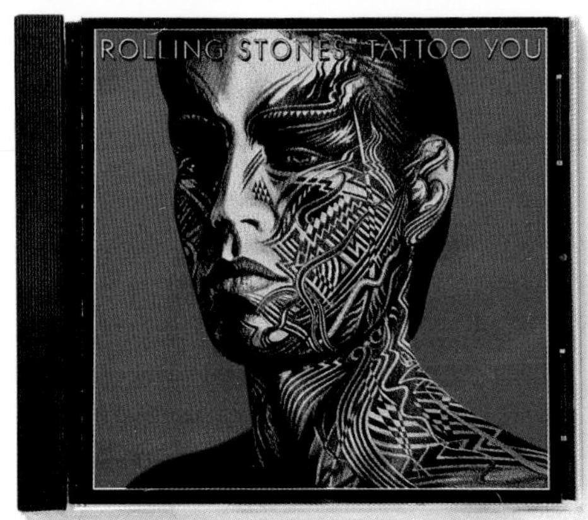
ROLLING STONES TATTOO YOU

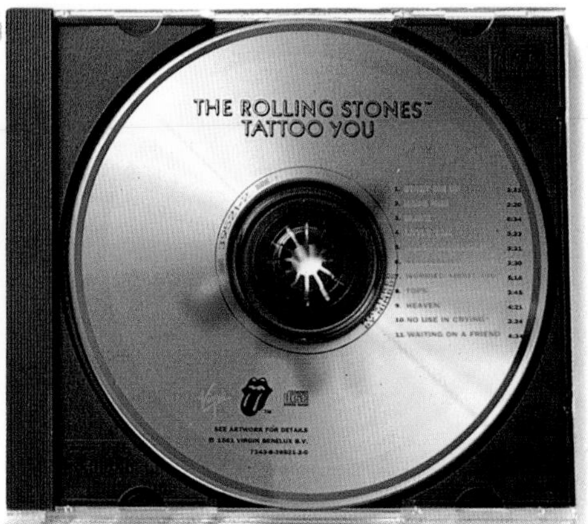
THE ROLLING STONES
TATTOO YOU

Kingmaker
CD 1
MADE IN UK
1. 10 YEARS ASLEEP 2. GENUINE LIAR
3. LADY MADONNA 4. WHEN LUCY'S DOWN (LIVE)
disc
Kingmaker
CD 2
1. 10 YEARS ASLEEP 2. SHIVER
3. HIGH AS A KITE (LIVE) 4. HARD TIMES (LIVE)
disc
THE FASTBACKS
Chrysalis
SPIDER
I WAS AGAIN
I AM THE WALRUS
GEMA
DAVID BYRNE

■ 1 RECORD COMPANY: EMIGRE ART DIRECTOR/DESIGNER: RUDY VANDERLANS PERFORMING ARTIST: BASEHEAD ALBUM TITLE: PLAY WITH TOYS ■ 2, 5 RECORD COMPANY: CHRYSALIS RECORDS ART DIRECTOR/DESIGNER: EDDIE DEIGHTON PERFORMING ARTIST: KINGMAKER ■ 3 RECORD COMPANY: EMIGRE ART DIRECTOR/DESIGNER: RUDY VANDERLANS PERFORMING ARTIST: VARIOUS ALBUM TITLE: EMIGRE SAMPLER NO. 2 ■ 4 RECORD COMPANY: SUB POP ART DIRECTOR/DESIGNER: ART CHANTRY PERFORMING ARTIST: MARK LANEGAN ALBUM TITLE: WHISKEY FOR THE HOLY GHOST ■ 6 RECORD COMPANY: LUCKY RECORDS ART DIRECTOR/DESIGNER: ART CHANTRY PERFORMING ARTIST: THE FASTBACKS ALBUM TITLE: BIKE, TOY, CLOCK, GIFT ■ 7 RECORD COMPANY: CHRYSALIS RECORDS ART DIRECTOR/DESIGNER: ANDREW GREETHAM PERFORMING ARTIST: CARTER USM ALBUM TITLE: POST HISTORIC MONSTERS ■ 8 RECORD COMPANY: CAPITOL RECORDS ART

DIRECTOR/DESIGNER: NORMAN MOORE DESIGN FIRM: DESIGN ART INC. PERFORMING ARTIST: HEART ALBUM TITLE: BRIGADE ■ 9 RECORD COMPANY: GIANT RECORDS ART DIRECTOR/DESIGNER: DEBORAH NORCROSS DESIGN FIRM: WARNER BROS. RECORDS IN-HOUSE ART DEPARTMENT PERFORMING ARTIST: BOINGO ALBUM TITLE: BOINGO ■ 10 RECORD COMPANY: NORMAL RECORDS ART DIRECTORS: KERSTIN VIEG, OLAF MEYER DESIGNER: OLAF MEYER PHOTOGRAPHER: KERSTIN VIEG PERFORMING ARTIST: TERRY LEE HALE ALBUM TITLE: O WHAT A WORLD ■ 11 RECORD COMPANY: CHUCKIE-BOY RECORDS ART DIRECTOR/DESIGNER: ART CHANTRY PERFORMING ARTIST: THE HOLIDAYS ALBUM TITLE: CHUCKIE-BOY ■ 12 RECORD COMPANY: LUAKA BOP RECORDS DESIGNERS: DAVID BYRNE, DOUBLESPACE NY DESIGN FIRM: DOUBLESPACE NY PERFORMING ARTIST: DAVID BYRNE ALBUM TITLE: REI MOMO ■ 13, 14 RECORD COMPANY: MCA RECORDS ART DIRECTOR: VARTAN DESIGNER/CONSTRUCTION: RON LARSON PERFORMING ARTIST: VARIOUS ALBUM TITLE: MUSIC FROM BEDROCK – SOUNDTRACK

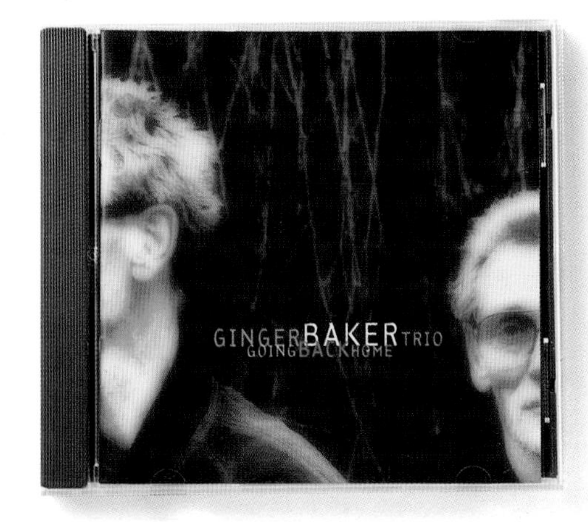
GINGER BAKER TRIO
GOING BACK HOME

BILL FRISELL
Electric Guitar
GINGER BAKER Drums, Vocals
CHARLIE HADEN
Acoustic Bass

GINGER BAKER TRIO
GOING BACK HOME

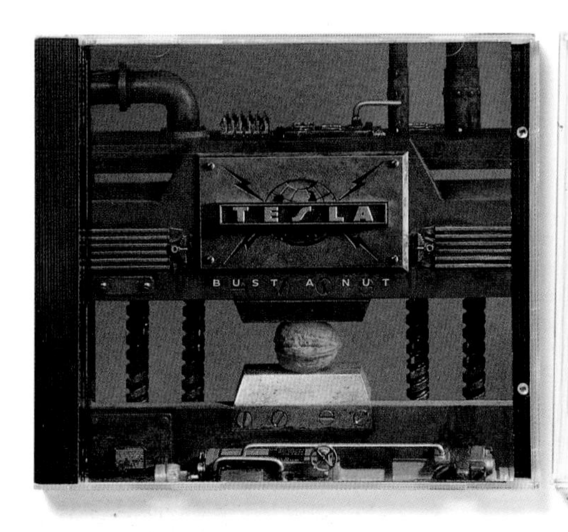
TESLA
BUST A NUT

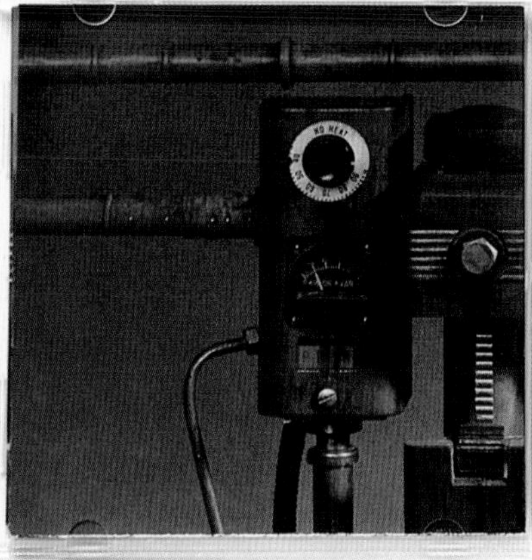

TESLA
BUST A NUT
GEFFEN
PRODUCED BY TERRY THOMAS FOR T2 LTD.
GEFD-24713

PRONG
CLEANSING

EPIC
PRONG
CLEANSING
UNBREAKABLE
EK 53019
ALL SONGS
WRITTEN BY PRONG
(ASCAP)

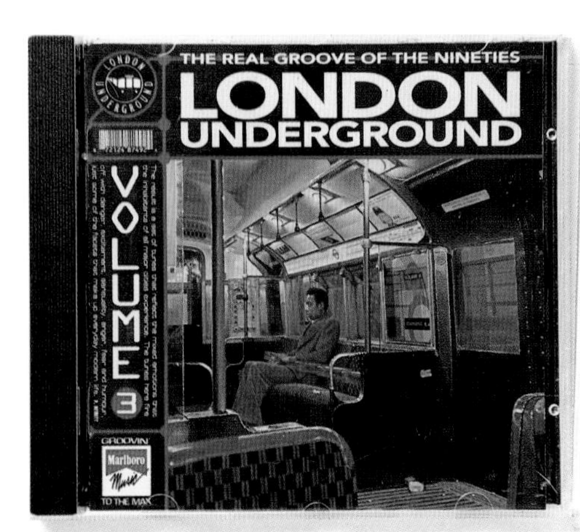
THE REAL GROOVE OF THE NINETIES
LONDON
UNDERGROUND
VOLUME 3
GROOVIN
Marlboro
TO THE MAX

0017492MRO

Marlboro
LC 8307 | 0017492MRO | A MARLBORO MUSIC RELEASE | SEE BOOKLETT FOR MORE DETAILS
LONDON
UNDERGROUND
VOLUME III

■ 1, 2 RECORD COMPANY: ATLANTIC RECORDS DESIGNER: GREENBERG KINGSLEY PERFORMING ARTIST: GINGER BAKER TRIO ALBUM TITLE: GOING BACK HOME ■ 3, 4 RECORD COMPANY: GEFFEN RECORDS ART DIRECTOR: HUGH SYME DESIGNER: HUGH SYME ILLUSTRATOR: HUGH SYME PERFORMING ARTIST: TESLA ALBUM TITLE: BUST A NUT ■ 5, 6 RECORD COMPANY: EPIC RECORDS ART DIRECTOR: CAROL CHEN DESIGNER: TRACY BOYCHUCK PHOTOGRAPHER: KEN SCHLES PERFORMING ARTIST: PRONG ALBUM TITLE: CLEANSING ■ 7, 8 RECORD COMPANY: MARLBORO MUSIC ART DIRECTOR: HANS HAMMERS JR. II DESIGNER: WOLFGANG V. GERAMB ILLUSTRATOR: MICHAEL MAU DESIGN FIRM: HEADCHARGE W.A. PERFORMING ARTIST: VARIOUS ALBUM TITLE: LONDON UNDERGROUND – VOLUME 3 ■ 9 RECORD COMPANY: COLUMBIA RECORDS ART DIRECTOR: SARA ROTMAN DESIGNER: SARA ROTMAN PERFORMING ARTIST: BILLY JOEL ALBUM TITLE: SHADES OF GREY ■ 10 RECORD COMPANY: HOLLYWOOD RECORDS ART DIRECTORS: JOE ELY, TERRY ALLEN PHOTOGRAPHERS: JOE ELY, TERRY ALLEN ILLUSTRATORS: JOE ELY, TERRY ALLEN DESIGNER: MARIA DEGRASSI PERFORMING ARTIST: VARIOUS ALBUM TITLE: SONGS FROM CHIPPY

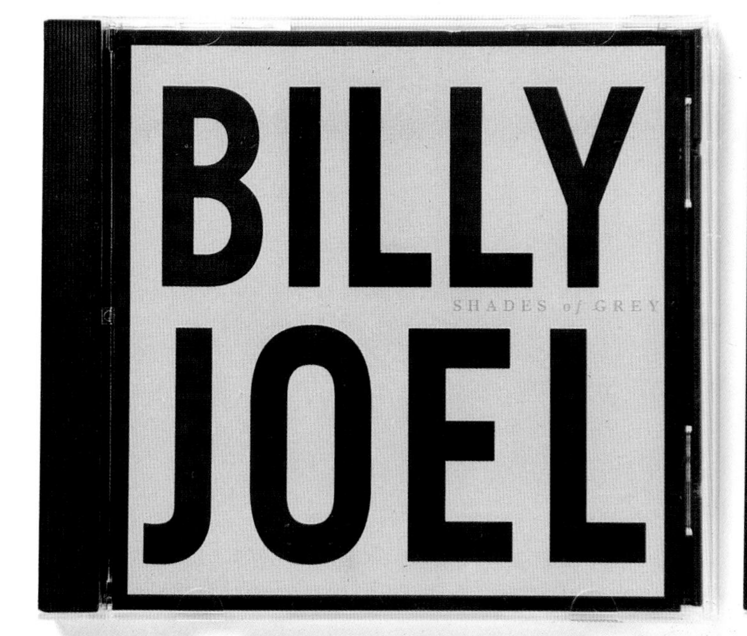

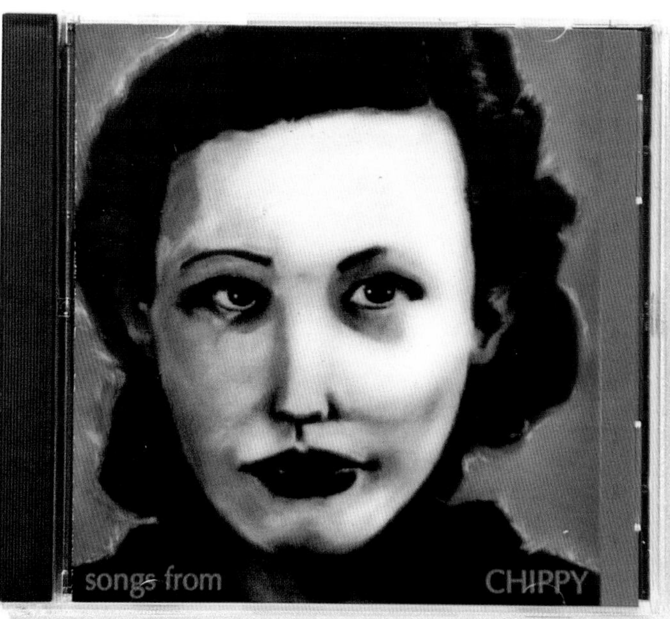

■ 1 RECORD COMPANY: COLUMBIA RECORDS ART DIRECTOR: TRACY BOYCHUK PHOTOGRAPHER: ANDREW ECCLES DESIGN FIRM: SONY MUSIC CREATIVE SERVICES PERFORMING ARTIST: DAVID SANCHEZ ALBUM TITLE: THE DEPARTURE ■ 2 RECORD COMPANY: SIRE/WARNER BROS. RECORDS ART DIRECTORS/DESIGNERS: STEPHANIE NASH, ANTHONY MICHAEL PHOTOGRAPHER: NICK KNIGHT DESIGN FIRM: MICHAEL NASH ASSOCIATES PERFORMING ARTIST: SEAL ALBUM TITLE: SEAL ■ 3 RECORD COMPANY: CASTLE VON BUHLER STUDIOS ART DIRECTOR/DESIGNER: FRITZ KLAETKE PHOTOGRAPHER: WILLIAM HUBER DESIGN FIRM: VISUAL DIALOGUE PERFORMING ARTIST: VARIOUS ALBUM TITLE: SOON ■ 4 RECORD COMPANY: WARNER BROS. RECORDS ART DIRECTOR: BOB SEIDEMAN ILLUSTRATOR: JOHN VAN HAMMERSVELD PERFORMING ARTIST: GRATEFUL DEAD ALBUM TITLE: SKELETONS FROM THE CLOSET ■ 5 RECORD COMPANY: REPRISE RECORDS ART DIRECTOR: JERI HEIDEN DESIGNERS: JERI HEIDEN, LYN BRADLEY PHOTOGRAPHER: FLORIA SIGISMONDI DESIGN FIRM: WARNER BROS. RECORDS IN-HOUSE ART DEPARTMENT PERFORMING ARTIST: JANE SIBERRY ALBUM TITLE: WHEN I WAS A BOY ■ 6 RECORD COMPANY: SONY MUSIC ART DIRECTOR/DESIGNER: VINCE FROST PHOTOGRAPHER: THE DOUGLAS BROTHERS DESIGN FIRM: FROST DESIGN PERFORMING ARTIST: EDDIE AND THE HOT RODS ALBUM TITLE: THE END OF THE BEGINNING ■ 7 RECORD COMPANY: EMI ELECTROLA GMBH COVER PAINTING: MANFRED "SCHMAL" BOECKER PERFORMING ARTIST: BAP ALBUM TITLE: DA CAPO ■ 8 RECORD COMPANY: NORMAL RECORDS ART DIRECTORS: KERSTIN

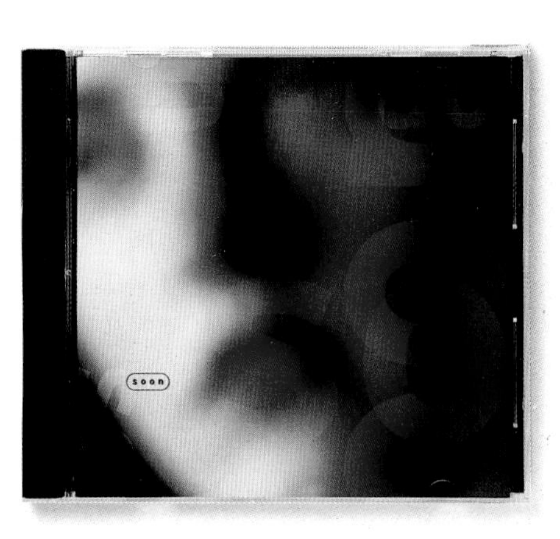

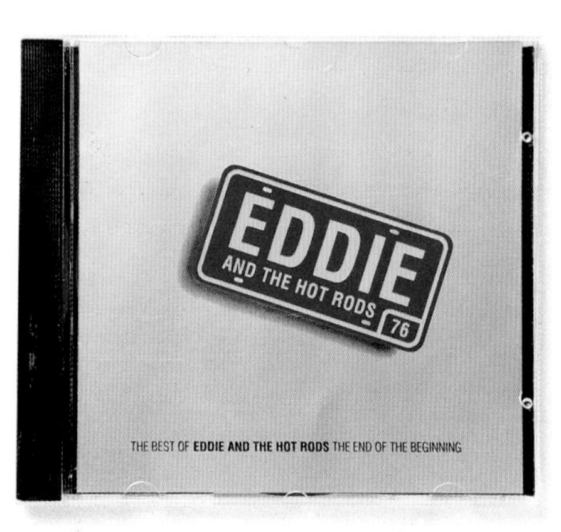

VIEG, OLAF MEYER DESIGNER: OLAF MEYER PHOTOGRAPHER: KERSTIN VIEG PERFORMING ARTIST: COSMIC PSYCHOS ALBUM TITLE: SLAVE TO THE CRAVE ■ 9 RECORD COMPANY: ELEKTRA RECORDS ART DIRECTOR/DESIGNER: LAURIE HENZEL PHOTOGRAPHER: MICHAEL LAVINE PERFORMING ARTIST: LUNA ALBUM TITLE: BEWITCHED ■ 10–12 RECORD COMPANY: MCA RECORDS ART DIRECTOR: VARTAN DESIGNER: MICHAEL DIEHL PERFORMING ARTIST: VARIOUS ALBUM TITLE: CHESS BLUES ■ 13 RECORD COMPANY: POLYGRAM GMBH ART DIRECTOR: GÜNTER WOLF – BEST OF... DESIGNER: Z-ART, VOLKER NAUMANN PHOTOGRAPHER: MARTIN BECKER PERFORMING ARTIST: JINGO DE LUNCH ALBUM TITLE: DEJA VOODOO ■ 14 RECORD COMPANY: SUB POP ART DIRECTOR/DESIGNER: ART CHANTRY PERFORMING ARTIST: LOVE BATTERY ALBUM TITLE: DAYGLO ■ 15 RECORD COMPANY: CAPRICORN RECORDS ART DIRECTOR: MARCIA BEVERLY DESIGNER: DEBORAH NORCROSS PHOTOGRAPHER: JEFF FRAZIER PERFORMING ARTIST: COL. BRUCE HAMPTON & THE AQUARIUM RESCUE UNIT ALBUM TITLE: COL. BRUCE HAMPTON & THE AQUARIUM RESCUE UNIT ■ 16 RECORD COMPANY: GEFFEN RECORDS ART DIRECTOR/DESIGNER: HUGH SYME PERFORMING ARTIST: COVERDALE/PAGE ALBUM TITLE: COVERDALE/PAGE ■ 17 RECORD COMPANY: NORMAL RECORDS ART DIRECTORS: KERSTIN VIEG, OLAF MEYER DESIGNER: OLAF MEYER PHOTOGRAPHER: KERSTIN VIEG PERFORMING ARTIST: MYRNA LOY ALBUM TITLE: TIME SAYS HELAY ■ 18 RECORD COMPANY: REPRISE RECORDS ART DIRECTORS: JERI HEIDEN, DEBORAH NORCROSS DESIGNER: DEBORAH NORCROSS PHOTOGRAPHER: ALASTAIR THAIN DESIGN FIRM: WARNER BROS. RECORDS IN-HOUSE ART DEPARTMENT PERFORMING ARTIST/ ALBUM TITLE: TOY MATINEE

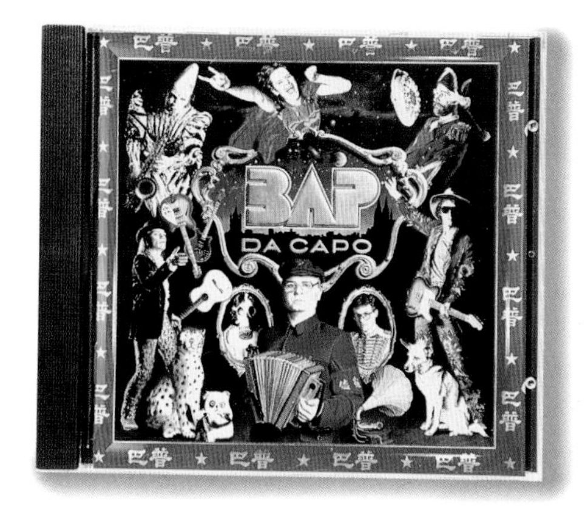
BAP
DA CAPO

COSMIC PSYCHOS SLAVE TO THE CRAVE
Live at the Palace · Melbourne

Luna
Bewitched

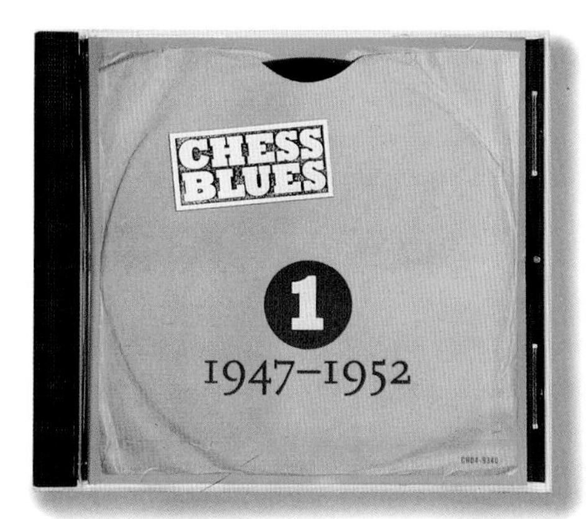
CHESS BLUES
1
1947–1952

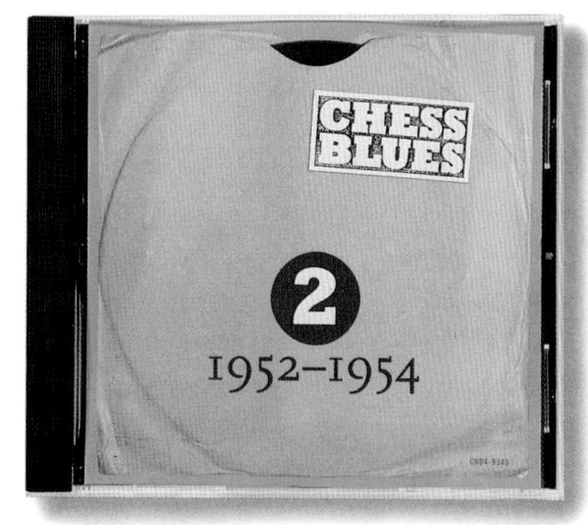
CHESS BLUES
2
1952–1954

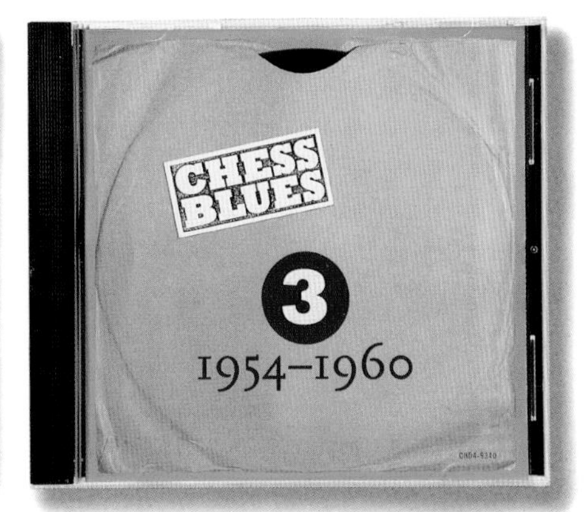
CHESS BLUES
3
1954–1960

Jingo de Lunch
Deja VooDoo

LOVE
+
SUB POP

COL. BRUCE HAMPTON & THE AQUARIUM RESCUE UNIT

COVERDALE · PAGE

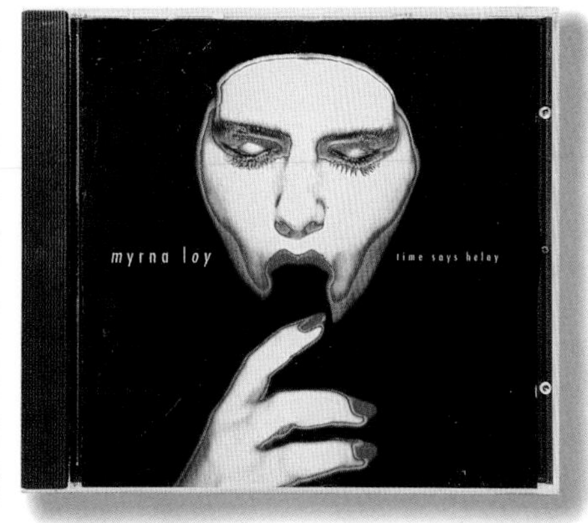
myrna loy
time says baby

toy matinee

■ 1 Record Company: WARNER BROS. RECORDS Art Directors: KIM CHAMPAGNE, JEFF GOLD Designer: KIM CHAMPAGNE Design Firm: WARNER BROS. RECORDS IN-HOUSE ART DEPARTMENT Performing Artist: ZZ TOP Album Title: RECYCLER ■ 2 Record Company: WARNER BROS. RECORDS Art Director/Designer: TOM RECCHION Illustrators: WARNER BROS. ARCHIVES Photographers: WARNER

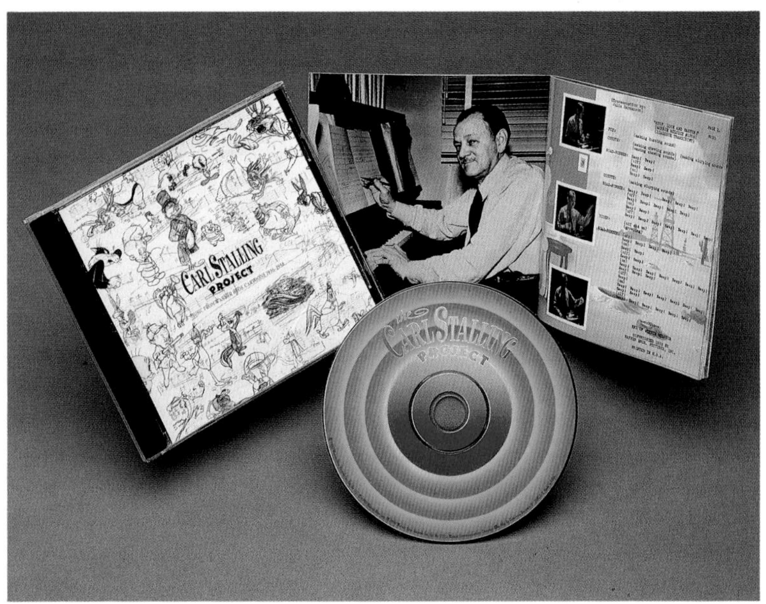

BROS. ARCHIVES Design Firm: WARNER BROS. RECORDS IN-HOUSE ART DEPT. Performing Artist: THE CARL STALLING PROJECT Album Title: MUSIC FROM WB CARTOONS 1936–1958 ■ 3 Record Company: CDCARD TM COMPANY, COURTESY OF THE BRIDGEMAN ART LIBRARY ARTISTS (TOP) Front Cover: WILLIAM ADOLPH BOUGUREAU (1825–1905, DETAIL) CHRISTIE'S LONDON (BOTTOM) Front Cover: ROSSO FIORENTINO (1494–1540, DETAIL) GALLERIA DEGLI UFFIZI, FLORENCE Performing Artists: VARIOUS Album Title: VARIOUS

■ 1 ART DIRECTORS/DESIGNERS: LAURIE ELLIS, JAN ELLIS ILLUSTRATOR: MARC BURCKHARDT DESIGN FIRM: ELLIS DESIGN CLIENT: SWEETPEA'S RESTAURANT COUNTRY: USA ■ 2 ART DIRECTOR/DESIGNER: LOUISE FILI ILLUSTRATOR: ANTHONY RUSSO DESIGN FIRM: LOUISE

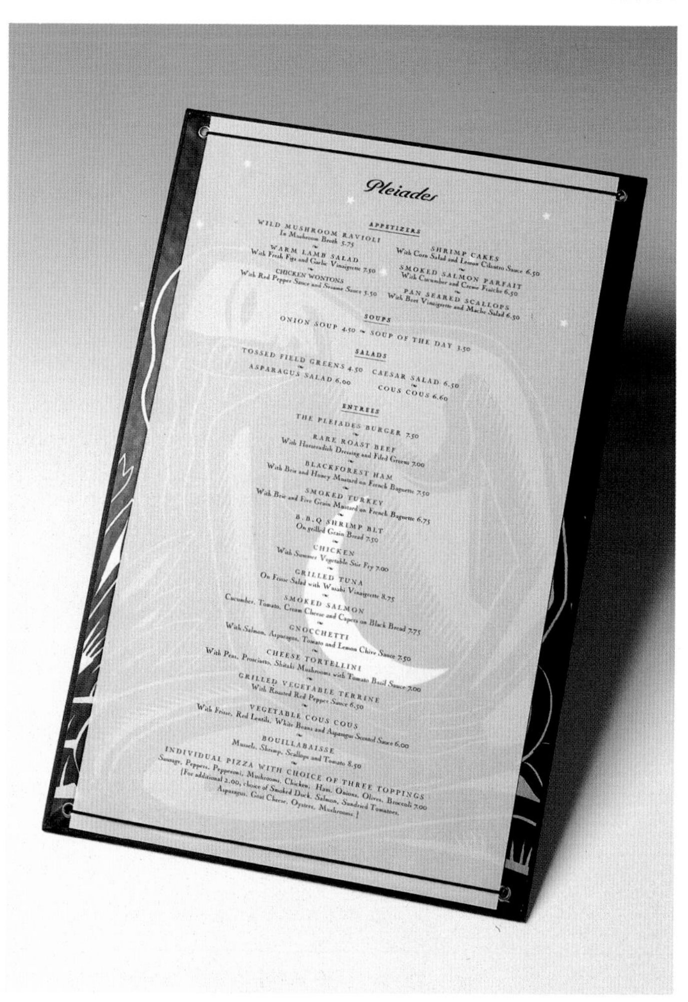

FILI LTD. CLIENT: PLEIADES COUNTRY: USA ■ 3 ART DIRECTORS: TOM ANTISTA, THOMAS FAIRCLOUGH DESIGNERS: TOM ANTISTA, THOMAS FAIRCLOUGH DESIGN FIRM: ANTISTA FAIRCLOUGH DESIGN, INC. CLIENT: TURNER HOME ENTERTAINMENT COUNTRY: USA

INFORMATION
DATED MATERIALS INSIDE
TURNER HOME ENTERTAINMENT
OPEN IMMEDIATELY
DATED MATERIALS INSIDE
INFORMATION
TURNER HOME ENTERTAINMENT
TURNER HOME ENTERTAINMENT

■ 1 ART DIRECTOR: MARGO CHASE DESIGNERS: MARGO CHASE, BRIAN HUNT PHOTOGRAPHER: VARIOUS DESIGN FIRM: MARGO CHASE DESIGN CLIENT: VIRGIN SOUND & VISION COUNTRY: USA ■ 2 ART DIRECTOR/DESIGNER: HOCK WAH YEO PRODUCT PHOTOGRAPHER: JESSE KUMIN/BIG TIME PRODUCTIONS ILLUSTRATOR: MARK FERRARI DESIGN FIRM: THE DESIGN OFFICE OF WONG & YEO CLIENT: MAGIC MOUSE PRODUCTIONS COUNTRY: USA ■ 3 ART DIRECTOR: HOCK WAH YEO DESIGNER: HOCK WAH YEO PRODUCT PHOTOGRAPHER: JESSE

KUMIN/BIG TIME PRODUCTIONS COMPUTER ARTISTS: DAVID SEEHOLZER, ROD PARONG DESIGN FIRM: THE DESIGN OFFICE OF WONG & YEO CLIENT: NOVA LOGIC COUNTRY: USA ■ 4 ART DIRECTOR: RON MIRIELLO DESIGNERS: MICHELLE ARANDA, DEAN AMSTUTZ ILLUSTRATOR: DEAN AMSTUTZ DESIGN FIRM: MIRIELLO GRAFICO, INC. CLIENT: GAMEMAKERS COUNTRY: USA ■ 5 ART DIRECTOR: PAUL WOODS DESIGNER: PEGGY KOCH ILLUSTRATOR: ROBIN JAREAUX DESIGN FIRM: SBG PARTNERS CLIENT: SYMANTEC CORPORATION COUNTRY: USA

CREATED BY
NOVA LOGIC
IBM CD-ROM
WOLFPACK

PENDULUM

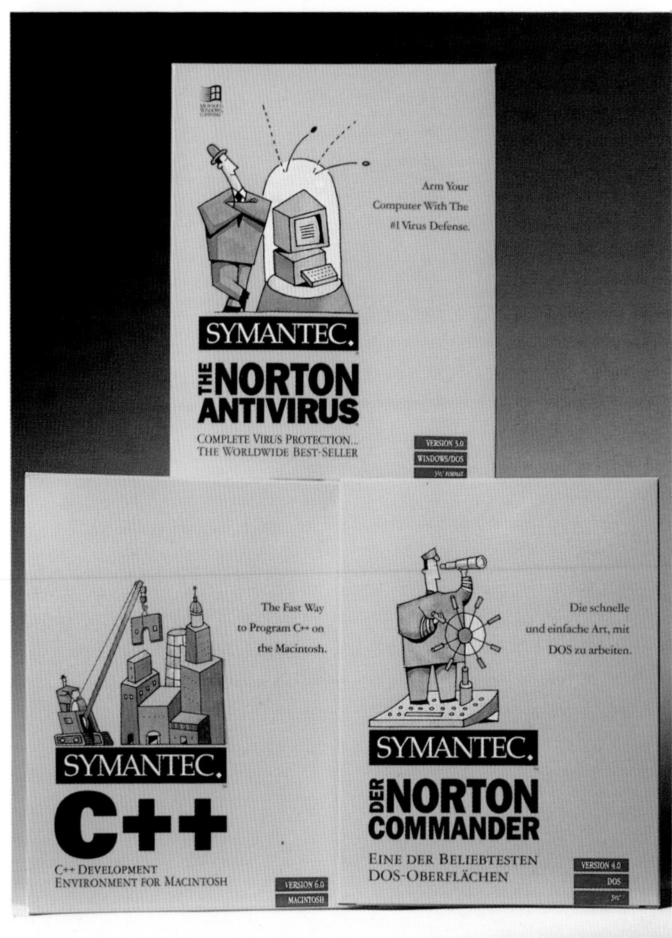
Arm Your Computer With The #1 Virus Defense.
SYMANTEC.
THE NORTON ANTIVIRUS
COMPLETE VIRUS PROTECTION...
THE WORLDWIDE BEST-SELLER
VERSION 3.0
WINDOWS/DOS
The Fast Way to Program C++ on the Macintosh.
SYMANTEC.
C++
C++ DEVELOPMENT ENVIRONMENT FOR MACINTOSH
VERSION 6.0
MACINTOSH
Die schnelle und einfache Art, mit DOS zu arbeiten.
SYMANTEC.
DER NORTON COMMANDER
EINE DER BELIEBTESTEN DOS-OBERFLÄCHEN
VERSION 4.0
DOS

■ 1 ART DIRECTOR: MITCHELL MAUK DESIGNERS: MITCHELL MAUK, CHRISTINE LASHAW, JULIE BERNATZ PHOTOGRAPHER: JULIE CHASE DESIGN FIRM: MAUK DESIGN CLIENT: BANCROFT WHITNEY COUNTRY: USA ■ 2 ART DIRECTORS: ROBERT WOOD, TAMMIE HUNT DESIGNER: ROBERT WOOD PHOTOGRAPHER: PETER MEDILIK DESIGN FIRM: FITCH INC. CLIENT: DIGITAL EQUIPMENT CORPORATION COUNTRY: USA

14" SVGA Color Monitor
digital
digital
STARION 200
STARION 200
FEATURES

■ 1 ART DIRECTOR: DAVID CURTIS DESIGNERS: DAVID CURTIS, RICK JANSEN DESIGN FIRM: CURTIS DESIGN CLIENT: MILLER BREWING CO. COUNTRY: USA ■ 2 ART DIRECTOR/DESIGNER: ANDREW CAWRSE DESIGN FIRM: CAWRSE & EFFECT CLIENT: COOPERS BREWERY COUNTRY: USA ■ 3 ART DIRECTOR: SAM J. CIULLA DESIGNERS: TRACY BACILEK, AMY RUSSELL ILLUSTRATORS (FROM LEFT TO RIGHT): DAVID DIAZ, JOHN JINKS, TERRY ALLEN, JONATHAN LUND DESIGN FIRM: LIPSON-ALPORT-GLASS & ASSOCIATES CLIENT: THE PERRIER

GROUP OF AMERICA COUNTRY: USA ■ 4 ART DIRECTOR: NEIL POWELL DESIGNERS: NEIL POWELL, ALAN LEUSINK DESIGN FIRM: DUFFY DESIGN CLIENT: THE STROH BREWERY COUNTRY: USA ■ 5 ART DIRECTOR: GLENN TUTSSEL DESIGNER: GARRICK HAMM ILLUSTRATOR: COLIN FREWIN DESIGN FIRM: TUTSSELS CLIENT: BASS COUNTRY: GREAT BRITAIN ■ 6 ART DIRECTORS: DEBBIE DOUGLAS, IAN MCILROY DESIGNER: GRAHAM WALKER DESIGN FIRM: EH6 DESIGN CONSULTANTS CLIENT: TENNENT CALEDONIAN BREWERIES COUNTRY: GREAT BRITAIN

Perrier
SPARKLING MINERAL WATER
Perrier

SBC
BARREL NO.
112
16 OZS.
LAGER BEER
St. Paul, Minnesota

CARLING
Black Label
LAGER
1994-95
CARLING
PREMIERSHIP
Special
EDITION

DRY
DRY

FERRARI-CARANO
SIENA
SONOMA COUNTY
1991

PRINDELO

יקבי רמת הגולן
GOLAN HEIGHTS WINERY
Chardonnay

AMÉ
A lively sparkling drink containing a unique and revitalising blend of eastern herbs, vitamins and fruit juices

aura
Each bottle sits for five years before it's available to public.
contains the finest wine with
inseng root.
The alcohol
level is 60%
by volume.
ginseng
Wine

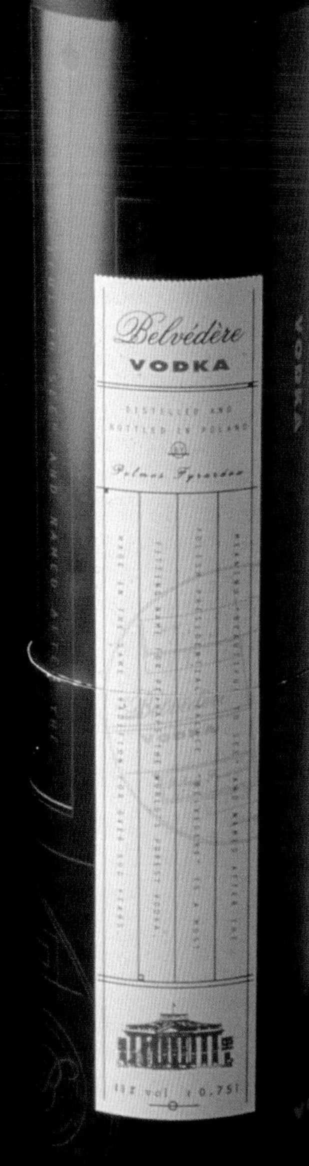
Belvédère
VODKA

■ 1 ART DIRECTOR: KOBE DESIGNERS: KOBE, ALAN LEUSINK DESIGN FIRM: DUFFY DESIGN CLIENT: ED PHILLIPS & SONS COUNTRY: USA ■ 2 CREATIVE DIRECTOR: JOHN BLACKBURN DESIGNER: BELINDA DUGGAN DESIGN FIRM: BLACKBURN'S

CLIENT: BERRY BROTHERS & RUDD LTD. COUNTRY: GREAT BRITAIN ■ 3 ART DIRECTOR: KEIZO MATSUI DESIGNERS: KEIZO MATSUI, YUKO ARAKI DESIGN FIRM: KEIZO MATSUI & ASSOCIATES CLIENT: YAGI SHUZO-BU CO., LTD. COUNTRY: JAPAN

RAHEL
KAPSELN
FÜR HAARE
UND NÄGEL
RAHEL
KAPSELN
FÜR HAARE
UND NÄGEL

MONT SOURCE
ELEMENT
II
FOR MEN
COLOGNE NATUREL
MONT SOURCE
ELEMENT
I
FOR MEN
COLOGNE NATUREL
MONT SOURCE
ELEMENT
III
FOR MEN
COLOGNE NATUREL

FIORUCCI
Bath Gel

STRONG WHITE 3-PLY
TISSUES FOR MEN
RECYCLED WHITE
TISSUES FOR MEN
WHITE 2-PLY
TISSUES FOR MEN

■ 1 ART DIRECTOR: SIGI MAYER DESIGN FIRM: PHARMA PERFORMANCE WERBEAGENTUR GMBH CLIENT: SIMONS GMBH COUNTRY: GERMANY ■ 2 ART DIRECTOR: JOHN MAROTA DESIGNERS: TOM ANTISTA, THOMAS FAIRCLOUGH DESIGN FIRM: ANTISTA FAIRCLOUGH DESIGN CLIENT: MONT SOURCE COUNTRY: USA ■ 3 ART DIRECTOR/DESIGNER: PHIL ELLETT ILLUSTRATORS: PHIL ELLETT, DARREN LEDWICH DESIGN FIRM: COZZOLINO

ELLETT DESIGN D'VISION CLIENT: MYER/GRACE BROS. COUNTRY: AUSTRALIA ■ 4 ART DIRECTOR: GLENN TUTSSEL DESIGNER: DAVE PEARMAN PHOTOGRAPHER: ANDY SEYMOUR DESIGN FIRM: TUTSSELS CLIENT: BOOTS THE CHEMIST COUNTRY: GREAT BRITAIN ■ 5 ART DIRECTOR: MARY LEWIS DESIGNERS: MARY LEWIS, LUCILLA SCRIMGEOUR DESIGN FIRM: LEWIS MOBERLY CLIENT: NEXT PLC COUNTRY: GREAT BRITAIN

■ 1 ART DIRECTOR/DESIGNER/ILLUSTRATOR: LINDA FOUNTAIN DESIGN FIRM: LINDA FOUNTAIN DESIGN CLIENT: STRUNG OUT JEWELRY COUNTRY: USA

■ 2 ART DIRECTOR: JOSE SERRANO DESIGNERS: JOSE SERRANO, MIKE BROWER DESIGN FIRM: MIRES DESIGN CLIENT: EKTELON COUNTRY: USA

EKTELON
EKTELON
EKTELON
EKTELON

■ 1, 2 ART DIRECTOR: JEFF WEITHMAN DESIGNER: JEFF WEITHMAN DESIGN FIRM: NIKE, INC. CLIENT: NIKE, INC. COUNTRY: USA ■ 3 ART DIRECTOR: STEVEN SANDSTROM DESIGNER: STEVEN SANDSTROM DESIGN FIRM: SANDSTROM DESIGN CLIENT: LEVI STRAUSS & CO. COUNTRY: USA ■ 4 ART DIRECTOR: JEFF WEITHMAN DESIGNER: JEFF WEITHMAN DESIGN FIRM: NIKE, INC. CLIENT: NIKE, INC. COUNTRY: USA

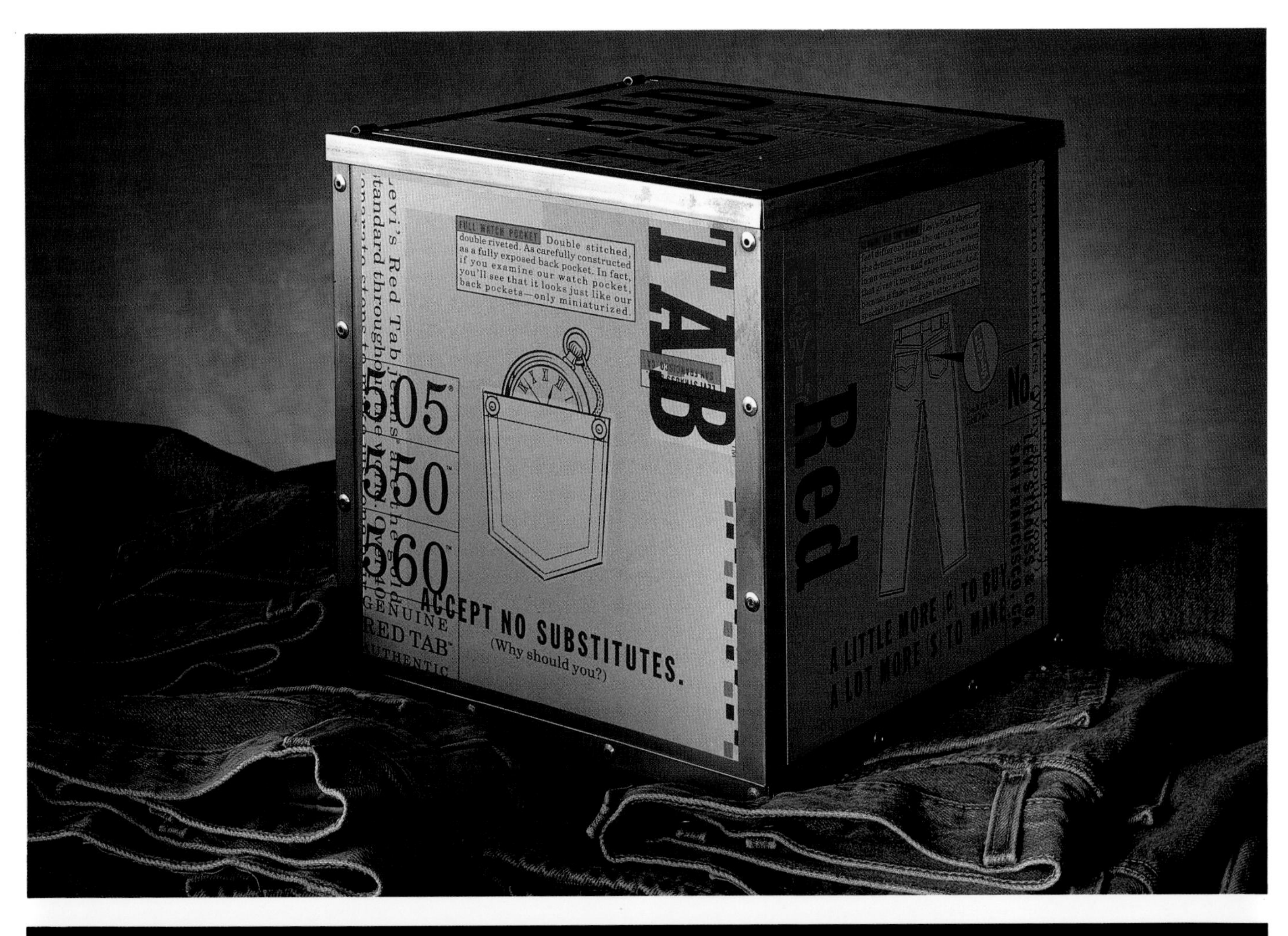
FULL WATCH POCKET Double stitched, double riveted. As carefully constructed as a fully exposed back pocket. In fact, if you examine our watch pocket, you'll see that it looks just like our back pockets—only miniaturized.
TAB
Red
505
550
560
ACCEPT NO SUBSTITUTES.
(Why should you?)

NIKE GOLF
NIKE
AIR

FRESH
FRENCH BREAD
BAKED FRESH
Bakery
EXTRA
SOUR DOUGH
GARLIC BREAD

茶
DIRECTIONS POUR HOT WATER

PESCHE

TINE
NORMANNA
TINE
NORZOLA
ROYAL BLUE
TINE
ROYAL BLUE

RED GEMS
TASTY
CLASS ONE
Firm, fresh, guaranteed sun ripened country tomatoes.
For best flavour, eat rich, red ripe. Store around 16°C.
10 KILOGRAMS
TOMATOES

m&m's
PLAIN CHOCOLATE CANDIES
m&m's
PLAIN CHOCOLATE CANDIES
m&m's
PEANUT CHOCOLATE CANDIES
m&m's
PLAIN CHOCOLATE CANDIES
m&m's
PLAIN CHOCOLATE CANDIES

■ 1 ART DIRECTORS: THOMAS MCNULTY, BRIAN JACOBSON DESIGNERS: DAVID LEONG, BRIAN JACOBSON ILLUSTRATOR: NIEL SHIBLY DESIGN FIRM: PROFILE DESIGN CLIENT: SAFEWAY STORES, INC. COUNTRY: USA ■ 2 ART DIRECTOR/DESIGNER: JESSIE HUANG PHOTOGRAPHER: KIRK KIU DESIGN FIRM: TOILET SEAT CLIENT: TEA FACTORY INC. COUNTRY: USA ■ 3 ART DIRECTOR/DESIGNER/DESIGN FIRM: ANGELO SGANZERLA ILLUSTRATOR: FRANCO TESTA CLIENT: ANDREA STAINER COUNTRY: ITALY ■ 4 ART DIRECTOR/DESIGNER: PER MAGNE LUND ARTIST: KJELL NUPEN DESIGN FIRM: CHRISTENSEN LUND CLIENT: TINE COUNTRY: NORWAY ■ 5 ART DIRECTORS/DESIGNERS: HELEN

WATTS, PETER WATTS DESIGN FIRM: WATTS GRAPHIC DESIGN CLIENT: PETER CUMMING COUNTRY: AUSTRALIA ■ 6 CREATIVE DIRECTOR: KAN TAI-KEUNG ART DIRECTORS: KAN TAI-KEUNG, EDDY YU CHI KONG DESIGNERS: EDDY YU CHI KONG, JOYCE HO NGAI SING DESIGN FIRM: KAN TAI-KEUNG DESIGN & ASSOC. LTD. CLIENT: EFFEM FOODS INC. COUNTRY: HONG KONG ■ 7 ART DIRECTOR/DESIGNER/DESIGN FIRM: FABIAN W. SCHMID CLIENT: VINCENZO DE GASPERI COUNTRY: ITALY ■ 8 CREATIVE DIRECTORS: DAVID YOUNG, JEFF LARAMORE ART DIRECTOR: CHRIS BEATTY ILLUSTRATOR: MARIO NOCHE DESIGN FIRM: YOUNG & LARAMORE CLIENT: RED GOLD TOMATOES COUNTRY: USA

■ 1 ART DIRECTOR: GLENN TUTSSEL DESIGNERS: GLENN TUTSSEL, MARCUS JONES ILLUSTRATOR: MARCUS JONES DESIGN FIRM/CLIENT: TUTSSELS COUNTRY: GREAT BRITAIN ■ 2 ART DIRECTOR: STEFANIE TINZ DESIGNERS: BERNHARD

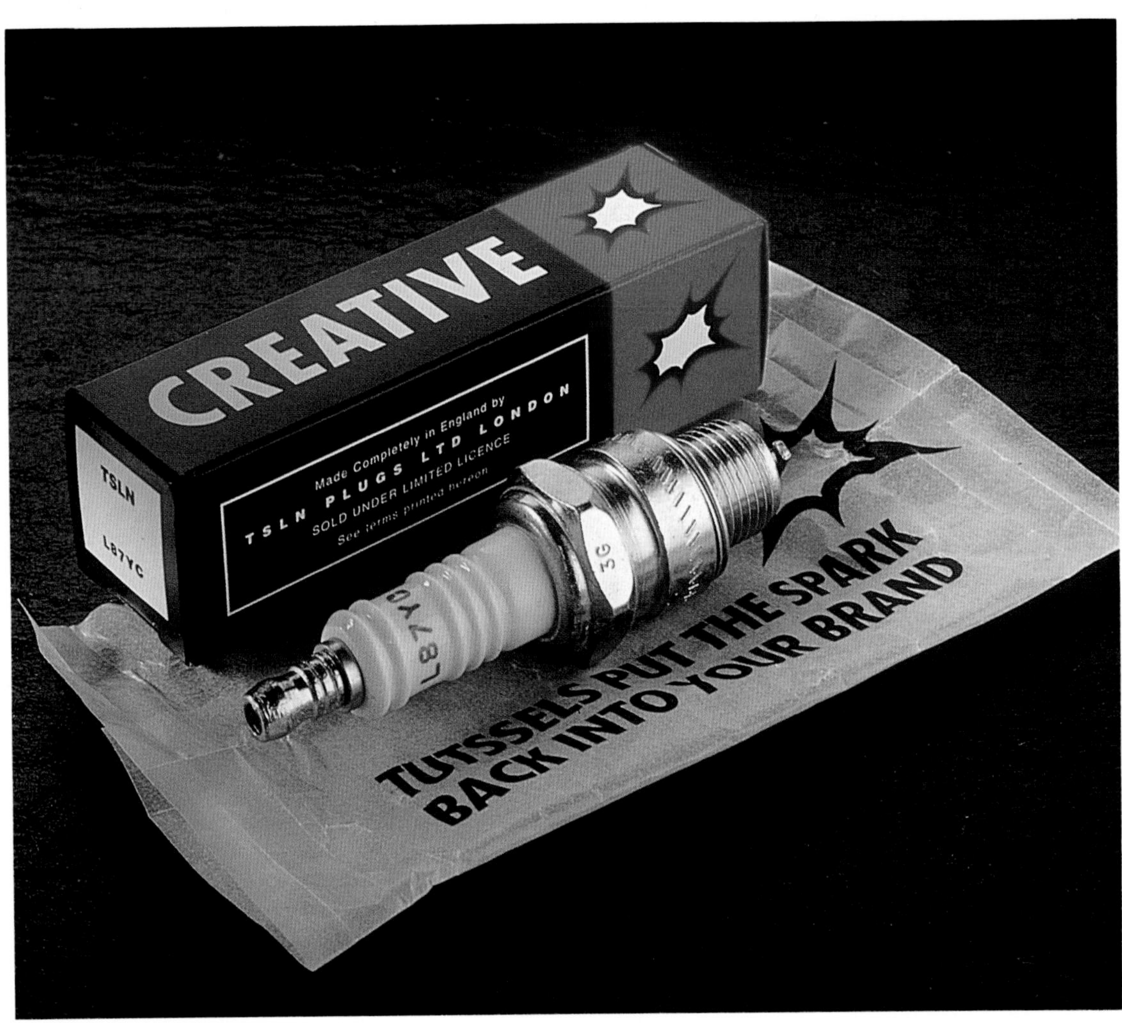

H. TINZ, BARBARA SIMMINGER, GERHARD ESKUCHE ILLUSTRATORS: BARBARA SIMMINGER, GERHARD ESKUCHE DESIGN FIRM: TINZ. DCC, DIVISION TINZ. PROMOTION CLIENT: M. KAINDL HOLZINDUSTRIE COUNTRY: AUSTRIA

Was Sie schon immer von der neuen Naturkollektion sehen wollten
KRONO
1
Kaindl
M. Kaindl Holzindustrie
WalserWeg12
A-5071 Wals / Salzburg
Tel. 0662 / 8588

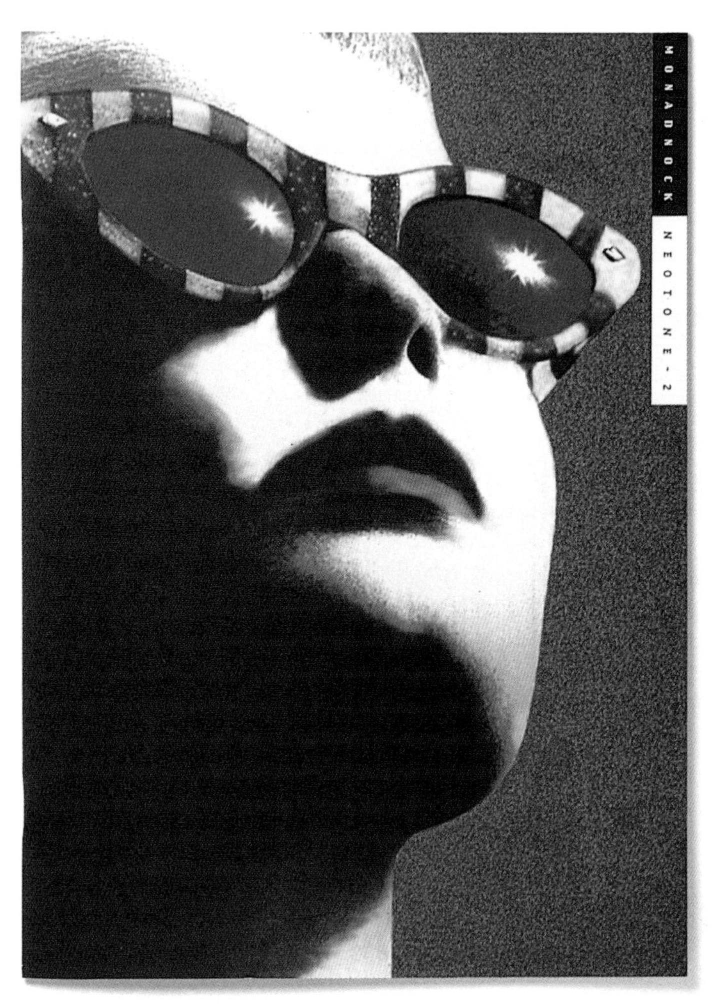

■ 1, 7–10. ART DIRECTOR: MICHAEL WEYMOUTH DESIGNER: TOM KRAFT PHOTOGRAPHER: VARIOUS COUNTRY: MONADNOCK PAPER MILLS, INC. ■ 2–6 ART DIRECTORS: JOHN PYLYPCZAK, DITI KATONA DESIGNERS: JOHN PYLYPCZAK, SCOTT A. CHRISTIE PHOTOGRAPHER: RON BAXTER SMITH DESIGN FIRM: CONCRETE DESIGN COMMUNICATIONS INC. CLIENT: BECKETT CAMBRIC COUNTRY: CANADA

OKAY.

SO BECKETT PAPER IS NEARLY 150 YEARS OLD. WE'RE NOT SPRING CHICKENS. BUT NEITHER ARE WE CORPORATE DINOSAURS. BECAUSE WE TAKE PRIDE IN BEING A PROGRESSIVE COMPANY. BUT ONE THING WILL NEVER CHANGE: THE BECKETT COMMITMENT TO PRODUCT INNOVATION AND QUALITY. CHECK OUT THE 11 NEW COLORS IN THE CAMBRIC PORTFOLIO AND THE ADDITION OF 80 LB. TEXT WEIGHT. YOU'LL DROOL ALL OVER THE SWATCHBOOK. IF YOU WON'T TAKE OUR WORD FOR IT,

TURN THE PAGE

AND READ WHAT EIGHT PEOPLE ARE SAYING ABOUT NEW BECKETT CAMBRIC.

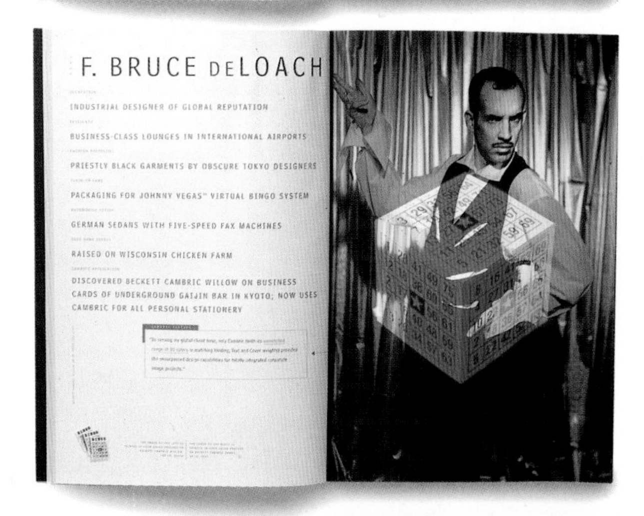

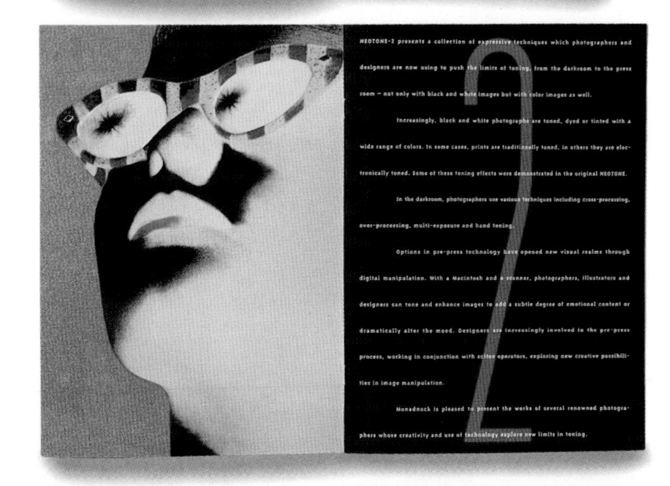

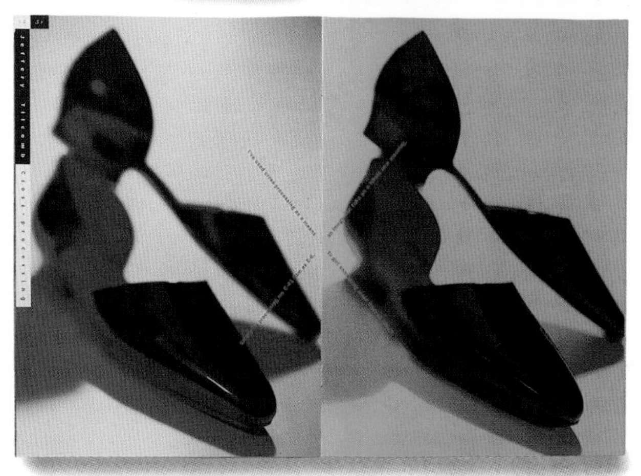

■ 1–6 ART DIRECTORS: PAT SAMATA, GREG SAMATA PHOTOGRAPHER: VARIOUS ILLUSTRATOR: VARIOUS DESIGN FIRM: SAMATA ASSOCIATES CLIENT: SIMPSON PAPER COMPANY COUNTRY: USA ■ 7 ART DIRECTORS: STEVEN TOLLESON, JENNIFER STERLING DESIGNERS: STEVEN TOLLESON, JENNIFER STERLING DESIGN FIRM: TOLLESON DESIGN CLIENT: FOX RIVER PAPER COMPANY COUNTRY: USA

BUSINESS CARD
BUSINESS CARD
BUSINESS CARD
CONFETTI
LETTERHEAD
ENVELOPE
CONFETTI BY FOX RIVER PAPER COMPANY
ISSUED AT
USE BEFORE

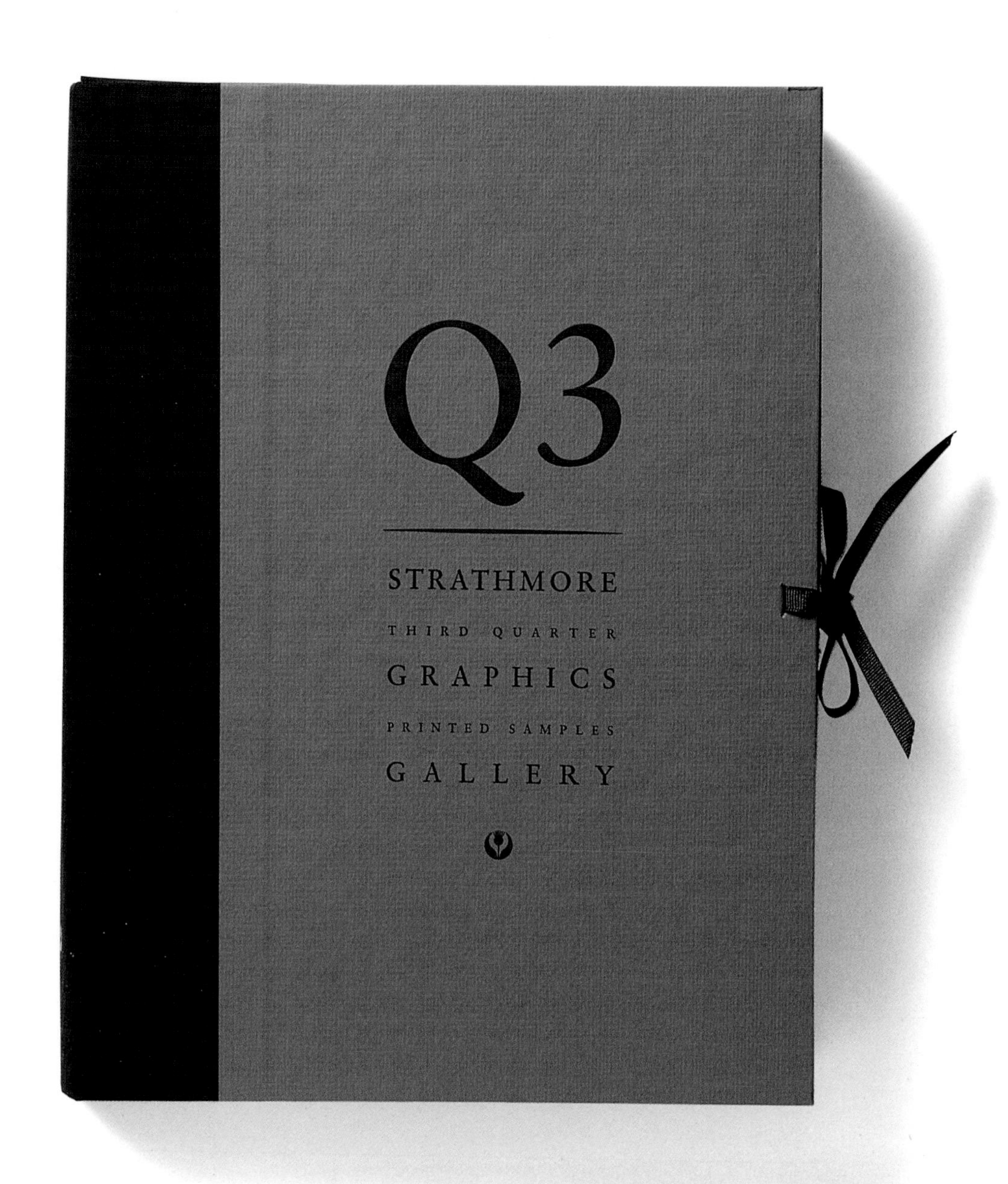

■ 1 DESIGNERS: ADRIENNE POLLARD, JEFF POLLARD PROJECT COORDINATOR: PAM WILLIAMS DESIGN FIRM: WILLIAMS + HOUSE CLIENT: STRATHMORE PAPER COMPANY COUNTRY: USA ■ 2 ART DIRECTOR: FRANK VIVA ILLUSTRATOR: FRANK VIVA DESIGNERS: FRANK VIVA, KAREN SATAK DESIGN FIRM: VIVA DOLAN COMMUNICATIONS & DESIGN CLIENT: ARJO WIGGINS FINE PAPERS COUNTRY: USA

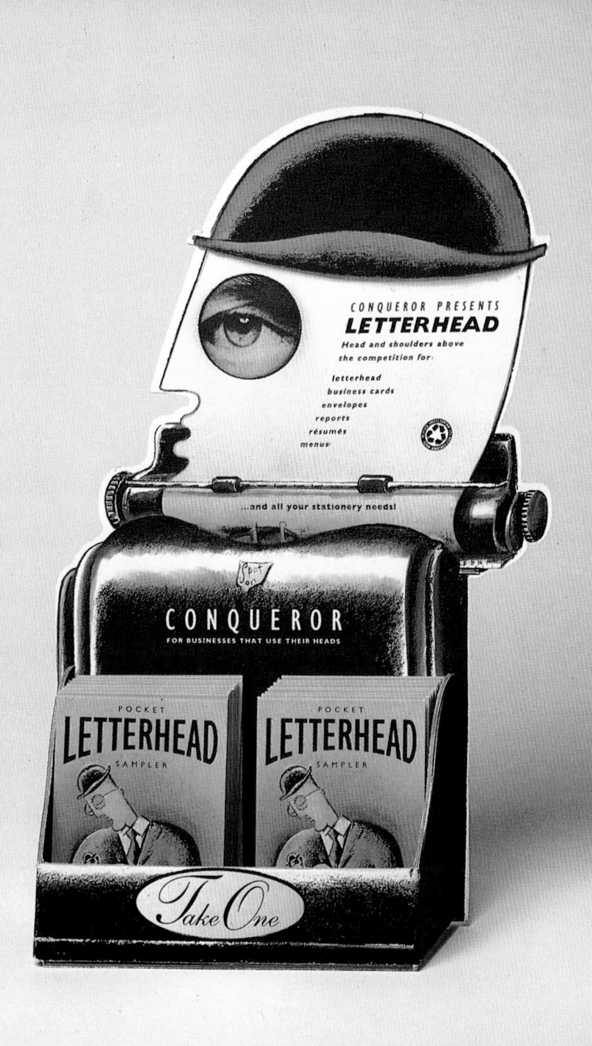
CONQUEROR PRESENTS
LETTERHEAD
Head and shoulders above
the competition for:
letterhead
business cards
envelopes
reports
résumés
menus
...and all your stationery needs!
CONQUEROR
FOR BUSINESSES THAT USE THEIR HEADS
POCKET
LETTERHEAD
SAMPLER
POCKET
LETTERHEAD
SAMPLER
Take One

■ 1, 7–10 CREATIVE DIRECTOR: JAMES A. SEBASTIAN ART DIRECTOR: MARGARET BIEDEL DESIGNERS: MARGARET BIEDEL, SARAH KLOMAN PHOTOGRAPHER: VARIOUS COPYWRITER: AUGUSTINE HOPE DESIGN FIRM: DESIGNFRAME CLIENT: STRATHMORE PAPER COUNTRY: USA ■ 2–6 ART DIRECTORS/DESIGNERS: STEVE PATTEE, KELLY STILES PHOTOGRAPHER: KING AU DESIGN FIRM: PATTEE DESIGN CLIENT: FOX RIVER COUNTRY: USA

fear
i kNOw

evil,
FORGOTTEN
can be very good...

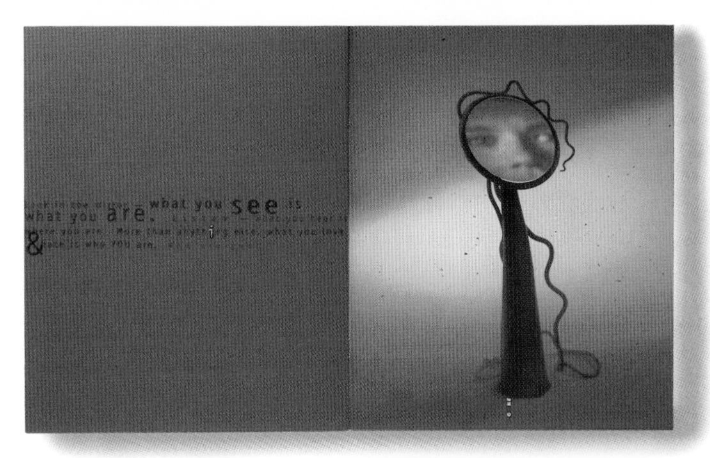
what you see is
what you are.
&

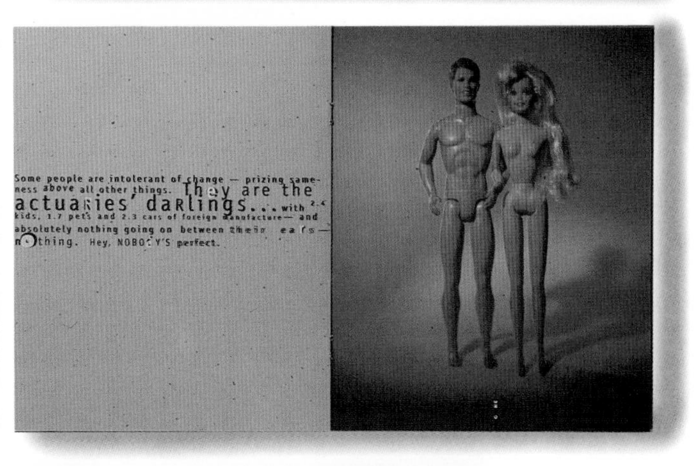
Some people are intolerant of change — prizing sameness above all other things. They are the
actuaries' darlings...
Hey, NOBODY'S perfect.

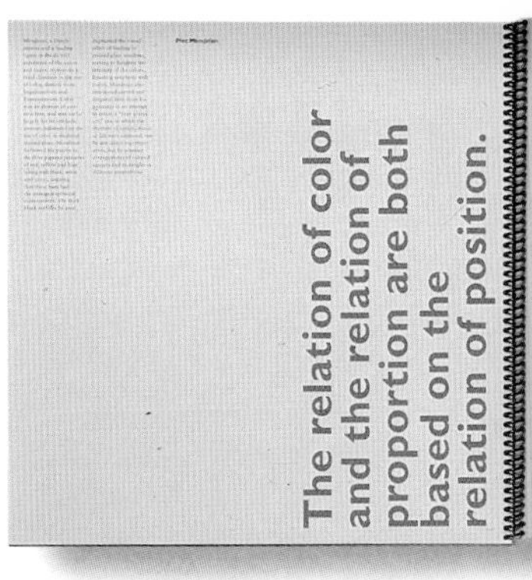
The relation of color
and the relation of
proportion are both
based on the
relation of position.

Complementary
colors make
a strange pair.
They are
opposite,
yet they require
each other.

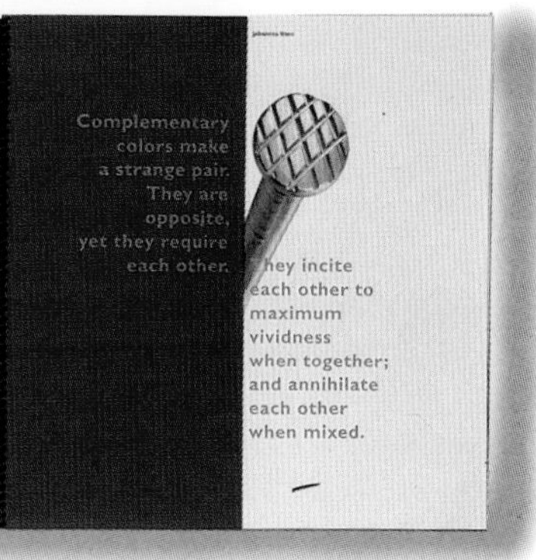
hey incite
each other to
maximum
vividness
when together;
and annihilate
each other
when mixed.

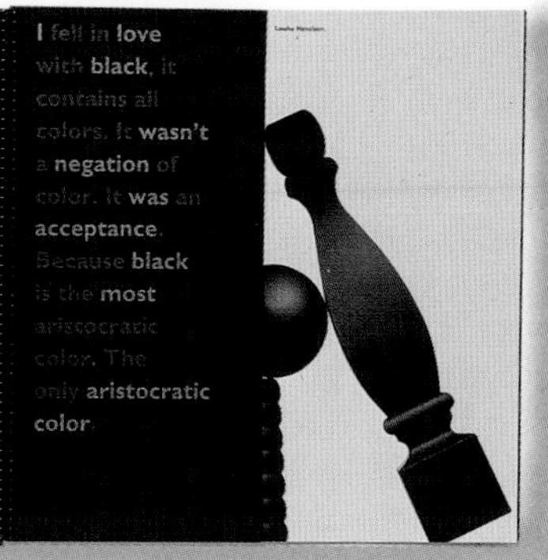
I fell in love
with black, it
contains all
colors. It wasn't
a negation of
color. It was an
acceptance.
Because black
is the most
aristocratic
color. The
only aristocratic
color.

whereas yellow
is blackened in
its shades, and
fades away when
lightened, red
when darkened
becomes brown,
and diluted with
white is no
longer red, but
another color
—pink.

The light-rich,
luminous texture of
these ornaments
seems to glow
off the page,
reproduced on a
smooth finish.
15

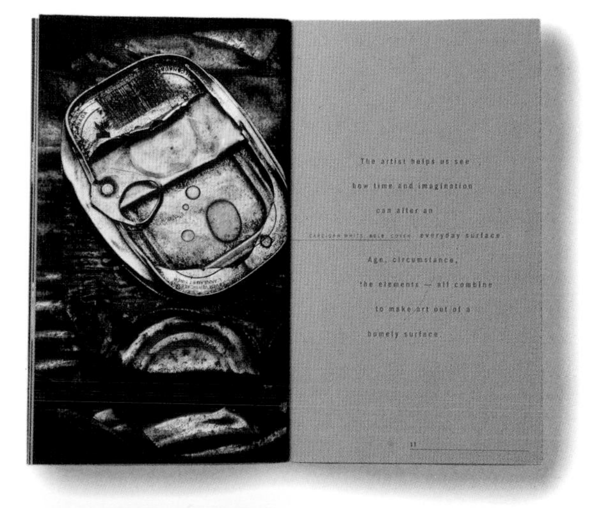
The artist helps us see
how time and imagination
can alter an
everyday surface.
Age, circumstance,
the elements — all combine
to make art out of a
homely surface.
11

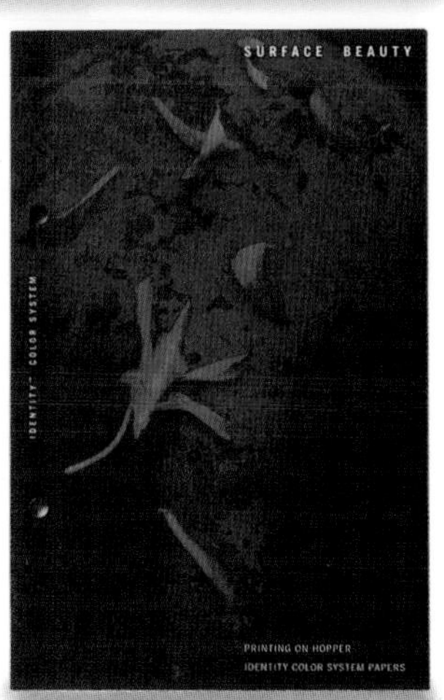
SURFACE BEAUTY
IDENTITY COLOR SYSTEM
PRINTING ON HOPPER
IDENTITY COLOR SYSTEM PAPERS

A silky smooth paper
puts the glow of
pure white milk at
center stage,
contained in glass
so faithfully reproduced
it shimmers off the page.
MILK
FOOD

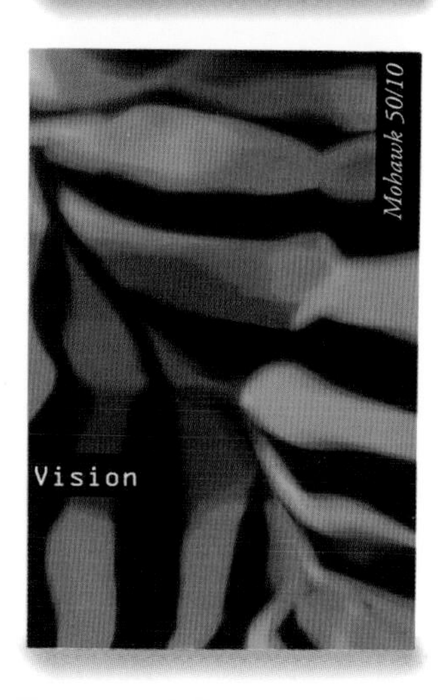
Mohawk 50/10
Vision

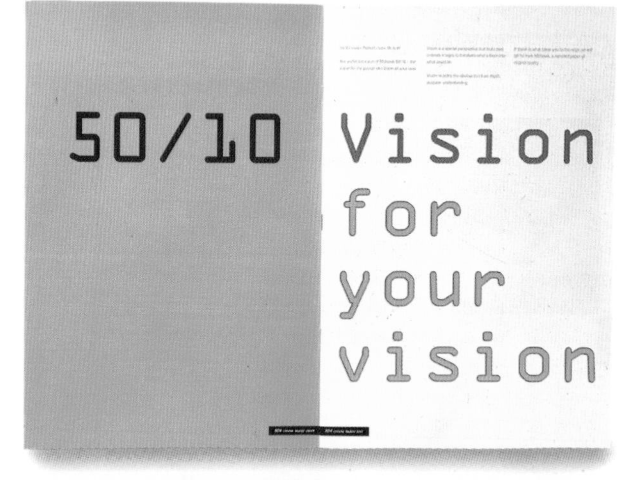
50/10
Vision
for
your
vision

50/10 Matte allures
with a rich velvet
touch that seduces your
sensory vision.

If your passion is tran
reality, Mohawk
that

■ 1–4 ART DIRECTORS: RIK BESSER, DOUGLAS JOSEPH DESIGNER: RIK BESSER PHOTOGRAPHER: TERRY HEFFERNAN DESIGN FIRM: BESSER JOSEPH PARTNERS CLIENT: HOPPER PAPER COMPANY COUNTRY: USA ■ 5–8 ART DIRECTOR: STEVE LISKA DESIGNER: KIM NYBERG

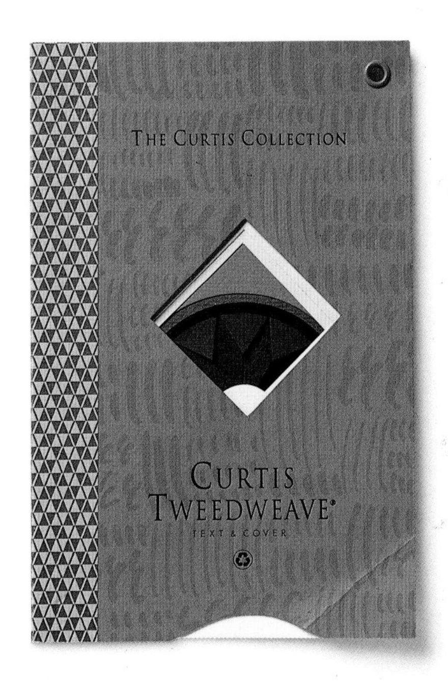

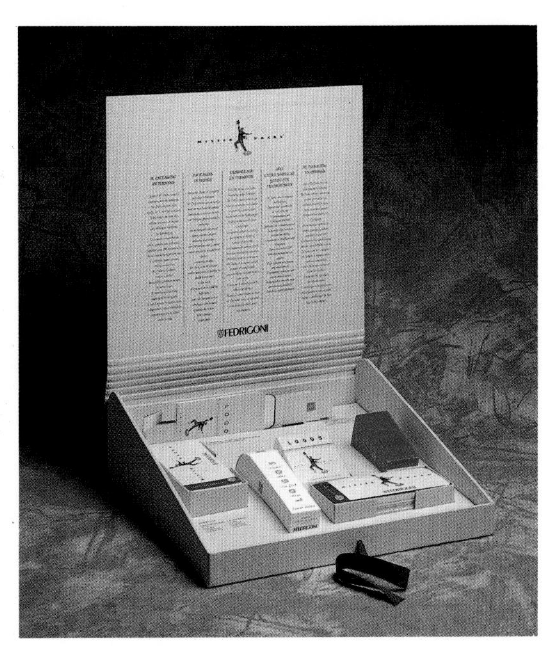

PHOTOGRAPHER: VARIOUS DESIGN FIRM: LISKA AND ASSOCIATES CLIENT: MOHAWK PAPER MILLS COUNTRY: USA ■ 9, 11 ART DIRECTOR/DESIGNER: REX PETEET DESIGN FIRM: SIBLEY/PETEET DESIGN CLIENT: JAMES RIVER PAPER COMPANY COUNTRY: USA ■ 10 ART DIRECTOR/DESIGNER: EDOARDO SERVENTE TEALDY DESIGN FIRM: MILANI S.R.L. CLIENT: CARTIERE FEDRIGONI COUNTRY: ITALY

REBUILD/TAKU SATOH DESIGN OFFICE INC.
1993 TAKARA SUPER CANCHU-HI

LOTTE
GREEN GUM
9 GUM STICKS
REBUILD/TAKU SATOH DESIGN OFFICE INC.
1993 LOTTE GUM MINT LINE

REBUILD/TAKU SATOH DESIGN OFFICE INC.
KOBU TSUKIJI BLDG. 5F. 3-10-9 TSUKIJI CHUO-KU TOKYO JAPAN

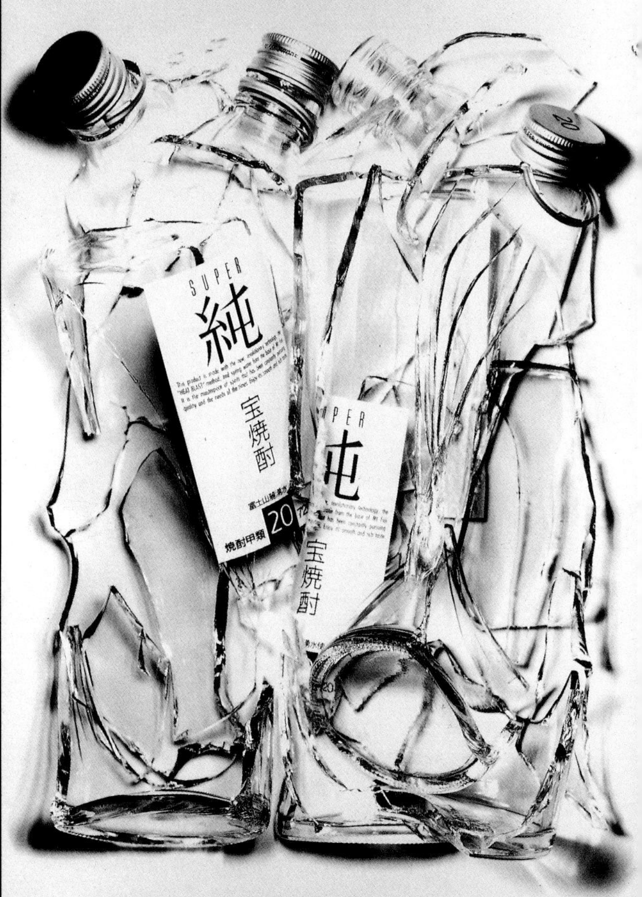
SUPER
純
宝焼酎
焼酎甲類
20
REBUILD/TAKU SATOH DESIGN OFFICE INC.
1992 TAKARA SUPER JUN

SOME
PEOPLE
OCTOBER
18-
NOVEM
BER
13
WRITTEN AND PERFORMED
BY DANNY
HOCH
DIRECTED
BY JO
BONNEY
THE
PUBLIC
THEATER

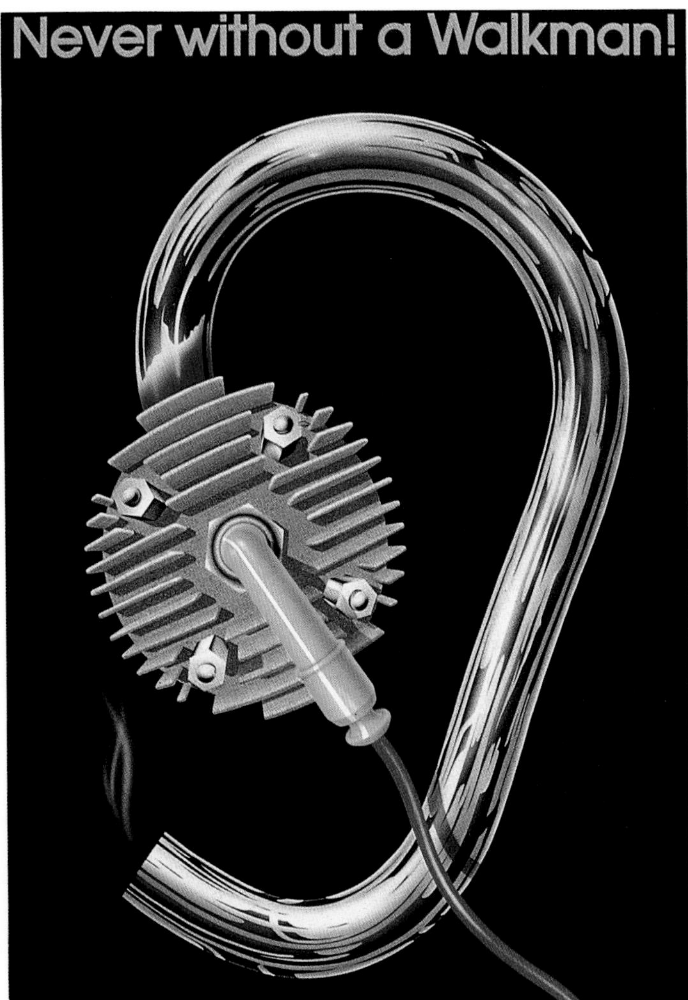
Never without a Walkman!

■ 1, 2 ART DIRECTOR: JOHN BATESON DESIGNERS: MICHAEL DENNY, DEBORAH OSBORNE, ANDREW ROSS PHOTOGRAPHER: TIM FLACH DESIGN FIRM: ROUNDEL DESIGN GROUP CLIENT: ZANDERS FEINPAPIERE AG COUNTRY: GERMANY ■ 3 ART DIRECTOR: ALBERT SHU SUNG WAN

DESIGNER/TYPOGRAPHER: JOSEPH YIM CHI HANG CONCEPT: JOSEPH YIM CHI HANG COMPUTER EFFECT: ANDY WONG YIN KEUNG PHOTOGRAPHER: HO WUN DESIGN FIRM: A. STUDIO & ASSOCIATES CO. LTD. CLIENT: HUGO MUSIC AUSTRALIA COMPANY COUNTRY: AUSTRALIA

HUGO
AUSTRALIA

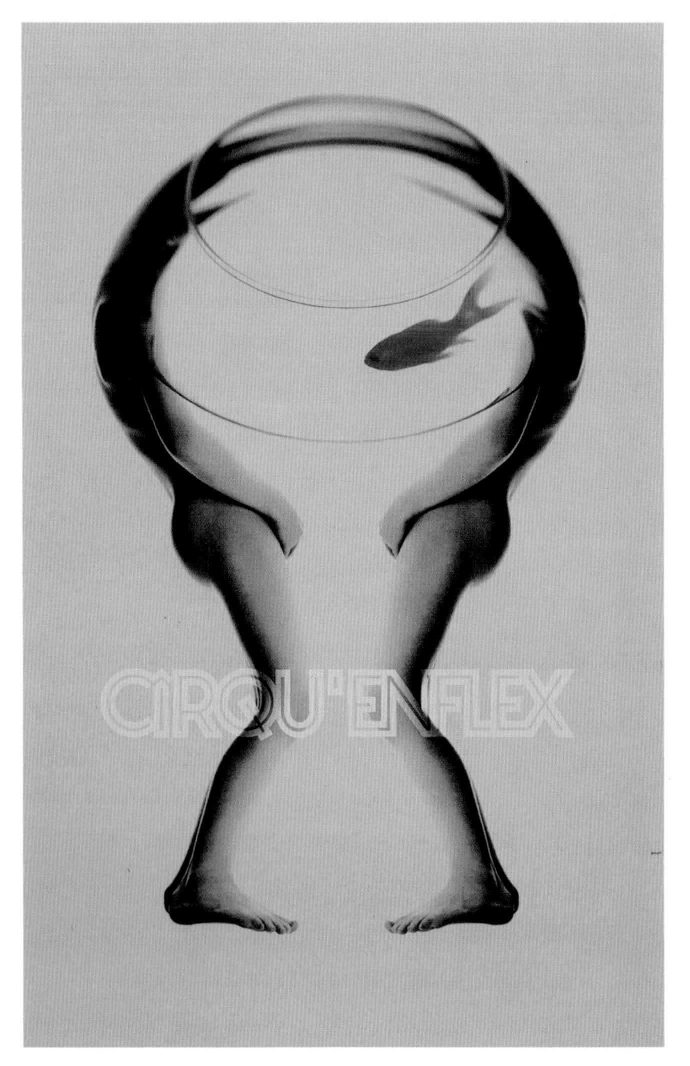
CIRQU'ENFLEX

AGDA in conjunction with DIA and Designers Saturday present Andrew Hoyne
2pm Saturday 30th July 1994
An Original Approach to Design
Workspace Commercial Furnishers
146 Dudley Street, West Melbourne
$18 AGDA & DIA members
$25 non members
For more info call 690 6299
Photograph by Rob Blackburn. Film courtesy of Witchtype.
Paper courtesy of Spicers. Printing courtesy of Vega Press.

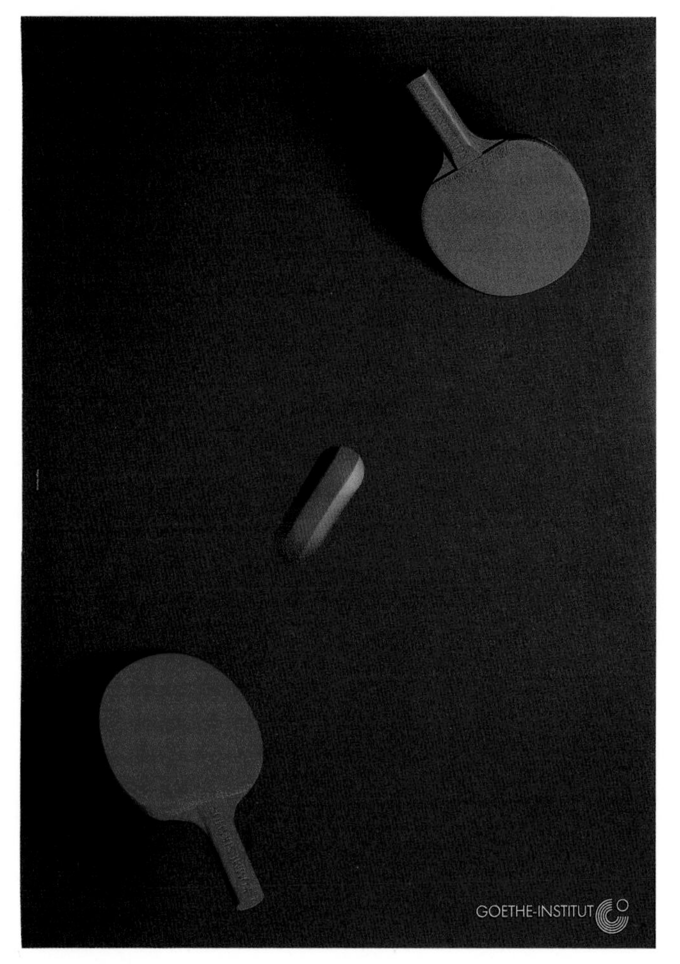

■ 1 ART DIRECTOR: HOCH DREI DESIGN FIRM: HOCH DREI DESIGNERS: WENDELIN HESS, BEAT MÜLLER PHOTOGRAPHER: HANS-JÖRG WALTER CLIENT: CIRQU'ENFLEX COUNTRY: SWITZERLAND ■ 2 ART DIRECTOR: ANDREW HOYNE DESIGNER: ANDREW HOYNE PHOTOGRAPHER: ROB BLACKBURN DESIGN FIRM: ANDREW HOYNE DESIGN CLIENT: AUSTRALIAN GRAPHIC DESIGN ASSOCIATION COUNTRY: AUSTRALIA ■ 3 ART DIRECTOR/DESIGNER: GERMAR WAMBACH CLIENT: SMITHKLINE BEECHAM PHARMA GMBH COUNTRY: GERMANY ■ 4 ART DIRECTOR: HOLGER MATTHIES DESIGNER: HOLGER MATTHIES PHOTOGRAPHER: HOLGER MATTHIES CLIENT: GOETHE INSTITUT COUNTRY: GERMANY

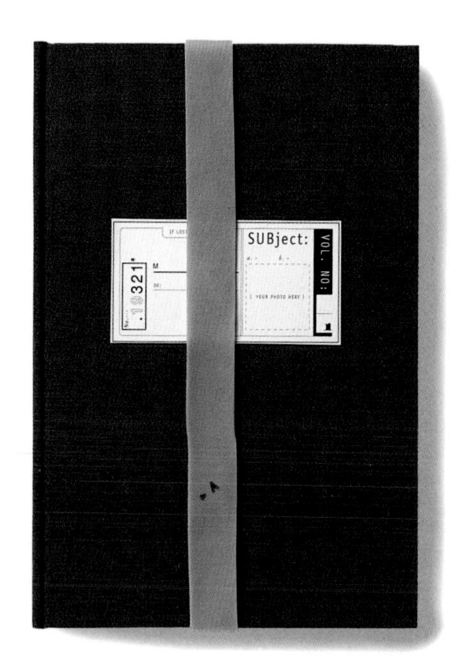
321
SUBject:
VOL. NO:

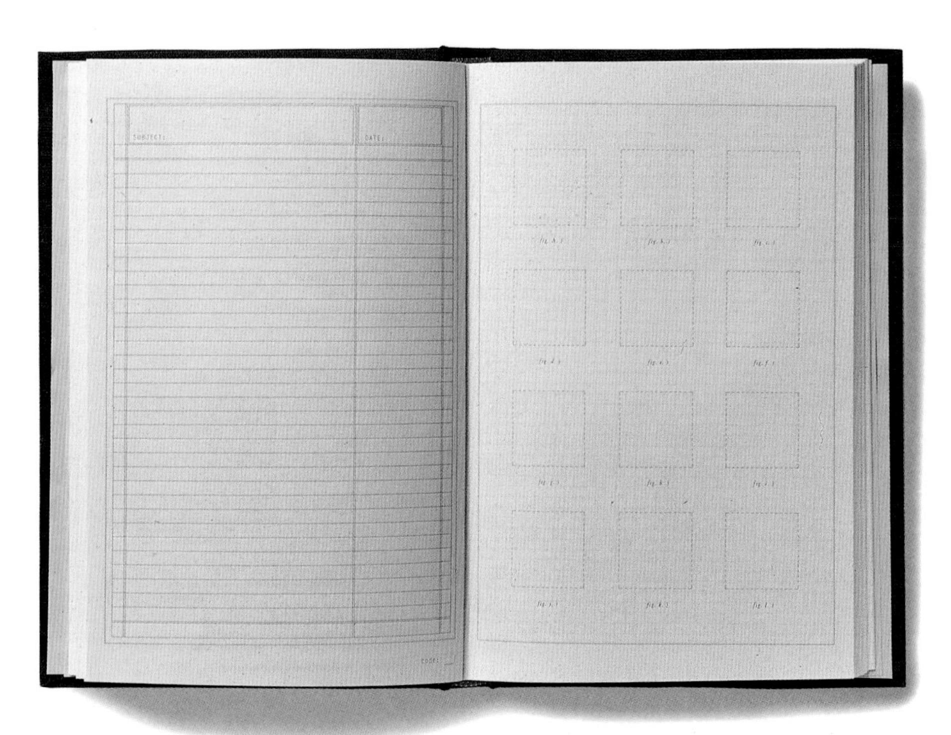

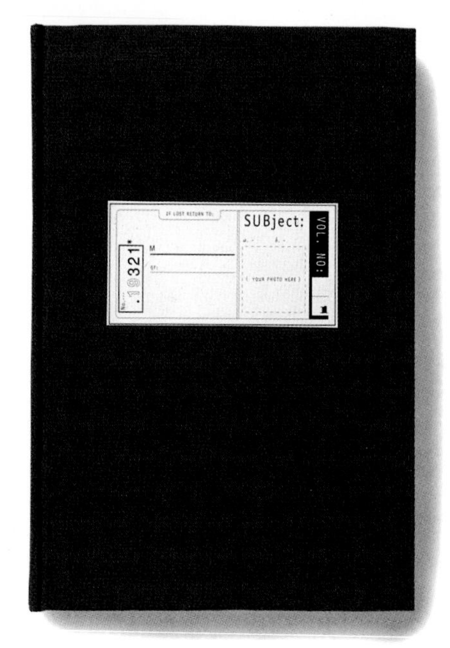
321
SUBject:
VOL. NO:

ALWAYS TIME FOR COCA-COLA
Coca-Cola
Coca-Cola

NICK at NITE
Classic TV
CLASSIC TV
NICK AT NITE IS

CLASSIC TV
NICK AT NITE IS
NICK at NITE
4

SPINERGY
SPINERGY
SPINERGY

SPINERGY
SPINERGY
ERGY
rev

■ (PRECEDING SPREAD) 1–3 ART DIRECTOR: STEVEN TOLLESON DESIGNERS: STEVEN TOLLESON, JEAN ORLEBEKE DESIGN FIRM: TOLLESON DESIGN CLIENT: ASYST TECHNOLOGIES COUNTRY: USA ■ 4 ART DIRECTOR: JOE DUFFY ILLUSTRATOR: JOE DUFFY DESIGNERS: JOE DUFFY, BRIDGET DUFFY (WATCH), MISSY WILSON (PACKAGE) DESIGN FIRM: DUFFY DESIGN CLIENT: THE COCA-COLA COMPANY COUNTRY: USA ■ (THIS SPREAD) 1, 2 ART DIRECTOR: SHARON WERNER DESIGNER: SHARON WERNER ILLUSTRATOR: SHARON WERNER

PHOTOGRAPHER: PAUL IRMITER DESIGN FIRM: WERNER DESIGN WERKS INC. CLIENT: NICK AT NITE COUNTRY: USA ■ 3, 4 ART DIRECTOR: ROBIN PERKINS DESIGNERS: ROBIN PERKINS, JEFF BREIDENBACH PHOTOGRAPHER: GREG WOSTREL DESIGN FIRM: CLIFFORD SELBERT DESIGN COLLABORATIVE CLIENT: SPINERGY, INC. COUNTRY: USA ■ 5 ART DIRECTOR: JOSE SERRANO DESIGNER: JOSE SERRANO ILLUSTRATOR: TRACY SABIN DESIGN FIRM: MIRES DESIGN, INC. CLIENT: FOUND STUFF PAPERWORKS COUNTRY: USA

■ 1 ART DIRECTOR/DESIGNER: JOHN SAYLES ILLUSTRATOR: JOHN SAYLES DESIGN FIRM: SAYLES GRAPHIC DESIGN CLIENT: ACCESS GRAPHICS COUNTRY: USA ■ 2 ART DIRECTOR/DESIGNER: CLEMENT YIP PRODUCT PHOTOGRAPHER: KIRK KIU DESIGN FIRM: Y DESIGN

ASSOCIATES CLIENT: MINOLTA COUNTRY: JAPAN ■ 3-6 ART DIRECTOR: CHARLES S. ANDERSON DESIGNERS: CHARLES S. ANDERSON, PAUL HOWART (3, 6), TODD PIPER-HAUSWIRTH (4, 6), JOEL TEMPLIN (5, 6), ERIK JOHNSON (6) PRODUCT PHOTOGRAPHERS: DON FORNER (3), ANDY KINGSBURY (4), DARRELL EAGER (5, 6) DESIGN FIRM: CHARLES S. ANDERSON DESIGN CO. CLIENT: CSA ARCHIVE COUNTRY: USA

CSA
3-D (PLASTI
JUNK:
3-D ARCHIVE IN A DRUM
toys
WE'VE TAKEN LINE ART INTO A WHOLE NEW DIMENSION
CSA ARCHIVE
3-D:

SLACKS
SLIP INTO SLACKS AND SLIP INTO SOMETHING MORE COMFORTABLE. BECAUSE AS YOUR FATHER ALREADY KNOWS, SLACKS ARE ALWAYS APPROPRIATE.
SLACKS COLOGNE

C.S.A. ARCHIVE
PRESENTS
GENUINE
LIMITED EDITION
CSA Archive

JAVA-JOE
HOT COFFEE
PERKED
1 cup
COFFEE TABLE
SERVED DAILY
WAKE UP AND SMELL THE CAPPUCCINO

shot in the USA an exhibition of photographs taken in America 4 July to 22 July 1994 The Association Gallery 9-10 Domingo Street London EC1 Telephone 071 608 1441
Opening hours
Monday to Friday
9.30am to 6.00pm
admission free
THE ASSOCIATION OF
PHOTOGRAPHERS
Kodak

■ 1 ART DIRECTOR: STEVE GIBBONS DESIGNERS: GILLIAN THOMAS, LOUISE EDWARDS DESIGN FIRM: THE PARTNERS CLIENT: ASSOCIATION OF PHOTOGRAPHERS COUNTRY: GREAT BRITAIN ■ 2 ART DIRECTOR: JANET KRUSE DESIGNER: TRACI DABERKO ILLUSTRATORS: VARIOUS CLIENT: PAT HACKETT/ARTIST REPRESENTATIVE COUNTRY: USA ■ (FOLLOWING SPREAD) 1 ART DIRECTOR:

CHARLES S. ANDERSON DESIGNERS: CHARLES S. ANDERSON, TODD PIPER-HAUSWIRTH, PAUL HOWART PHOTOGRAPHER: DARRELL EAGER DESIGN FIRM: CHARLES S. ANDERSON DESIGN CO. CLIENT: PRINT CRAFT, INC. COUNTRY: USA ■ 2 DESIGNER: MICHAEL SCHWAB ILLUSTRATOR: MICHAEL SCHWAB DESIGN FIRM: SCOTT DESIGN CLIENT: DALLAS SOCIETY OF VISUAL COMMUNICATIONS COUNTRY: USA

"C" OUR EXCITING NEW CAPABILITIES
The addition of a 28" x 40" 6-Color Heidelberg CD press not only allows us to print on up to 40 pt. board, the in-line aqueous Tower Coater seals the sheet completely with almost no spray powder and has a faster drying time than varnish. And our new saddle stitcher does everything but slice bread – it can trim, collate, drill and stack over twelve thousand books per hour. That's up to 160 pages plus cover, all in one efficient pass!
READY FOR THE FUTURE
The new acquisition of the latest in high-tech equipment allows Print Craft to better meet the needs of today's modern customer.
c/1
Capabilities
PRINT CRAFT INCORPORATED
TEL: (612) 633-8122 / FAX: (612) 633-1862
WHAT WE CAN DO FOR YOU?
PRINTCRAFT INCORPORATED
P
THE FOUR "C's" OF QUALITY PRINTING
Capabilities, Craftsmanship, Color And Capacity
Don't Just Take Our Word For It, "C" For Yourself!

GRAPHIC ARTIST
MICHAEL SCHWAB
DALLAS
7:00 P. M.
MARCH 2

CRAFTED WITH PRIDE IN AMERICA

BNA
DESIGN

■ 1 ART DIRECTOR: TOM SCHIFANELLA DESIGNERS: JEFFERSON RALL, JENNIFER HARMAN DESIGN FIRM: ROBIN SHEPHERD STUDIOS COUNTRY: USA ■ 2 ART DIRECTOR: JASON O'HARA DESIGNER: JASON O'HARA PHOTOGRAPHER: ALAN DOAK ILLUSTRATOR: JEREMY BENNETT DESIGN FIRM: BNA DESIGN CLIENT: BNA DESIGN COUNTRY: NEW ZEALAND ■ 3 ART DIRECTOR: STEVEN TOLLESON DESIGNERS: STEVEN TOLLESON, JEAN ORLEBEKE DESIGN FIRM: TOLLESON DESIGN CLIENT: ASYST TECHNOLOGIES COUNTRY: USA

4-WAY

UNIVERSAL
Ossip
Optometry
Broad Ripple

■ 1, 2 CREATIVE DIRECTORS: JEFF LARAMORE, DAVID YOUNG ART DIRECTOR: CHRIS BEATTY SCULPTOR: DAVID KIRBY BELLAMY DESIGN FIRM: YOUNG + LARAMORE CLIENT: OSSIP OPTOMETRY COUNTRY: USA ■ 3 ART DIRECTOR: JASON O'HARA DESIGNER: JASON O'HARA PHOTOGRAPHER: ALAN DOAK ILLUSTRATOR: JEREMY BENNETT DESIGN FIRM: BNA DESIGN CLIENT: BNA DESIGN COUNTRY: NEW ZEALAND

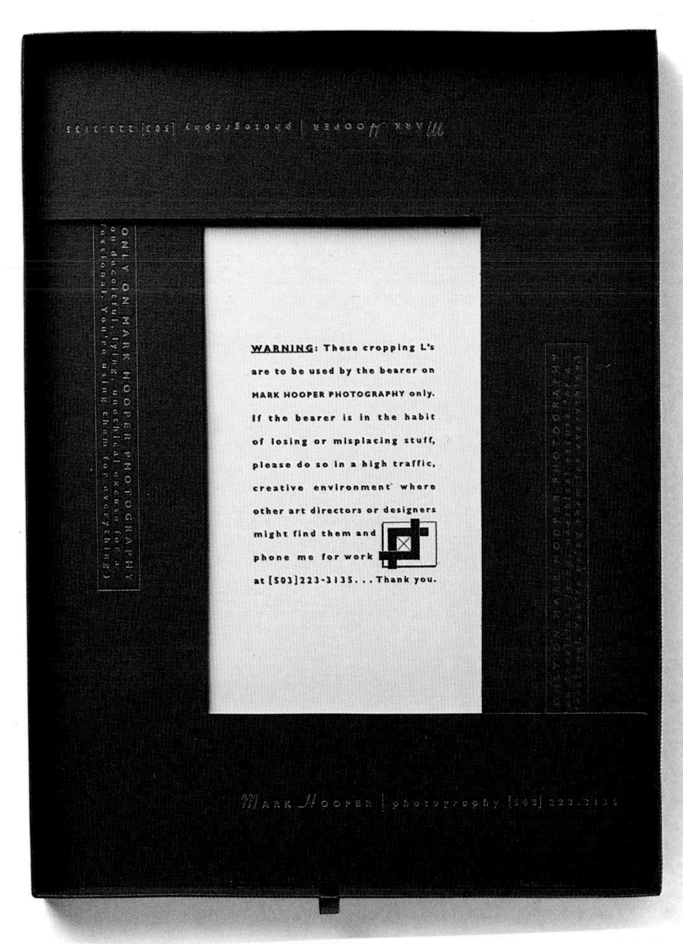
WARNING: These cropping L's
are to be used by the bearer on
MARK HOOPER PHOTOGRAPHY only.
If the bearer is in the habit
of losing or misplacing stuff,
please do so in a high traffic,
creative environment where
other art directors or designers
might find them and
phone me for work
at [503]223-3135. . . Thank you.

■ 1, 2 ART DIRECTOR/DESIGNER: STEVEN SANDSTROM PHOTOGRAPHER: MARK HOOPER DESIGN FIRM: SANDSTROM DESIGN CLIENT: MARK HOOPER PHOTOGRAPHY COUNTRY: USA ■ 3, 4 ART DIRECTORS: DOUG AKAGI, DAVID BIGMAN DESIGNERS: DOUG AKAGI, KIMBERLY POWELL PHOTOGRAPHER: VARIOUS ILLUSTRATOR: VARIOUS DESIGN FIRM: J. WALTER THOMPSON CLIENT: AMERICAN HAWAII CRUISES COUNTRY: USA

For aeons, the islands of Hawaii lay undiscovered, except by an occasional seabird. Then came the Polynesians of ancient times. Followed by Captain James Cook a scant 215 years ago. And thus, the world first learned of these precious jewels serenely anchored in the middle of the Pacific. No other place on earth offers such wild and other worldly beauty. No other place can touch you so magically with the flavor of an exotic culture. But to find all this, you must take a different course than others. To the still-undisturbed parts of Hawaii, explored year-round only by American Hawaii Cruises. Follow our seven-day route on this map, and you'll discover far more than four islands and five ports. You'll find the Hawaii you've always dreamed of.
A CRUISE of the LESS EXPLORED HAWAII
Shore Excursions & Commentary
TO HANA
KAUAI
NIIHAU
LEHUA
NAWILIWILI
OAHU
HONOLULU
MOLOKAI
LANAI
MAUI
KAHULUI
MOLOKINI
KAHOOLAWE
HAWAII
KONA
HILO
AMERICAN HAWAII CRUISES

AMERICAN HAWAII CRUISES
ITINERARY AND PARTICULARS
Special Theme Cruises
Our Shore Excursions
A SAMPLING
Hotel Vacation Extensions
FOR RESERVATIONS, MORE INFORMATION OR OUR FREE BROCHURE
SEE YOUR TRAVEL AGENT
AMERICAN HAWAII CRUISES

■ 1 ART DIRECTORS: ANDREI SHELUTTO, IGOR GUROVICH DESIGNERS: ANDREI SHELUTTO, IGOR GUROVICH PHOTOGRAPHER: EDUARD BASILIJA DESIGN FIRM: IMA-PRESS PUBLISHERS CLIENT: IMA-PRESS ASSOCIATION COUNTRY: RUSSIA ■ 2 ART DIRECTOR: ROLF JANSSON

DESIGNER: ILLUSTRATOR/CLIENT: ROLF JANSSON COUNTRY: NORWAY ■ 3 ART DIRECTOR/LETTERING/CLIENT: JILL BELL COUNTRY: USA ■ 4, 5 ART DIRECTOR/DESIGNER: RANDY HUGHES DESIGN FIRM: CLARITY COVERDALE FURY CLIENT: LAMINATION CONCEPTS COUNTRY: USA

Hva så ?
Rolf Jansson er illustratør...

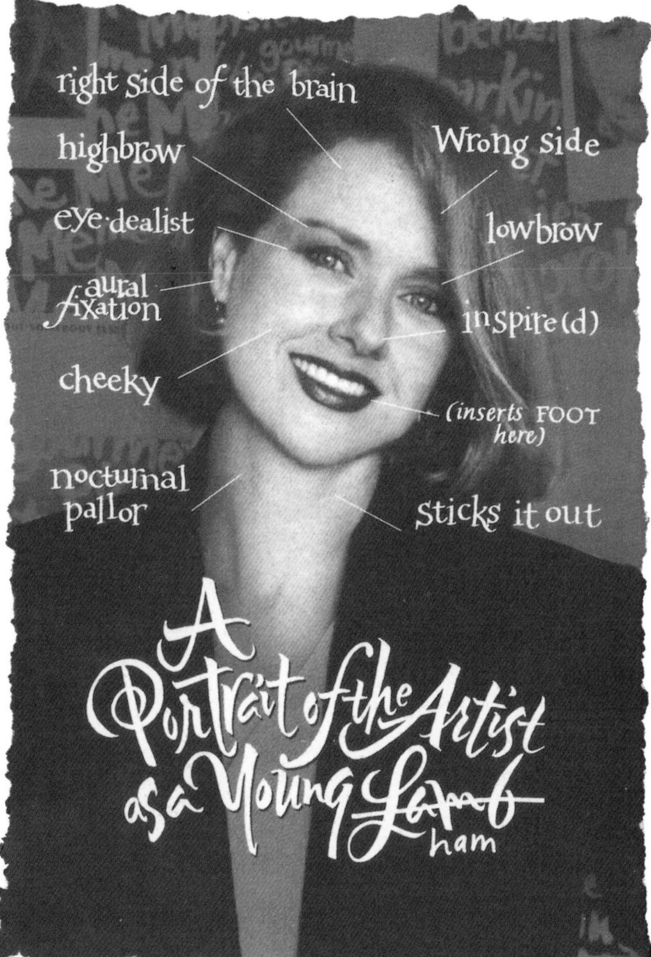
right side of the brain
highbrow
Wrong side
eye·dealist
lowbrow
aural fixation
inspire(d)
cheeky
(inserts FOOT here)
nocturnal pallor
sticks it out
A Portrait of the Artist as a Young Lamb ham

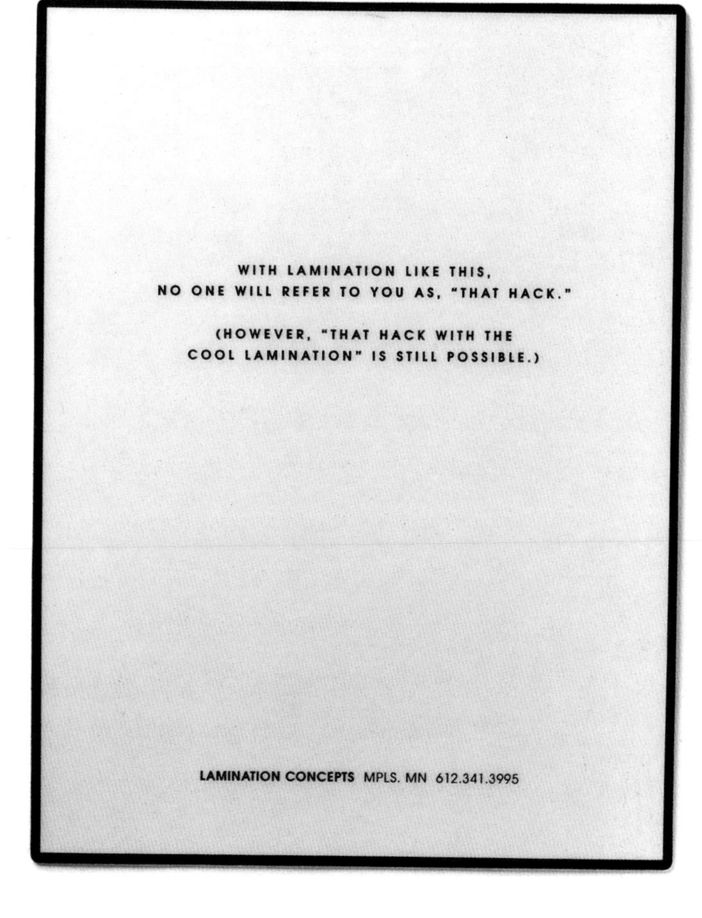
WITH LAMINATION LIKE THIS, NO ONE WILL REFER TO YOU AS, "THAT HACK."
(HOWEVER, "THAT HACK WITH THE COOL LAMINATION" IS STILL POSSIBLE.)
LAMINATION CONCEPTS MPLS. MN 612.341.3995

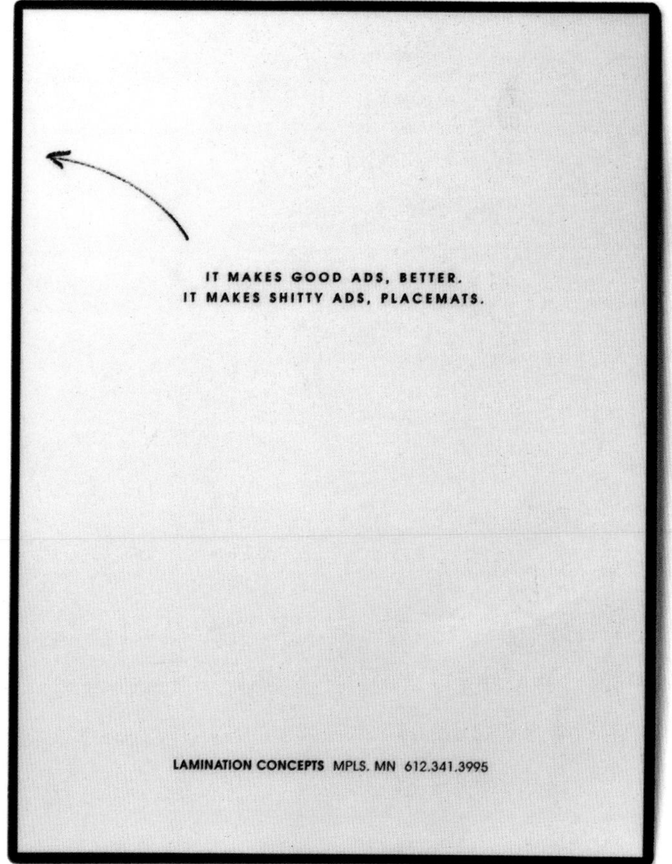
IT MAKES GOOD ADS, BETTER.
IT MAKES SHITTY ADS, PLACEMATS.
LAMINATION CONCEPTS MPLS. MN 612.341.3995

dobber
№ 47984
GUARANTEED TO LAST
MANUFACTURED BY
dobber
Nº 1 ESSENTIAL CLOTHING SUPPLIES
REGULAR CONSTRUCTION
BY DOBBER

■ 1 ART DIRECTOR: MIKE SALISBURY DESIGNER: MIKE SALISBURY PHOTOGRAPHER/ILLUSTRATOR: MIKE SALISBURY DESIGN FIRM: MIKE SALISBURY COMMUNICATIONS CLIENT: THE VILLAGE COUNTRY: USA ■ 2 ART DIRECTOR: NIKKO AMANDONICO DESIGNER: PAUL BARRY DESIGN FIRM: ENERGY PROJECT CLIENT: DOBBER COUNTRY: ITALY ■ 3 ART DIRECTOR/DESIGNER: XAVIER CORRETJÉ DESIGN FIRM: ACR-CORRETJÉ CLIENT: VIDEOCOMUNICACION S.A. COUNTRY: SPAIN ■ 4 ART DIRECTOR: KRISTIN BRESLIN SOMMESE DESIGNER: GRETCHEN LEARY PRODUCT PHOTOGRAPHER: DICK ACKLEY CLIENT: RED BARON COLLECTIBLES (STUDENT PROJECT) COUNTRY: USA ■ 5 DESIGNER/PHOTOGRAPHER: ANDY THOMPSON/BENDER & BENDER PHOTOGRAPHY COUNTRY: USA ■ 6 ART DIRECTOR: KRISTIN BRESLIN SOMMESE DESIGNER/PHOTOGRAPHER: CHRISTIAN WERNER PRODUCT PHOTOGRAPHER: DICK ACKLEY CLIENT: THE TREE HOUSE (STUDENT PROJECT) COUNTRY: USA

ESSES

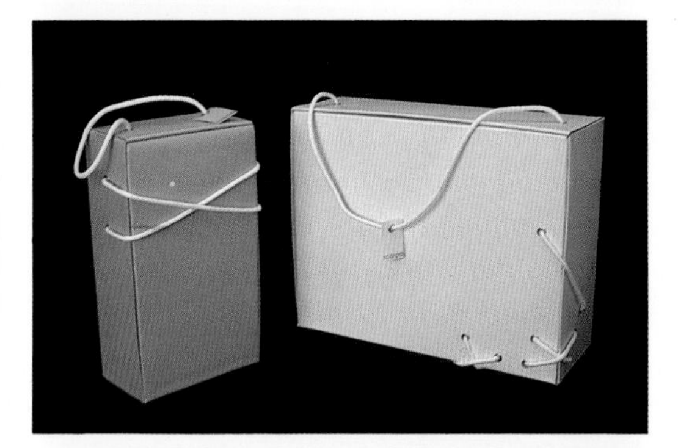

"Paper Is Our Bag"
FRENCH
Paper Co., Niles, MI

WORKS
NILES, MI
"FRENCH DUR-O-TONE"
PAPERS THAT PULL
THEIR OWN WEIGHT

■ 1 ART DIRECTOR: DOO H. KIM DESIGNERS: DONGIL LEE, SEUNGHEE LEE, JUNGHEE HAN DESIGN FIRM: DOOKIM DESIGN CLIENT: ESSES COUNTRY: KOREA ■ 2 ART DIRECTOR: MASSIMO VIGNELLI DESIGNERS: MASSIMO VIGNELLI, DAVID LAW DESIGN FIRM: VIGNELLI ASSOCIATES LTD. CLIENT: BROOKSTONE COUNTRY: USA ■ 3 ART DIRECTOR/DESIGNER: LANA RIGSBY PRODUCT PHOTOGRAPHER: TERRY VINE DESIGN FIRM: RIGSBY DESIGN CLIENT: ZOOT RESTAURANT COUNTRY: USA ■ 4 ART DIRECTOR: KRISTIN BRESLIN SOMMESE DESIGNER:

BRIDGETTE KLOECKER PRODUCT PHOTOGRAPHER: DICK ACKLEY COUNTRY: USA ■ 5, 6 ART DIRECTOR: CHARLES S. ANDERSON DESIGNERS: CHARLES S. ANDERSON, PAUL HOWART (6) PRODUCT PHOTOGRAPHER: DARRELL EAGER (6) ILLUSTRATOR: CSA ARCHIVE (6) DESIGN FIRM: CHARLES S. ANDERSON DESIGN CLIENT: FRENCH PAPER CO. COUNTRY: USA ■ 7 ART DIRECTOR/DESIGNER: BILL THORBURN PHOTOGRAPHERS: DON FREEMAN, THOMAS BRUMMETT DESIGN FIRM: THE KUESTER GROUP CLIENT: POTLATCH PAPER COMPANY COUNTRY: USA

■ 1 ART DIRECTOR: AVITAL KELLNER-GAZIT DESIGNER: AVITAL KELLNER-GAZIT DESIGN FIRM: STUDIO REISINGER CLIENT: GOLAN HEIGHTS WINERY COUNTRY: ISRAEL ■ 2, 3 ART DIRECTOR: RAMESH MULYE DESIGNER: RAMESH MULYE DESIGN FIRM: LIGHT LINE STATION CLIENT: HUNNAR PAPER PRODUCTS COUNTRY: INDIA ■ 4 ART DIRECTOR: RAFAEL KOSAKOWSKI DESIGNER: RAFAEL KOSAKOWSKI DESIGN

FIRM/CLIENT: SUPERSOULDESIGN COUNTRY: AUSTRIA ■ 5 ART DIRECTOR: TAKENOBU IGARASHI DESIGNERS: TAKENOBU IGARASHI, ROSS B. MCBRIDE PRODUCT PHOTOGRAPHER: MASARU MERA DESIGN FIRM: IGARASHI STUDIO CLIENT: THE MUSEUM OF MODERN ART COUNTRY: USA ■ 6, 7 ART DIRECTOR: GECCHELIN LORENZO DESIGNER: PAOLO TATAVITTO DESIGN FIRM: COMPETITION S.R.L. COUNTRY: ITALY

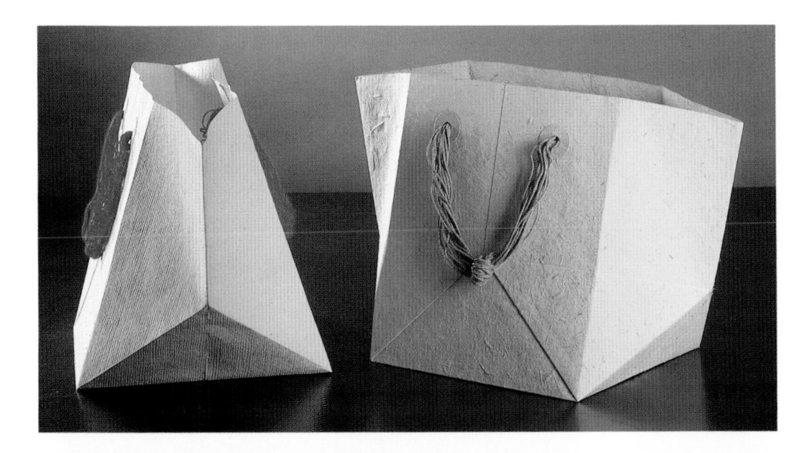

STOLEN
GOODS

The Museum of Modern Art
The Museum of Modern Art
The Museum of Modern Art

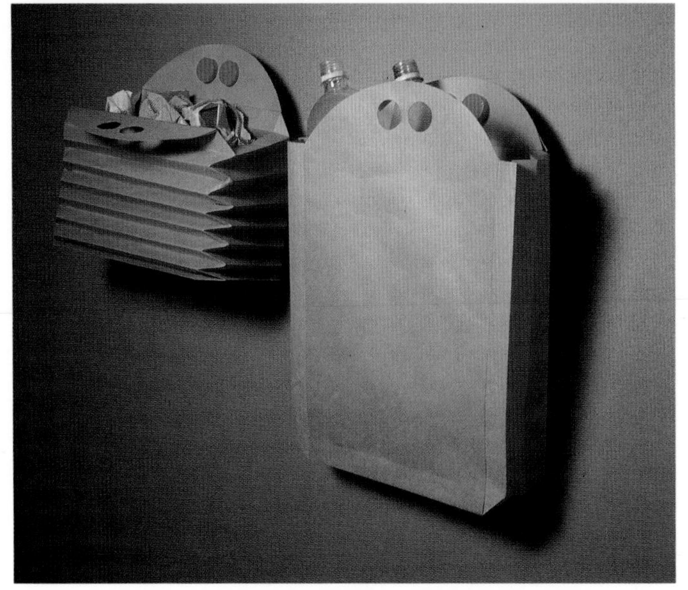

KEEP THE HOME FIRES BURNING
1940's
NEW ZEALAND POST
FIRST DAY COVER
NEW ZEALAND
PHILATELIC BUREAU
WANGANUI NZ
3 NOVEMBER 1993
45c
80c
$1.00
$1.50
$1.80

NEW ZEALAND
45 CENTS
The 1920's: Flaming Youth.

NEW ZEALAND
50 CENTS
The 1920's: Birth of Broadcasting.

NEW ZEALAND
80 CENTS
The 1920's: All Blacks — The Invincibles.

NEW ZEALAND
$1.00
The 1920's: The Swaggie.

NEW ZEALAND
$1.50
The 1920's: The motor car brings freedom.

NEW ZEALAND
$1.80
The 1920's: The arrival of the air age.

19 NEW ZEALAND 30's
buttons and bows
the new femininity
45 CENTS

19 NEW ZEALAND 30's
the great depression
UNEMPLOYED WORKERS
ORGANISE
50 CENTS

19 NEW ZEALAND 30's
phar lap
80 CENTS

19 NEW ZEALAND 30's
state housing
$1.00

19 NEW ZEALAND 30's
free milk for schools
$1.50

19 NEW ZEALAND 30's
the talkies
TICKETS
CIVIC
RICHMAN
THE RITZ
$1.80

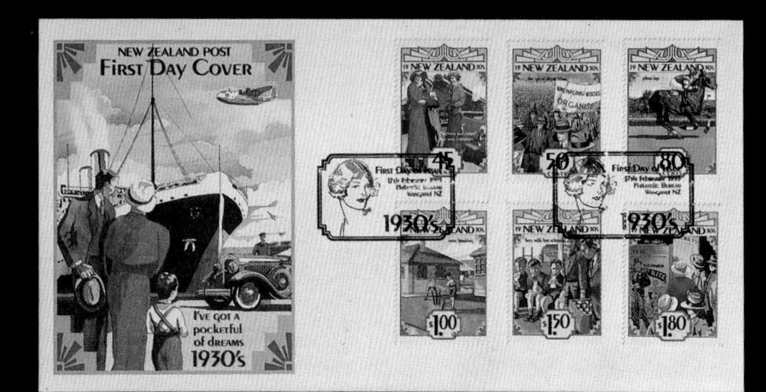
NEW ZEALAND POST
First Day Cover
I've got a pocketful of dreams
1930's
First Day of Issue
1930's

D-DAY
25p GROUNDCREW RELOADING RAF BOSTONS 6 JUNE 1944

D-DAY
25p COASTAL BOMBARDMENT BY HMS WARSPITE 6 JUNE 1944

D-DAY
25p COMMANDOS LANDING ON GOLD BEACH 6 JUNE 1944

D-DAY
25p INFANTRY REGROUPING ON SWORD BEACH 6 JUNE 1944

D-DAY
25p ADVANCING INLAND FROM OUISTREHAM 6 JUNE 1944

Canada
43
International Civil Aviation
L'aviation civile internationale

Canada 43 International Civil Aviation L'aviation civile internationale
Canada 43 International Civil Aviation L'aviation civile internationale
Canada 43 International Civil Aviation L'aviation civile internationale
Canada 43 International Civil Aviation L'aviation civile internationale
Canada 43 International Civil Aviation L'aviation civile internationale
Canada 43 International Civil Aviation L'aviation civile internationale
Canada 43 International Civil Aviation L'aviation civile internationale
Canada 43 International Civil Aviation L'aviation civile internationale
Canada 43 International Civil Aviation L'aviation civile internationale
Canada 43 International Civil Aviation L'aviation civile internationale
Canada 43 International Civil Aviation L'aviation civile internationale
Canada 43 International Civil Aviation L'aviation civile internationale
Canada 43 International Civil Aviation L'aviation civile internationale
Canada 43 International Civil Aviation L'aviation civile internationale
Canada 43 International Civil Aviation L'aviation civile internationale
Canada 43 International Civil Aviation L'aviation civile internationale
Canada 43 International Civil Aviation L'aviation civile internationale
Canada 43 International Civil Aviation L'aviation civile internationale
Canada 43 International Civil Aviation L'aviation civile internationale
Canada 43 International Civil Aviation L'aviation civile internationale
Canada 43 International Civil Aviation L'aviation civile internationale
Canada 43 International Civil Aviation L'aviation civile internationale
Canada 43 International Civil Aviation L'aviation civile internationale
Canada 43 International Civil Aviation L'aviation civile internationale

■ 1 ART DIRECTOR: DICK SHEAFF DESIGNER: MARK HESS ILLUSTRATOR: MARK HESS CLIENT: U.S. POSTAL SERVICE COUNTRY: USA ■ 2 ART DIRECTOR: SWEDEN POST STAMPS DESIGN FIRM: SWEDEN POST STAMPS DESIGNER: EVA EDE ILLUSTRATORS: RENÉ DESSIRIER

CLASSIC
COLLECTION

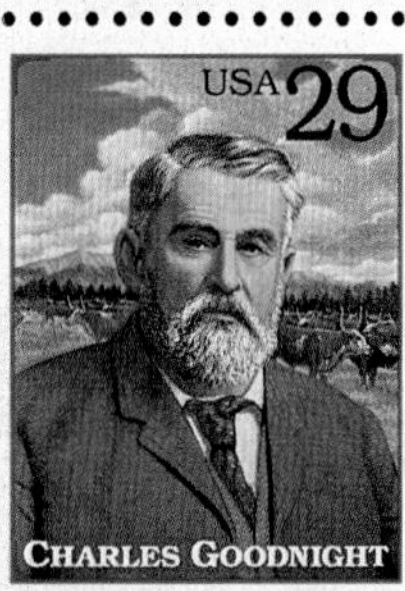

(TOP CENTER), P. HILLESTRÖM (BOTTOM LEFT), N. LAFRENSEN (BOTTOM CENTER), F. GÉRARD (BOTTOM RIGHT) COUNTRY: SWEDEN ■ 3 ART DIRECTORS: NAOMI ESHEL, MEIR ESHEL DESIGNERS: NAOMI ESHEL, MEIR ESHEL PHOTOGRAPHER: ICONS LTD

Manipulation: ICONS LTD. Design Firm: NAOMI & MEIR – GRAPHIC DESIGN Client: ISRAEL POSTAL AUTHORIT

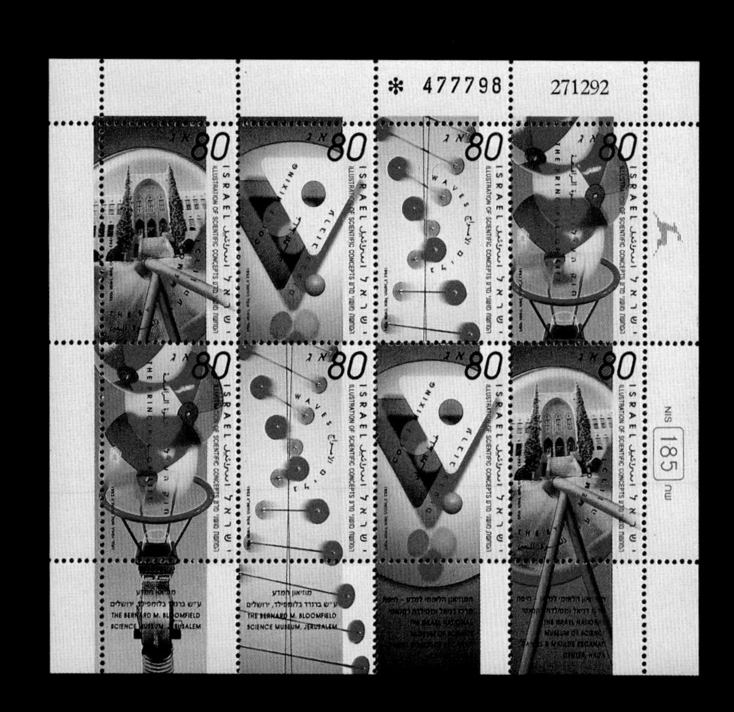

(THIS PAGE) **1–4** ART DIRECTOR: CHARLES S. ANDERSON DESIGNERS: CHARLES S. ANDERSON (1–3), PAUL HOWART (1–3), ERIK JOHNSON (1–3), JOEL TEMPLIN (4) PRODUCT PHOTOGRAPHER: PAUL IRMITER (1–3) DESIGN FIRM: CHARLES S. ANDERSON DESIGN CO. CLIENT: CSA ARCHIVE COUNTRY: USA ■ (PAGE 240) ILLUSTRATOR: SHINICHIRO WAKAO COUNTRY: JAPAN

INDEX

VERZEICHNIS

INDEX

GRAPHIS PUBLICATIONS

GRAPHIS PUBLIKATIONEN

PUBLICATIONS GRAPHIS

ADVERTISING
TYPE
THE BEST IN DIGITAL CLASSIC TEXT FONTS
BOOK DESIGN
INFORMATION ARCHITECTS
Richard Saul Wurman
Information Architects Richard Saul Wurman
GRAPHIS PHOTO
MUSIC CDS
GRAPHIS MUSIC CDS
Fine Art
PHOTOGRAPHY
THE ART OF THE SHOPPING BAG
EPHEMERA
GRAPHIS EPHEMERA

G R A P H I S B O O K S

BOOK ORDER FORM: USA, CANADA, SOUTH AMERICA, ASIA, PACIFIC

BOOKS	ALL REGIONS
□ GRAPHIS ADVERTISING 96	US$ 69.95
□ GRAPHIS ALTERNATIVE PHOTOGRAPHY 95	US$ 69.95
□ GRAPHIS ANNUAL REPORTS 4	US$ 69.95
□ GRAPHIS BOOK DESIGN	US$ 75.95
□ GRAPHIS CORPORATE IDENTITY 2	US$ 75.95
□ GRAPHIS DESIGN 96	US$ 69.95
□ GRAPHIS EPHEMERA	US$ 75.95
□ GRAPHIS FINE ART PHOTOGRAPHY	US$ 85.00
□ GRAPHIS INFORMATION ARCHITECTS	US$ 69.95
□ GRAPHIS MUSIC CDS	US$ 75.95
□ GRAPHIS NUDES	US$ 89.95
□ GRAPHIS PHOTO 95	US$ 69.95
□ GRAPHIS POSTER 95	US$ 69.95
□ GRAPHIS PRODUCTS BY DESIGN	US$ 69.95
□ GRAPHIS SHOPPING BAGS	US$ 69.95
□ GRAPHIS TYPOGRAPHY 1	US$ 69.95
□ GRAPHIS TYPE SPECIMENS	US$ 49.95
□ **GRAPHIS PAPER SPECIFIER SYSTEM (GPS)**	US$ 395.00

** ADD $30 SHIPPING/HANDLING FOR GPS; AFTER DEC. 1, 1995, GPS IS $495.00

NOTE! NY RESIDENTS ADD 8.25% SALES TAX

□ CHECK ENCLOSED (PAYABLE TO GRAPHIS)
(US$ ONLY, DRAWN ON A BANK IN THE USA)

USE CREDIT CARDS (DEBITED IN US DOLLARS)

□ AMERICAN EXPRESS □ MASTERCARD □ VISA

CARD NO. EXP. DATE

CARDHOLDER NAME

SIGNATURE

(PLEASE PRINT)

NAME

TITLE

COMPANY

ADDRESS

CITY

STATE/PROVINCE ZIP CODE

COUNTRY

SEND ORDER FORM AND MAKE CHECK PAYABLE TO:
GRAPHIS US, INC.,
141 LEXINGTON AVENUE, NEW YORK, NY 10016-8193, USA

BOOK ORDER FORM: EUROPE, AFRICA, MIDDLE EAST

BOOKS	EUROPE/AFRICA MIDDLE EAST	GERMANY	U.K.
□ GRAPHIS ADVERTISING 96	SFR. 123.–	DM 149,–	£ 52.00
□ GRAPHIS ALTERNATIVE PHOTO 95	SFR. 123.–	DM 149,–	£ 52.00
□ GRAPHIS ANNUAL REPORTS 4	SFR. 137.–	DM 162,–	£ 55.00
□ GRAPHIS BOOK DESIGN	SFR. 137.–	DM 162,–	£ 55.00
□ GRAPHIS CORPORATE IDENTITY 2	SFR. 137.–	DM 162,–	£ 55.00
□ GRAPHIS DESIGN 96	SFR. 123.–	DM 149,–	£ 52.00
□ GRAPHIS EPHEMERA	SFR. 137.–	DM 162,–	£ 55.00
□ GRAPHIS FINE ART PHOTOGRAPHY	SFR. 128.–	DM 155,–	£ 69.00
□ GRAPHIS INFORMATION ARCHITECTS	SFR. 123.–	DM 149,–	£ 52.00
□ GRAPHIS MUSIC CDS	SFR. 137.–	DM 162,–	£ 55.00
□ GRAPHIS NUDES	SFR. 168.–	DM 168,–	£ 62.00
□ GRAPHIS PHOTO 95	SFR. 123.–	DM 149,–	£ 52.00
□ GRAPHIS POSTER 95	SFR. 123.–	DM 149,–	£ 52.00
□ GRAPHIS PRODUCTS BY DESIGN	SFR. 123.–	DM 149,–	£ 52.00
□ GRAPHIS SHOPPING BAGS	SFR. 123.–	DM 149,–	£ 52.00
□ GRAPHIS TYPOGRAPHY 1	SFR. 137.–	DM 162,–	£ 55.00
□ GRAPHIS TYPE SPECIMENS	SFR. 75.–	DM 89,–	£ 37.00

(FOR ORDERS FROM EC COUNTRIES V.A.T. WILL BE CHARGED IN ADDITION TO ABOVE BOOK PRICES)

FOR CREDIT CARD PAYMENT (DEBITED IN SWISS FRANCS):

□ AMERICAN EXPRESS □ DINER'S CLUB

□ VISA/BARCLAYCARD/CARTE BLEUE

CARD NO. EXP. DATE

CARDHOLDER NAME

SIGNATURE

□ PLEASE BILL ME (ADDITIONAL MAILING COSTS WILL BE CHARGED)

(PLEASE PRINT)

LAST NAME FIRST NAME

TITLE

COMPANY

ADDRESS

CITY POSTAL CODE

COUNTRY

PLEASE SEND ORDER FORM TO:
GRAPHIS PRESS CORP.
DUFOURSTRASSE 107, CH-8008 ZÜRICH, SWITZERLAND

Graphis 296
The Digital Revolution: R/GA Softimage Silicon Graphics European Mindscapes Multimedia
Graphis 295
Carson Chiat/Day Apeloig Leih Agency Legorreta Gorham
Graphis
Ishioka Fletcher Arnett ABV Achilli & Piazza CD Boxed Sets

G R A P H ' I S   M A G A Z I N E

SUBSCRIBE TO GRAPHIS: USA, CANADA, SOUTH AMERICA, ASIA,

MAGAZINE	USA	CANADA	SOUTHAMERICA/ ASIA/PACIFIC
☐ ONE YEAR (6 ISSUES)	US$ 89.00	US$ 99.00	US$ 125.00
☐ TWO YEARS (12 ISSUES)	US$ 159.00	US$ 179.00	US$ 235.00
☐ AIRMAIL SURCHARGE (6 ISSUES)	US$ 59.00	US$ 59.00	US$ 59.00

☐ 25% DISCOUNT FOR STUDENTS WITH COPY OF VALID, DATED STUDENT ID AND PAYMENT WITH ORDER

☐ CHECK ENCLOSED

USE CREDIT CARDS (DEBITED IN US DOLLARS)

☐ AMERICAN EXPRESS

☐ MASTERCARD

☐ VISA

CARD NO. EXP. DATE

CARDHOLDER NAME

SIGNATURE

☐ PLEASE BILL ME

(PLEASE PRINT)

NAME

TITLE

COMPANY

ADDRESS

CITY

STATE/PROVINCE ZIP CODE

COUNTRY

SEND ORDER FORM AND MAKE CHECK PAYABLE TO:
GRAPHIS US, INC.,
141 LEXINGTON AVENUE,
NEW YORK, NY 10016-8193, USA

SERVICE BEGINS WITH ISSUE THAT IS CURRENT WHEN ORDER IS PROCESSED. (C9B0A)

SUBSCRIBE TO GRAPHIS: EUROPE, AFRICA, MIDDLE EAST

MAGAZINE	EUROPE/AFRICA MIDDLE EAST	GERMANY	U.K.
☐ ONE YEAR (6 ISSUES)	SFR. 164.–	DM 190,–	£ 68.00
☐ TWO YEARS (12 ISSUES)	SFR. 295.–	DM 342,–	£ 122.00
☐ AIRMAIL SURCHARGES	SFR 65.–	DM 75,–	£ 30.00
☐ REGISTERED MAIL	SFR 20.–	DM 24,–	£ 9.00

☐ CHECK ENCLOSED (PLEASE MAKE SFR.–CHECK PAYABLE TO A SWISS BANK)

☐ STUDENTS MAY REQUEST A 25% DISCOUNT BY SENDING STUDENT ID

FOR CREDIT CARD PAYMENT (ALL CARDS DEBITED IN SWISS FRANCS):

☐ AMERICAN EXPRESS ☐ DINER'S CLUB

☐ VISA/BARCLAYCARD/CARTE BLEUE

CARD NO. EXP. DATE

CARDHOLDER NAME

SIGNATURE

☐ PLEASE BILL ME

(PLEASE PRINT)

LAST NAME

FIRST NAME

TITLE

COMPANY

ADDRESS

CITY POSTAL CODE

COUNTRY

NOTE TO GERMAN SUBSCRIBERS ONLY:
ICH ERKLÄRE MICH EINVERSTANDEN, DASS MEINE NEUE ADRESSE DURCH DIE POST AN DEN VERTRIEB WEITERGELEITET WIRD.

PLEASE SEND ORDER FORM AND MAKE CHECK PAYABLE TO:
GRAPHIS PRESS CORP.
DUFOURSTRASSE 107
CH–8008 ZÜRICH, SWITZERLAND

SERVICE BEGINS WITH ISSUE THAT IS CURRENT WHEN ORDER IS PROCESSED. (C9B0A)